Prehistoric Ceramics Research Group: Occasional Paper 5

Prehistoric Pottery:
Some Recent Research

Edited by

Alex Gibson

PREHISTORIC
CERAMICS
RESEARCH
GROUP

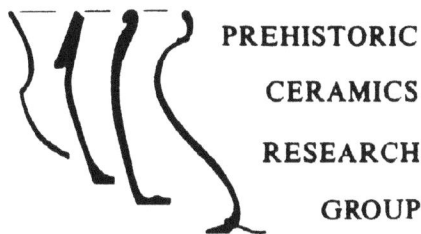

BAR International Series 1509
2006

Published in 2016 by
BAR Publishing, Oxford

BAR International Series 1509

Prehistoric Ceramics Research Group: Occasional Paper 5
Prehistoric Pottery: Some Recent Research

ISBN 978 1 84171 943 6

BAR Publishing is the trading name of British Archaeological Reports (Oxford) Ltd.
British Archaeological Reports was first incorporated in 1974 to publish the BAR
Series, International and British. In 1992 Hadrian Books Ltd became part of the BAR
group. This volume was originally published by Archaeopress in conjunction with
British Archaeological Reports (Oxford) Ltd / Hadrian Books Ltd, the Series principal
publisher, in 2006. This present volume is published by BAR Publishing, 2016.

Printed in England

BAR
PUBLISHING

BAR titles are available from:

BAR Publishing
122 Banbury Rd, Oxford, OX2 7BP, UK
EMAIL info@barpublishing.com
PHONE +44 (0)1865 310431
FAX +44 (0)1865 316916
www.barpublishing.com

Contents

List of Contributors

Embaie Ferrow
Department of Geology,
Lund University,
Sweden

Daniel Fuglesang
Classical Archaeology & Ancient History,
Lund University
Sweden

Alex Gibson
Department of Archaeological Science
University of Bradford
Bradford
UK

Frances Healy
School of History and Archaeology
University of Wales, College Cardiff
Cardiff

Aleksander Kośko
Adam Mickiewicz University,
Poznań,
Poland

Jerzy Langer
Adam Mickiewicz University,
Poznań,
Poland

Anders Lindahl
Laboratory for Ceramic Research,
Quaternary Geology,
Lund University,Sweden

Sławomir Pietrzak
Adam Mickiewicz University,
Poznań,
Poland

Sarah Ralph
Department of Archaeology
University of Cambridge
Downing Street
Cambridge

Pia Sköld
Laboratory for Ceramic Research,
Quaternary Geology,
Lund University
Sweden

Ben Stern
Department of Archaeological Science
University of Bradford
Bradford
UK

Ole Stilborg
Laboratory for Ceramic Research,
Quaternary Geology,
Lund University
Sweden

Marzena Szmyt
Adam Mickiewicz University,
Poznań,
Poland

Yuri B. Tsetlin
History of Ceramics Laboratory,
Institute of Archaeology,
Russian Academy of Sciences.
Dm.Ulianov str., 19,
Moscow 117036,
Russia;

Jan Turek
Alzirska 639
Praha 6 Vokovice
160 00
Czech Republic

Prehistoric Pottery: Recent Research – An Introduction

Alex Gibson

In October 2004 over 70 delegates from across Europe (and one from the USA) met in the Department of Archaeological Sciences at the University of Bradford for the second International Conference on Prehistoric Ceramics. The conference was the second major biannual conference to be organised by the *Prehistoric Ceramics Research Group*, and once again was in collaboration with the *Prehistoric Society*. The call for papers was deliberately broad in its scope – recent research – and such is the amount of work currently taking place on Prehistoric Ceramics across Europe (and indeed further afield) that the conference organisers were inundated with offers of papers.

Such a wide-ranging call can often lead to a conference that is disjointed, even eclectic, with little cohesion other than an interest in ceramics. This may be viewed as unfortunate by some yet may also be welcomed by others. Personally, I am the welcoming sort for after the conference I certainly felt that my horizons had been widened and the range of research and analytical techniques being employed with regard to Prehistoric Ceramics is truly impressive. Ceramics, for long stylistically analysed to provide basic typologies for regional and chronological studies, can now be seen to provide the source for much greater scientific, economic, artistic, sociological and ecological databases.

I have previously and for a long time called for an holistic approach to ceramic studies looking away from the 'class 1a to class 5c' kinds of typologies. Useful though (some of) these might be, they ignore the human influence on and the social and economic strategies involved in ceramic production. They ignore the socio-economic information provided by chemical analyses, the use-histories and belief-systems indicated by use-wear and ethnographic analyses, the evidence for long distance networking and the deliberate selection of tempers provided by geological analyses, the evidence for technological development provided by technological studies into all aspects of ceramic manufacture, from clay preparation and temper acquisition to fashioning, decoration, firing and post-firing surface treatments. Indeed this can be taken further to the study of repair, deliberate destruction and the secondary use of damaged ceramics as grog, items of structured deposition such as deposits in pits and graves or even secondary artefacts. They also ignore the information on belief systems and even mythologies that might be gleaned from studies of such facets as temper selection, ethnographic practices and terminologies, decorative techniques and motifs, and relationships with other aspects of material culture (even materiality) that can be provided from an ethnographic and theoretical basis. Such holistic studies have been labelled '*Ceramic Ecology*' by scholars in the USA while the term '*Chaîne Opératoire*' is favoured by French researchers. The terms do not matter, what is important is the joint realisation that the multi-faceted study of ceramics can produce so much more information on past populations than, I would argue, any other artefact type. Pots = People, sometimes literally (fig. 1).

In such a developing subject as is modern ceramic studies, therefore, it is logical to assume that papers will be wide-ranging and varied. It is hoped that in the papers presented in this volume, readers will find much to stimulate the mind and their own directions of study even if the subject matter is not directly relevant to their own specific fields. This is the unifying beauty of ceramic research.

Fig 1: Copy of a chalcolithic anthropomorphic vase from Romania by the potter Mădălina Mihăilă.

Acknowledgements

The 2004 Bradford Conference was supported and made possible thanks to generous financial assistance from English Heritage and The Prehistoric Society. The University of Bradford, Department of Archaeological Sciences offered free use of their facilities and I am grateful to the Dean, Professor Carl Heron for his support and to Mr John McIlwaine for ensuring that everything ran smoothly. Thanks are also warmly extended to the Department of Archaeological Sciences and the students of the University of Bradford Archaeological Society for hosting the pre-conference wine reception and buffet. I am also extremely grateful to my wife, Jane, for hosting and preparing the post-conference lunch for foreign delegates in our home in Ilkley. Finally thanks are extended to the volume's referee for turning the typescript round so quickly and for useful and pertinent comments.

Alex Gibson
Hon Chairman, PCRG

CHAPTER 1

The Origin of Graphic Modes of Pottery Decoration

Yuri B. Tsetlin

General approach

The origin of decoration is a problem which has been discussed many times in the scientific literature but usually decoration in general is discussed as a specific cultural phenomenon. There are three main theories of the origin of decoration – 'magical', 'biological' and 'technical'.

The 'magical' theory was first advanced by the Russian cultural historian L.K.Popov (1880). Later many other scholars adopted this point of view (*inter alia* Grosse 1894: Schtenberg 1936: Voevodsky 1936). They thought that any kind of decoration was a materialized reflection of the external world in a symbolic (magical) form.

The 'biological' theory originates from the famous Greek philosophers Plato and Aristotle. Many cultural historians and archaeologists had developed the theory during the 19th and the beginning of the 20th century (see for example, Stephan 1907: Osborn 1916). They all believed that the 'sense of the beautiful' is a natural human aspiration as with the earliest of biological species. Indeed this instinctive 'sense of the beautiful' and an aspiration to 'beauty' were the real objective foundations of people's desires to decorate themselves and their possessions, and this was a source of decoration as a special field in fine arts. Some of these scholars considered ancient decoration as a materialized reflection of people's 'sense of rhythm' developed by a long practice of various kinds of human activity (Bücher 1896: Filippov 1937).

The founder of the 'technical' theory for the origins of decoration was the German architect G. Semper (1860-1863). Afterwards this theory obtained a very wide acceptance among scholars who thought that ancient decoration had appeared as the result of human imitation of technological traces on the surfaces of goods; in other words on the 'technological' basis (*Anon 1958*). As regards pottery decoration they thought that it had appeared as a result of the imitation of woven and basketry containers.

As I said earlier all these theories considered the problem of the origin of decoration first of all as a general cultural phenomenon without the analysis of its internal structure. Now, from the point of view of a historical-and-cultural scientific approach, it is possible to consider the same problem taking into account its internal structure.

A historical-and-cultural approach to this problem includes the study of formation processes of each of the components of the decorative tradition's structure. There are three such components: *technical-and-technological, stylistic* and *semantic*. The origin of the *technical-and-technological* component includes the investigation of the origin of various modes of pottery decoration, the origin of the *stylistic* component includes the study of the formation of decorative patterns, and the origin of the *semantic* one includes the research into the formation of certain senses of decoration on the surface of clay vessels. Thus, a full answer to the question of the origin of pottery decoration could be achieved only by means of the investigation of the whole spectrum of these problems. But at the present time this is impossible. For this reason I would like to consider here the question of the origin of the first structural component of pottery decorative traditions, namely *the origin of various modes of making pottery decoration.* It is known that about 15 such modes combined into five main directions of pottery decoration development (Tsetlin 2000, 251 – 2). Graphic pottery decoration could be created by the following six modes:

1. By impressions resulting from the relief in moulds during vessel manufacture
2. By beating out the surface of vessels with relief paddles.
3. By rolling the surface of vessels with wide relief stamps.
4. By smoothing the surface of vessels with various coarse tools.
5. By printing or impressing decoration with single stamps.
6. By cutting (incising) decoration with single- or multi-toothed edges.

What could be the probable sources or origins of all these modes of pottery decoration? Let us consider them step by step.

Printing of relief concave-forms on the surfaces of vessels.

It is well known now from both ethnographic and archaeological data that special forming moulds can be used for forming clay vessels. Ancient potters used both concave moulds as well as convex ones. When they used a concave mould clay was put inside and in this case traces of the structure of the mould's material became printed on the outside surface of vessel. Sometimes these prints were smoothed during the later treatment of vessels, but in other cases they were preserved on the surfaces of finished pots. In some ancient cultures such relief surfaces became traditional, and that is why we may need to consider it as an essential feature of a

Fig 1. Traces of relief concave-forms on clay vessels:
1-2 – Traces of leather concave mould on clay vessels, Dyakov Lob (Bobrinsky, 1978, p. 196, Fig. 77,6) and Nastas'ino – Early Iron Age, Eastern Europe. 3 – Traces of wattled concave mould on a vessel, Tell Magzalia, Mesopotamia, 7th Millennium BC (Bader, 1989, p.101, Table 37:1). 4 – Traces of coarse fabric concave mould on clay vessel, Tell Shair, Mesopotamia, 6th millennium BC.

vessel's surface: in other words it is a special kind of pottery decoration.

What kinds of materials were used by ancient potters to make concave moulds? Probably, they were various, but it has only been possible to identify moulds made of leather and of fabric. Leather moulds with relief surfaces were made of an animal's rumen skin (Fig 1:1,2) and fabric moulds (Fig 1:3) were made of a coarse material similar to sacking (Bobrinsky 1978, 193 – 209). Moreover, according to some archaeological and ethnographic data, basketry moulds made from various plant materials could also be used for making pots (Fig 1:4) (Kozhin 1967, 140 – 1; Holmes 1883, 449). It is appropriate to remember here that leather and basketry containers were widely used both by ancient peoples who had their own tradition of pottery production and those who had not.

All these facts allow one to assume that pots with such relief prints on the surfaces were made as an imitation of the leather, fabric or coarse plant fibre containers. Thus, those concave moulds had a dual function, on the one hand they were used for pottery forming, and on the other hand they served as special 'tools' for the making of surface decoration. That is why such pots can be deemed to have *technological-and-decorated* surfaces and belong

to a *partly-formed* state of pottery decoration. But similar designs on clay vessels could also be created in other ways.

Beating out the surfaces of vessels with relief paddles.
Not all of the vessels with clear imprints of leather or fabric were made in concave moulds. They were often the result of the beating out of the vessel's surface using various relief paddles on special anvils. According to the impressions observed on archaeological ceramics such relief could be achieved firstly by beating out the surfaces with paddles covered with coarse leather (Fig 2:1) (Bobrinsky, 1978, 206, fig. 86:4), fabric or cord (see, for example, Fig 2:2), and secondly by the use of special carved paddles (Fig 2:3-6) (Bobrinsky, 1978, 208, fig. 88:2).

From the technological point of view, the beating out of the surfaces of clay vessels using paddles serves to compact the vessel walls and to bind elements (such as rings or coils) from which the vessels had been made. This also increased the strength of vessels. Clearly the same results can be attained (and were attained in antiquity) by using smooth paddles and without leaving any relief traces on the vessels' surfaces. Therefore, by using relief paddles we have to consider that the potters had decided to combine two different tasks –

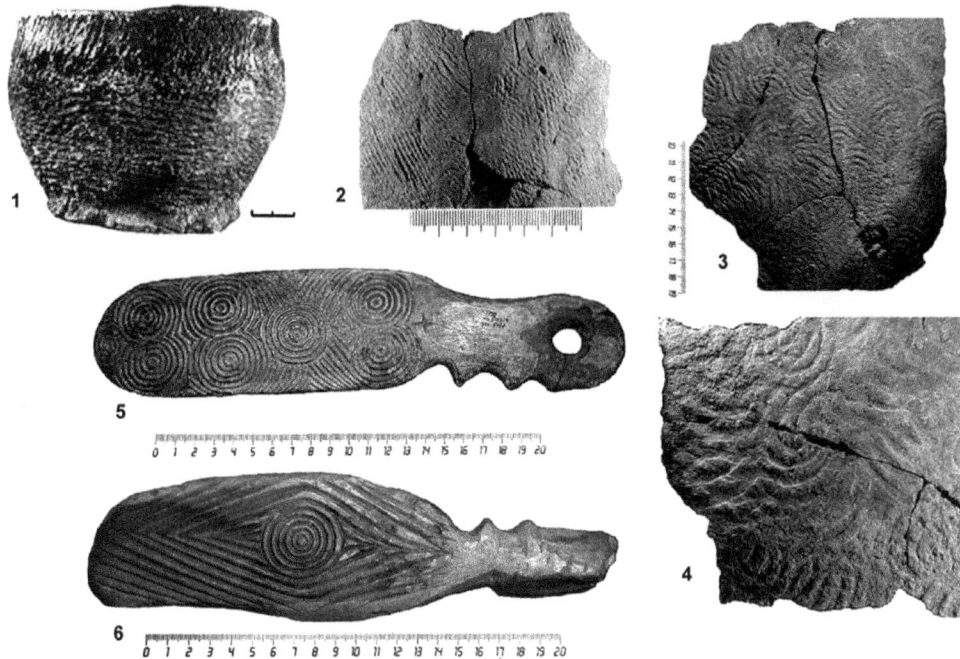

Fig. 2. Traces of beating out the vessels with relief paddles:
1 – Traces of beating out with paddle covered with rumen leather, Grafskaya Gora – Early Iron Age, Eastern Europe (Bobrinsky, 1978, p. 206, Fig. 86,4.). 2 – Traces of beating out with paddle wrapped around with twisted cord, Nastas'ino – Early Iron Age, Eastern Europe. 3-4 – Traces of beating out with carved paddle, Ekven, Chukchi Peninsula, 1st millennium AD. 5-6 – Carved paddles of walrus ivory for beating out clay vessels, Ekven, Chukchi Peninsula, 1st millennium AD.

technological and decorative at the same time. It is important to emphasize that potters often used paddles covered with the same kinds of leather that had been used for the leather moulds. These facts evidently show that the origin of these modes of pottery decoration was the result of the potters' intentions to make their pots resemble moulded forms. The vessels beaten out with relief paddles have a *technological-and-decorated* surface and reflect a *partly-formed* state of pottery decoration.

In addition, ancient potters also used some other modes for making relief-decorated pots. One of these is by *rolling* the surface of vessels with wide relief stamps.

Rolling of clay vessels with wide relief stamps
The use of wide stamps for treating pots' surfaces is well known from ethnography and archaeology (Bobrinsky, 1978, 231 – 4). Such decoration is typical, for example, on the vessels of the Gorodetskaya and Dyakovo cultures from the Early Iron Age located in the forest zone of Eastern Europe - the so-called 'matted' ceramics (Smirnov & Trubnikova, 1965, Table 6:11,12). The making of such decoration clearly shows the potters' intentions to create a special design on a vessel's surface. As Bobrinsky has written: 'more probably it appeared as an imitation of the beating out of the vessel's surface

with a paddle covered with an animal's rumen leather' (Bobrinsky, 1978, 231).

To solve the problem of the origin of this mode of surface treatment, it is necessary to focus our attention on the following observations:

1	each of the impressions has a squared shape,
2	the bases of some of the impressions are flat,
3	the size of squarish facets averages about 0,5x0,5cm or 0,5x1,0cm, and
4	the impressions were made by a stamp made from a hard material.

It is also necessary to compare the impressions on archaeological ceramics (Fig 3:1) with the experimental impressions made by wide carved stamps in clay (Fig 3:2 – 3), with examples of bast matting (Fig 3:4) (Razumovskaya, 1967, 116, Table I:8,9) and with the impressions of matting in clay (Fig 3:5). It is important to note that bast strips from 3 – 10mm wide were used for making bast shoes (Zelenin, 1991, 202 – 4). According to the above data it is possible to conclude that the structure and the size of impressions on both the ancient ceramics and on the experimental samples rolled with carved stamps are very similar to the bast impressions but not to leather.

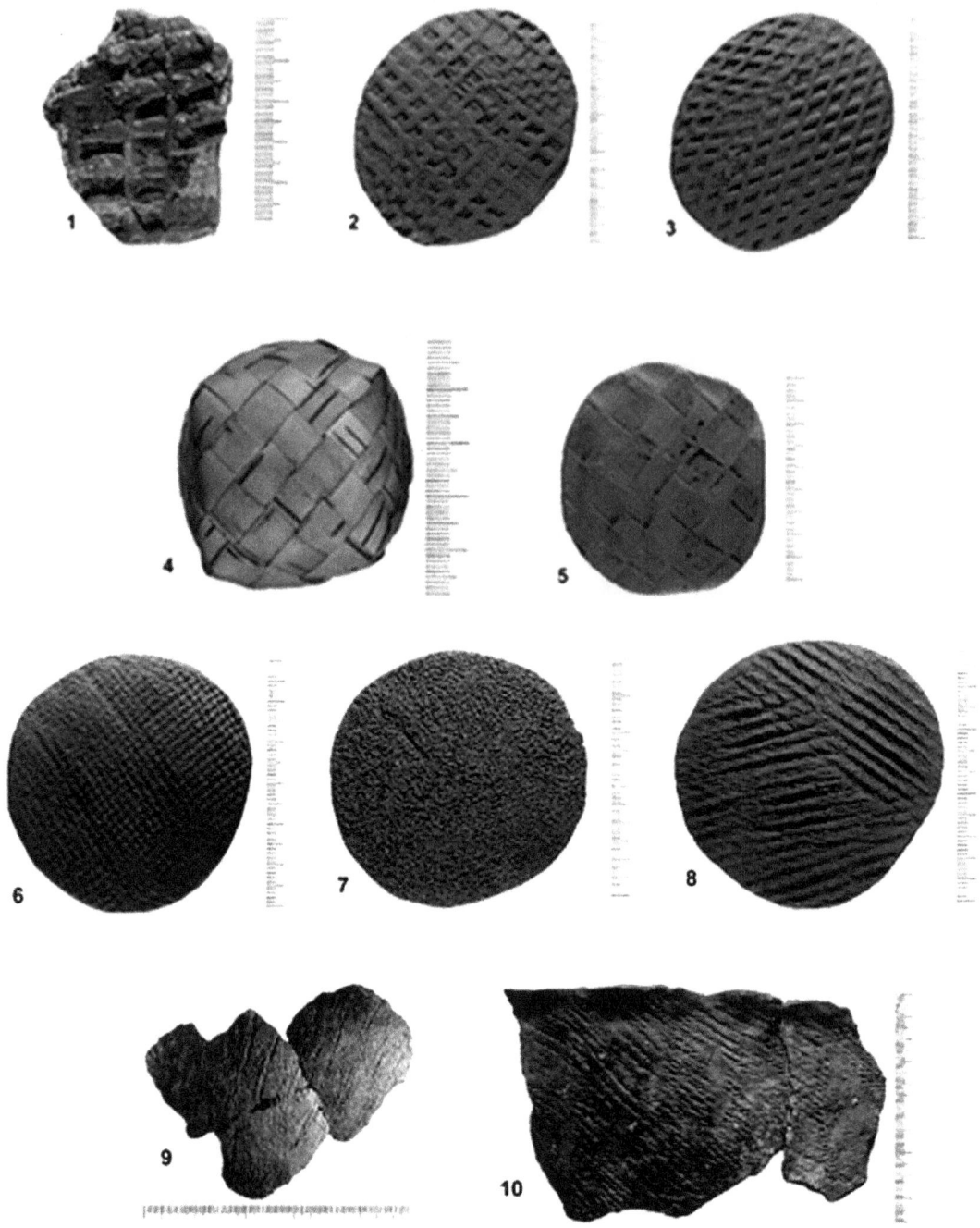

Fig. 3. Traces of rolling of clay vessels with wide relief stamps and sample of bast mat:
1 – Traces of rolling with wide relief stamp, Nastas'ino – Early Iron Age, Eastern Europe. 2-3 – Traces of rolling with wood carved stamps (experimental samples).4 – Woven basket of bast. 5 – Traces of rolling with wattled stamp (clay experimental sample). 6 – Traces of rolling with wide stamp covered with coarse fabric like mat (clay experimental sample). 7 - Traces of rolling with wide stamp covered with animal's rumen leather (clay experimental sample). 8 – Traces of rolling with wide stamp wrapped around with twisted cord (clay experimental sample). 9-10 - Traces of rolling with wide relief stamp wrapped around with twisted cord, Nastas'ino, Early Iron Age, Eastern Europe.

All these facts show that in this case the use of wide relief stamps for surface treatment was a deliberate attempt by the potter to simulate a basketry or bast effect. This kind of surface treatment could not only be made with carved stamps but also with paddles or rolls covered with fabric (Fig 3:6), leather (Fig 3:7), or twisted cord (Fig 3:8). This last-named tool was used for the treatment of some vessels from the Dyakovo culture (Fig 3:9-10) and it is quite possible that in this case the ancient potters had intended to imitate earlier moulded pots.

Because the use of wide stamps had a special decorative

Fig. 4. Traces of coarse smoothing of clay vessels:
1 – Traces of coarse smoothing with animal's rumen leather, Brest-Trishin cemetery, Iron Age, Eastern Europe (Bobrinsky, 1978, p. 233, Fig. 97, 5). 2 – Traces of coarse smoothing with wisp of grass, Lithuanian group of Stroked Ware Culture. 3-5 – Traces of coarse smoothing with comb stamp: 3 – Odoevskie Fermy, Eneolithic Age, Eastern Europe, 4 - Nastas'ino, Early Iron Age, Eastern Europe, 5 – Jomon Culture, 10-7th millennium BC, Japan.

function, the surface of such clay vessels must be characterised in all cases as being in a *fully-formed* state of decoration.

But similar prints on clay vessels could also be made by smoothing the surfaces with special tools.

Coarse smoothing of clay vessels
From the archaeological data we can recognise a few methods of coarse smoothing:

a   with an animal's rumen leather (Fig 4:1) (Bobrinsky, 1978, 232 – 3, fig 97:4),
b   with a wisp of grass or straw (Fig 4:2), and
c   with comb stamps (Fig 4:3 – 5).

Coarse smoothing was widely practised among the people of the Stroked Ware Culture in Lithuania and Bellarus from the Iron Age (Bobrinsky, 1978, 218) but ceramics with this kind of smoothing had originally appeared in the Neolithic (Loze, 1988, Table XLIX, fig 12,15).

From the technological point of view coarse and flat smoothing are quite the same technique yet produce different results and for this reason we can consider coarse smoothing as a special fully-formed mode of pottery decoration. In the opinion of Alexander

Bobrinsky 'the smoothing with grass or straw probably appeared as a result of the imitation of an earlier method of smoothing using an animal's rumen leather' (Bobrinsky, 1978, 218). This idea can possibly be developed by considering coarse smoothing as one of the final evolutionary steps away from the incipient moulded impressions.

Decoration of clay vessels with single stamps
The use of single stamps must in all cases be a special mode of pottery decoration. It was most widely distributed in pottery production from the Neolithic, at least in Eastern Europe. Moreover there were a multitude of archaeological cultures dating from the Early Neolithic with ceramics covered in continuous stamped decoration. These facts allow us to suppose that such decoration could appear in any sphere of pottery production in complete, fully developed state. The difficulties in reconstructing the prehistory of stamped decoration rise from the almost complete absence of any archaeological objects (besides pottery) employing such decoration and for this reason we have to use some ethnographic data to help determine its origins.

According to the ethnographic data from Siberia collected and studied by the Russian scholar S.V.Ivanov (Ivanov 1961, 369 – 429) it is known that special stamps were used to decorate the objects of *soft* materials, such

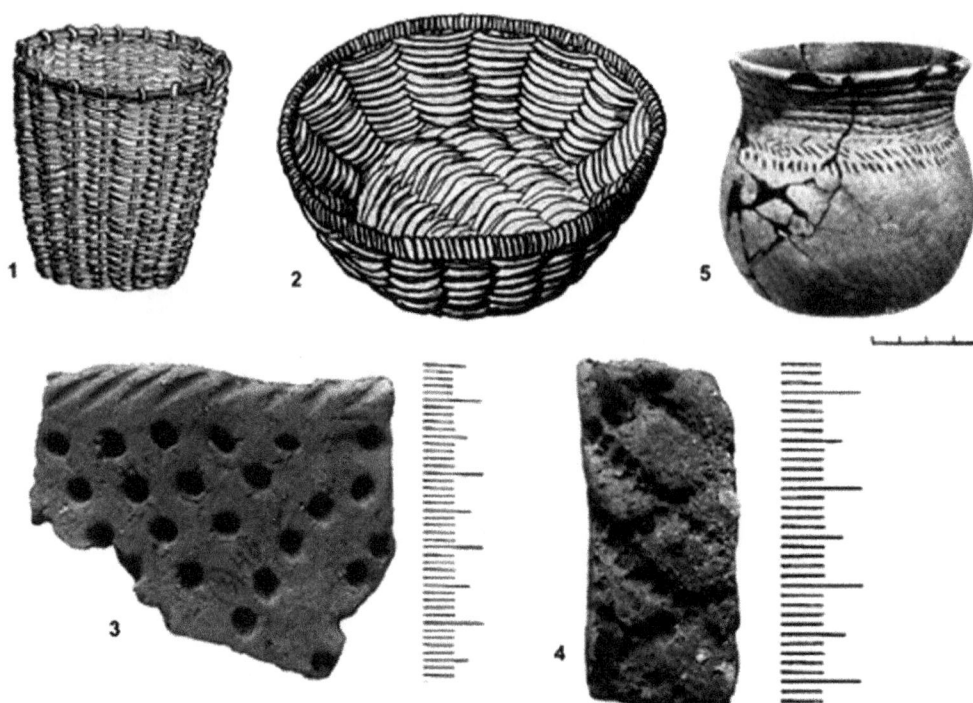

Fig. 5. Baskets and traces of single stamps on clay vessels:
1-2 – Various kinds of wickered rims of baskets (Donets E., Rachkov P. 1994, p. 71, Fig. 61; p. 86, Fig. 75). 3-4 – Traces of flat and comb prints on the rims of Neolithic vessels which imitate wickered baskets' rims (3 – Ivanovskoe III, Pit-and-Comb Ware Culture; 4 – Ivanovskoe VII, Volosovo Culture). 5 – Traces of cord prints on the rim and neck of a vessel from the Olochinskiy cemetery, Fatyanovo Culture (Kraynov, 1964, Tabl. XXIV.1).

as birchbark (50%), leather (25%), and clay (25%). Thus stamping as a special mode of decoration in all cases is connected by its use on soft materials. There are some other examples of the close connection between all these kinds of materials. For example, baskets often have bound and thickened rims to make them stronger (Fig 5:1 – 2) (Donets & Rachkov, 1994, 71, fig 61; 86, fig 75). At the same time a lot of clay vessels have similar features. Here I have in mind the impressions of flat, comb or cord stamps over the edges of thickened pot rims (Fig 5:3 – 4). It is most likely that in these cases ancient potters were imitating the earlier tradition of braiding over the whole rims of woven vessels in order to make them stronger.

The links between the use of single stamps and leather containers already discussed above are confirmed by many Bronze Age vessels which are decorated on the neck with horizontal lines of cord impressions (Fig 5:5). Furthermore, Helena V.Volkova (1998) has demonstrated experimentally that cord was used very widely during the manufacture of clay vessels of the Fatyanovo culture belonging to the family of Corded Wares and Battle Axes Cultures.

All these facts lead me to suggest that ancient potters borrowed the use of single stamps from the traditions of basketry and leatherwork.

Incision of decoration on clay vessels with single- or multi-toothed tools

The difference between incised and stamped decoration is mainly one of dynamics. Incised as well as stamped decoration appeared from the very beginning of pottery production, but stamped decoration was not so common in the Early Neolithic. Nevertheless, incised decoration is known on the vessels of the Sotto and Hassuna cultures, from Jarmo, Jericho B, the Cretan Neolithic, and so forth dating to the 7th-5th millennium BC (see for example, Fig 6:1 – 3).

To resolve the problem regarding the origin of incised decoration on ceramics, we need to determine what other kinds of materials had been decorated in this way. An ethnographic study in Siberia showed that the native Siberians had used incision to decorate objects of bone (48%), wood (33%), birchbark (15%) and metal (4%) (Ivanov, 1961, 369 – 429). Generally speaking, therefore, incision was used to decorate hard materials (85%) and as less common on softer ones (15%) such as bichbark. Furthermore, during the Neolithic and earlier (in the 10th - 7th millennium BC) incised decoration was also widely distributed on stone vessels from the Near East and other regions (Mellaart 1975, 129 – 32: Redman 1978, 74, fig 3-12:Q,R: Bader 1989, 201 – 33: Rosenberg & Davis 1992, 1 – 18: Stordeur 2000, 33 – 60: Özkaya, San & Yildizhan 2002, 739 – 57).

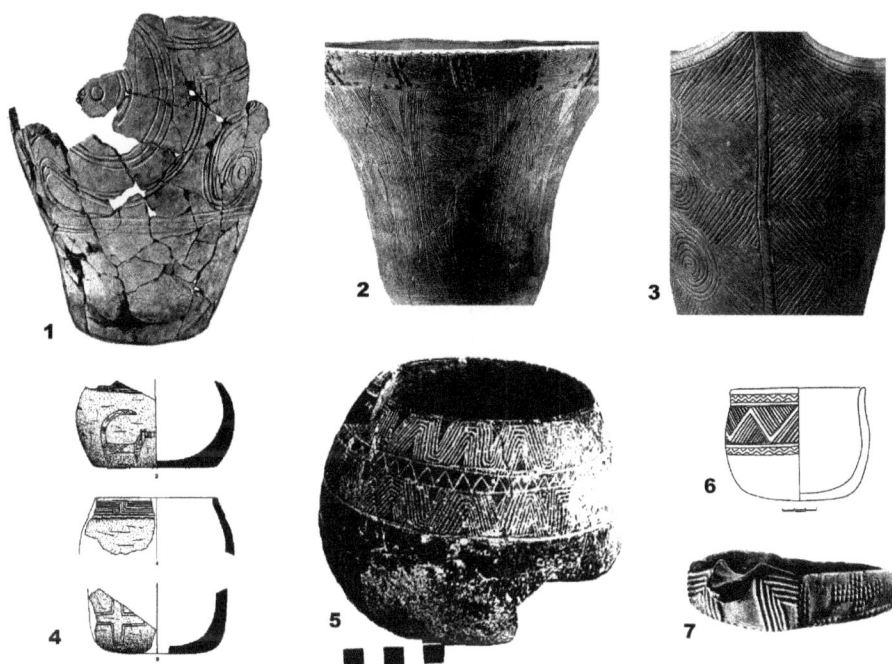

Fig. 6. Clay and stone vessels with carved decoration:
1-3 – Clay vessels with carved decoration: 1 – Neolithic culture of Lower Amur, (Okladnikov, 1984, p. 120, Table LXII.2); 2–3 – Jomon Culture, 5th-3rd and 2nd-1st millennium BC (Clay Objects of Ancient Japan, 2001, p. 29, Fig. 28; p. 60, Fig. 86). 4-7 – Earliest stone vessels with carved decoration from the Near East and Cyprus (4 – Rosenberg and Davis, 1992, p.15, Fig. 8: 2, 4, 6; 5 – Özkaya, San & Yildizhan, 2002, p.748, Fig. 9, 10; 6 – Stordeur, 2000, p. 52, Fig. 10: 12; 7 – Khirokitia – Mellaart, 1975, p. 132, Fig. 77.).

In summarizing the archaeological and ethnographic data it is possible to conclude that incised or carved decoration was mostly typical on hard materials such as stone, bone, and wood. So, it is most likely that incision as a mode of decoration had appeared very early outside of pottery production and was later adopted by potters from craftsmen working with hard non-clay materials – probably, such as the stone vessels (Fig 6:4 – 7).

Main results

First of all it is necessary to emphasize that the conformation of modes of graphic pottery decoration was a long process developed in two main directions: *first* – the making of clay vessels with technological-and-decorated surfaces and *second* – the making of clay vessels with deliberately decorated surfaces.

The *First Direction* includes the modes with a dual nature. On the one hand these modes were a necessary part of pottery making, and on the other hand they added the special design to clay vessels by which the users could define their own vessels from foreign ones.

The conformation process of the subsequent modes of graphic pottery decoration took place within the first direction:

1   The use of relief concave moulds, the impre-

ssions from which were preserved on the surface of the pots.

2   Beating out the visual surfaces of clay vessels with relief paddles, the use of these modes reflecting a *partly-formed* state of pottery decoration development.

The *Second Direction* included the formulation of modes of deliberate decoration. Here the first aim was to make an absolutely new design by covering pots' surfaces with special decoration. This was done by the following methods:

3   Rolling the visible surfaces with wide relief stamps.

4   Coarse smoothing of visible surfaces.

5   Stamping of decoration on the visible surfaces using single stamps.

6   Incising or cutting decoration into the visible surfaces of vessels using single-tooth or multi-toothed tools.

These modes reflected an already fully-formed state in the development of pottery decoration. Furthermore, it is necessary to note that on the basis of modes formed inside the first direction there later appeared two other modes (3 and 4) used for making decorated surfaces which represent mould materials.

The next question arising from these results is why do the

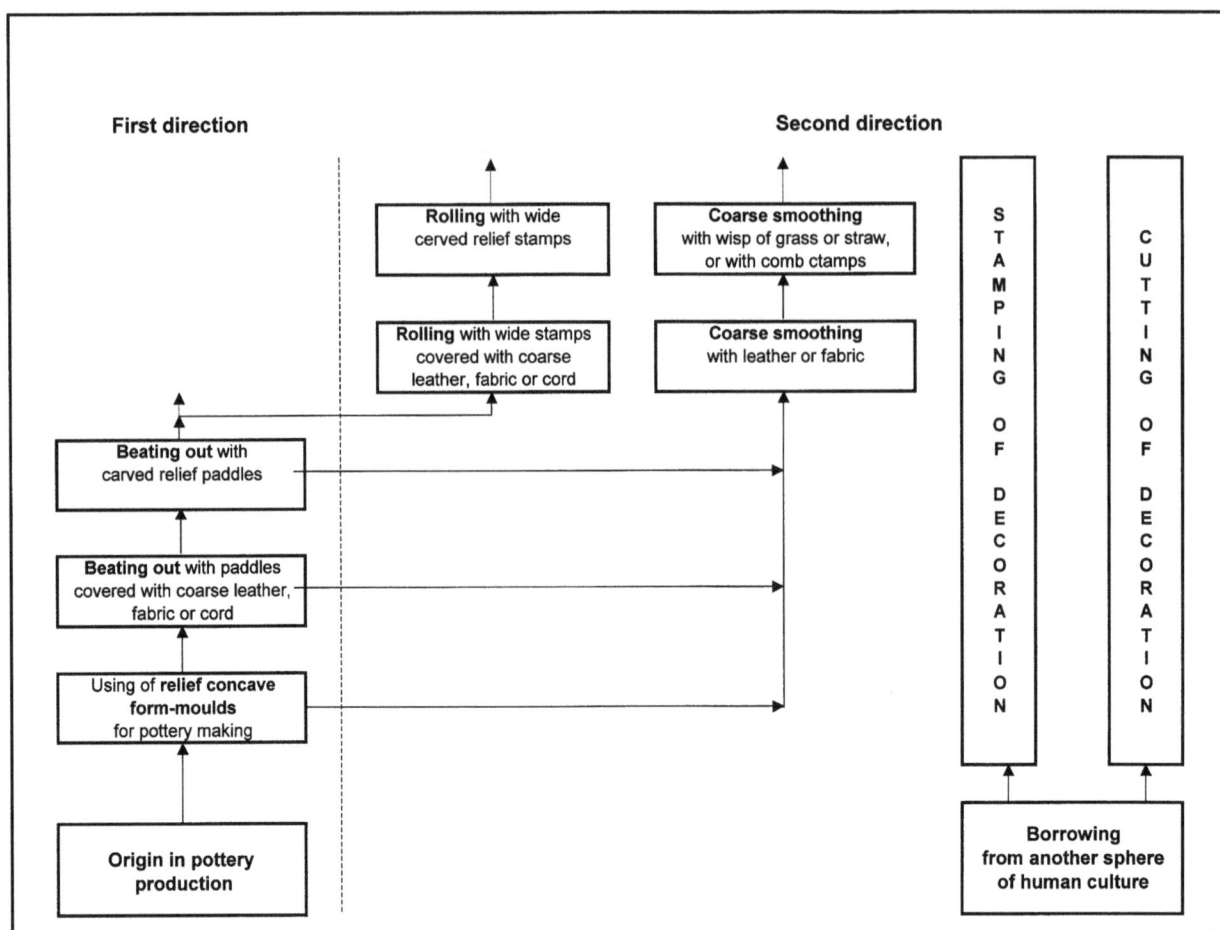

Fig. 7. Main directions and steps of origin and development of graphic modes of pottery decoration

main modes of making the technological-and-decorated surfaces of clay vessels apparently belong to some later time than the modes of making of material decorated surfaces? Indeed both the impressions of concave moulds and of beating out vessels with relief paddles (first direction), and of rolling decoration with wide relief stamps (second direction) were widely spread on vessels from the Bronze and Iron Ages, but clay vessels with coarse smoothing surfaces and with stamped and carved decoration appeared from the Neolithic. The reason for this apparent contradiction is that (as I had noted above) all modes of making graphic technological-and-decorated surfaces on clay vessels were formed during the history of pottery production itself, but the main modes of making a really graphic decoration were introduced into pottery production in a finished state from other fields of human culture. Therefore a general evolution of the modes of graphic pottery decoration might be represented by the following steps (Fig 7).

The modes appearing in pottery production
First direction

Step 1a The use of relief concave moulds for pottery making.

Step 2 Beating out the visible surfaces of clay vessels with paddles covered with coarse leather, fabric or cord.

Step 3 Beating out the visible surfaces of clay vessels with carved relief paddles.

Second direction

Step 4a Rolling of visible clay surfaces with wide stamps covered with coarse leather, fabric, or cord.

Step 5 Rolling of visible clay surfaces with wide carved relief stamps.

Step 4b Coarse smoothing of visible clay surfaces with leather or fabric.

Step 5b Coarse smoothing of visible clay surfaces with wisps of grass or straw or with comb stamps.

The modes borrowed from other fields of human culture
Second direction

Step 1b The use of single stamps for impressed pottery decoration.

Step 1c The use of single- or multi-toothed tools for incised pottery decoration.

8

All these steps are seen both in a general succession of the modes of pottery decoration and their long-time coexistence in other media during a real human history process.

On the basis of all the considered data it is possible to conclude firstly, that the graphic decoration of clay vessels had originally appeared from an objective technical-and-technological basis and could only later be explained as subjective, being derived from real social conditions, and secondly, was a mechanism by which new modes of decoration could be seen as an aspiration of ancient potters to imitate earlier and contemporary non-clay and clay artefacts.

Acknowledgements

I would like to express my gratitude to Dr. Helena V.Volkova (History of Ceramics Laboratory, Institute of Archaeology, Moscow, Russia), my long time colleague, for very useful discussions on ancient pottery decoration, Dr. Marie Le Miere (CNRS - Archeorient, Lyon, France) for continuous help with archaeological literature, Dr. Kirill A.Dneprovsky (Moscow State Museum of Oriental Art, Russia) for his kind permission to use the photographs of carved paddles and pottery sherds from Ekven (Chukchi Peninsula), and to Dr. Alex Gibson (Bradford University, United Kingdom) for his kind invitation to the conference "Prehistoric Ceramics: Resent Research" and for his hospitality in Bradford and Ilkley.

References

Anon, 1958. *A History of Technology.* Vol 1. London.

Bader, O.N., 1989. *Earliest Cultivators in Northern Mesopotamia. The Investigations of Soviet Archaeological Expedition in Iraq at Settlements Tell Magzaliya, Tell Sotto, Kűl Tepe.* Moscow. (in Rus.)

Bobrinsky, A.A., 1978. *Pottery of the Eastern Europe. Sources and Methods of Study.* Moscow. (in Rus.)

Bobrinsky, A.A., 1987. *Bronze Age in the Forest Zone of the USSR. Archaeology of the USSR.* Moscow. (in Rus.)

Bücher, K., 1896. *Arbeit und Rhythmus.* Leipzig.

Bücher, K., 2001. *Clay Objects of Ancient Japan. From Jomon and Yayoi Periods.* Tokyo: National Museum.

Donets E. & Rachkov, P., 1994. *Wicker-work of Withe and Bast.* Moscow. (in Rus.)

Filippov, A.V., 1937. *Creation of Decoration with Many Kinds of Variants.* Moscow. (in Rus.)

Grosse, E., 1894. *Die Anfänge der Kunst.* Leipzig.

Holmes, W.H., 1883. *Origin and Development of Form and Ornament in Ceramic Art.* Bureau of Ethnology, 437 – 65. Washington: Smithsonian Institution.

Ivanov, S.V., 1961. *Ornament. Historical-and-Ethnographical Atlas of Siberia.* Moscow-Leningrad. (in Rus.)

Kozhin, P.M., 1967. Ceramics of Pueblo Indians. In: *Culture and Life of American Peoples,*140 – 46. Sbornik Museya Anthropologii i Ethnographii, 24. Leningrad (in Rus.)

Kraynov, D.A., 1964. The Sites of Fatyanovo Culture. Yaroslavle-and-Kalinin Group. *Svod Archeologicheskih Istochnikov,* B1-20. Moscow. (in Rus.)

Loze, I.A., 1988. *Stone Age Population in the Lubanskaya Plain. Mesolithic, early and Middle Neolithic.* Riga. (in Rus.)

Schtenberg, L.Ya., 1936. *Primitive Religion in the Light of Ethnography.* Leningrad. (in Rus.)

Mellaart, J., 1975. *The Neolithic of the Near East.* New York: Scribner.

Okladnikov, A.P., 1984. *Ceramics of Kondon's Ancient Population (Amur Basin).* Novosibirsk. (in Rus.)

Osborn, H.F., 1916. *Men of the Old Stone Age.* New York: Scribner.

Özkaya V., San O. & Yildizhan, H., 2002. Excavations at Kortik Tepe: 2000. *Salvage Project of the Archaeological Heritage of the Ilisu and Carchemish Dam Reservoirs Activities in 2000,* 739 – 57. Ankara.

Popov, L.K., 1880. *Of Primitive Human Life.* St.Peterburg. (in Rus.)

Razumovskaya, R.S., 1967. Wattled goods of the north-western Indians. In: *Culture and Life of American Peoples,* 93 – 123. Sbornik Museya Anthropologii i Ethnographii. 24. Leningrad. (in Rus.)

Redman, Ch.L., 1978. *The Rise of Civilization. From Early Farmers to Urban Society in the Ancient Near East.* San Francisco: W H Freeman.

Rosenberg, M. & Davis, M.K., 1992. Hallan Çemi Tepesi, an early aceramic Neolithic site in Eastern Anatolia: Some preliminary observations concerning material culture. *Anatolia,* 18, 1 – 18.

Schternberg, L.Ya., 1936. *Primitive Religion in the Light of Ethnography.* Leningrad. (in Rus.)

Semper, G. 1860-1863. *Der Stil in den Technischen und Tektonishen Künsten.* Bd. 1-2, Berlin. (second edition – 1872).

Smirnov, A.P. & Trubnikova, N.V., 1965. Gorodetskaya Culture. *Svod Archeologicheskih Istochnikov,* D1-14. Moscow. (in Rus.)

Stephan, E., 1907. *Südseekundst. Beitrag zur Kunst des Bismarck-Archipels und zur Urgeschichte der Kunst überhaupt.* Berlin.

Stordeur, D., 2000. Jerf el Ahmar et l'Émergence du Néolithique en Proche Orient: Premiers Paysans du Monde. *Naissances des Agricultures,* 33 – 60. Paris.

Tsetlin, Y.B., 2000. The criteria of definition between decorated and undecorated ceramics. *Tverskoy Archeologicheskiy Sbornic,* 4.1, 251 – 9. (in Rus.)

Voevodsky, M.V., 1936. On the investigation of pottery technology of primitive-and- communist society in the region of forest zone of the European part of the RSFSR. *Soviet Archaeology,* 1, 51-77. Moscow-Leningrad. (in Rus.)

Volkova, H.V., 1998. Role of Experiment in the

Reconstruction of Fatyanovo Pottery Technology. *Tverskoy Archaeologicheskiy Sbornik*, 3, 125 – 34. (in Rus.)

Zelenin, D.K., 1991. *The Ethnography of Eastern Slavonic*. Moscow. (1st edition in 1927 in German)

CHAPTER 2

Pottery Deposition at Hambledon Hill

Frances Healy

Introduction

Hambledon Hill lies in north-east Dorset, at NGR ST 849 122, 35 km from coast to which it is linked by the river Stour. It is at the western margin of Cranborne Chase, where Mesolithic, Neolithic and Bronze Age settlement, land use, and ceremonial practice have been exceptionally well documented by the pioneering work of General Pitt-Rivers in the nineteenth and early twentieth centuries (Bowden 1984) and by more recent investigations (Barrett *et al.* 1991; Green 2000). The hill forms part of the north-west scarp of the Wessex chalk, at its boundary with the very different landscape of south-western England: to the west and north-west the chalk gives way to Greensand, Gault and the low-lying Blackmoor Vale, based mainly on Kimmeridge and Oxford Clays, beyond which rises the Jurassic ridge (Fig 1). The hill is a striking landform, consisting of a central dome from which extend three main spurs (Fig 2). The entire hill, almost 2km long, is occupied by a complex of earthworks built in the fourth millennium cal BC, including two long barrows, one of the largest causewayed enclosures in Britain (the main enclosure, on the central dome), and one of the smallest (the Stepleton enclosure, on the tip of the southern spur). In addition to these there are cross-dykes cutting off the spurs, and linear outworks around the less steep parts of the hill, one of them extending along the west side of the northern spur, almost obscured by the ramparts of an Iron Age hillfort. Alex Bayliss' Bayesian modelling of 161 radiocarbon dates has shown that the earthworks were built episodically over a period of 310–370 years, between 3680–3630 and 3340–3300 cal BC, the older ones remaining in use as the later ones were constructed (Fig 3; Bayliss *et al.* forthcoming).

Roger Mercer's large-scale investigations, conducted between 1974 and 1986, have yielded a wealth of evidence (Mercer & Healy forthcoming). This paper is primarily concerned with the Neolithic Bowl pottery which, at 26032 sherds/96785g, is one of the largest assemblages of this tradition in Britain, second only to that from Windmill Hill in Wiltshire (Smith 1965; Zienkiewicz 1999). In the 1980s the assemblage was the subject of a magisterial analysis by Isobel Smith (forthcoming), in the course of which she selected 43 sherds, representative of the fabrics which she had identified, for thin-sectioning undertaken by Timothy Darvill in the course of his PhD research (1983; forthcoming). In the 1990s the pottery was quantified and recorded in greater detail by Rachael Seager Smith. The results and interpretations offered here are based on the

work of all three. The assemblage is morphologically similar to that from Maiden Castle, also in Dorset (Cleal 1991): essentially of the South-Western style, dominated by unshouldered, neutral forms with simple rims, and with fairly frequent lugs. There are also elements of the heavier-rimmed Decorated style more prevalent farther east (Smith forthcoming).

Fabrics

The main fabric groups are shown in Figs 4 & 5, compared in the first of these with the results of Cleal's review of Bowl fabrics in Wessex, the sample for which did not include the Hambledon Hill material. Flint, virtually ubiquitous in Wessex, is the most frequent temper in both samples. Even the flint-tempered wares from Hambledon, however, seem to have been brought to the hill rather than made there, since the clay matrix of the six thin-sectioned sherds was matched in Kimmeridge Clay from the Blackmoor Vale some 2km to the north-west Fig 1), rather than in Clay-with-Flints from the hilltop itself (Darvill forthcoming); in the Maiden Castle area, samples from the Clay-with-Flints equally failed to match fabrics from the enclosure (Cleal 1991, 173). It is worth noting the caveat of Morris and Woodward (2003, 297) that even vessels in potentially local fabrics like this may have been transported some distance.

Of the two main non-flint fabric groups at Hambledon, one, red pellets, is of unknown source and the other, calcareous, is non-local. The first is characterised by a natural inclusion: numerous small, roughly spherical, iron-rich clay pellets set in a fine-grained slightly micaceous clay matrix with a light scatter of well-sorted subangular quartz grains. Iron staining is widespread within the matrix as a whole. The main added filler is flint, although crushed land mollusc shell, chalk, sandstone, crushed quartz or quartzite and fresh shell were also used (Darvill forthcoming). It is noteworthy that, diverse as these inclusions are, none of them derives from the Jurassic ridge to the north and west. In pots of this fabric group 'surface treatment seems usually to have been confined to a perfunctory hand-smoothing, with little attempt to reduce irregularities. Some bowls are markedly asymmetrical and clumsy, and the standard appears low in comparison with products attributed to other fabric groups' (Smith forthcoming). The fabric is difficult to match among published Neolithic Bowl assemblages. The closest is Cleal's fabric FFe:1 from Maiden Castle, with moderate to dense flint and rare to sparse dusty red, rounded ferruginous inclusions. This,

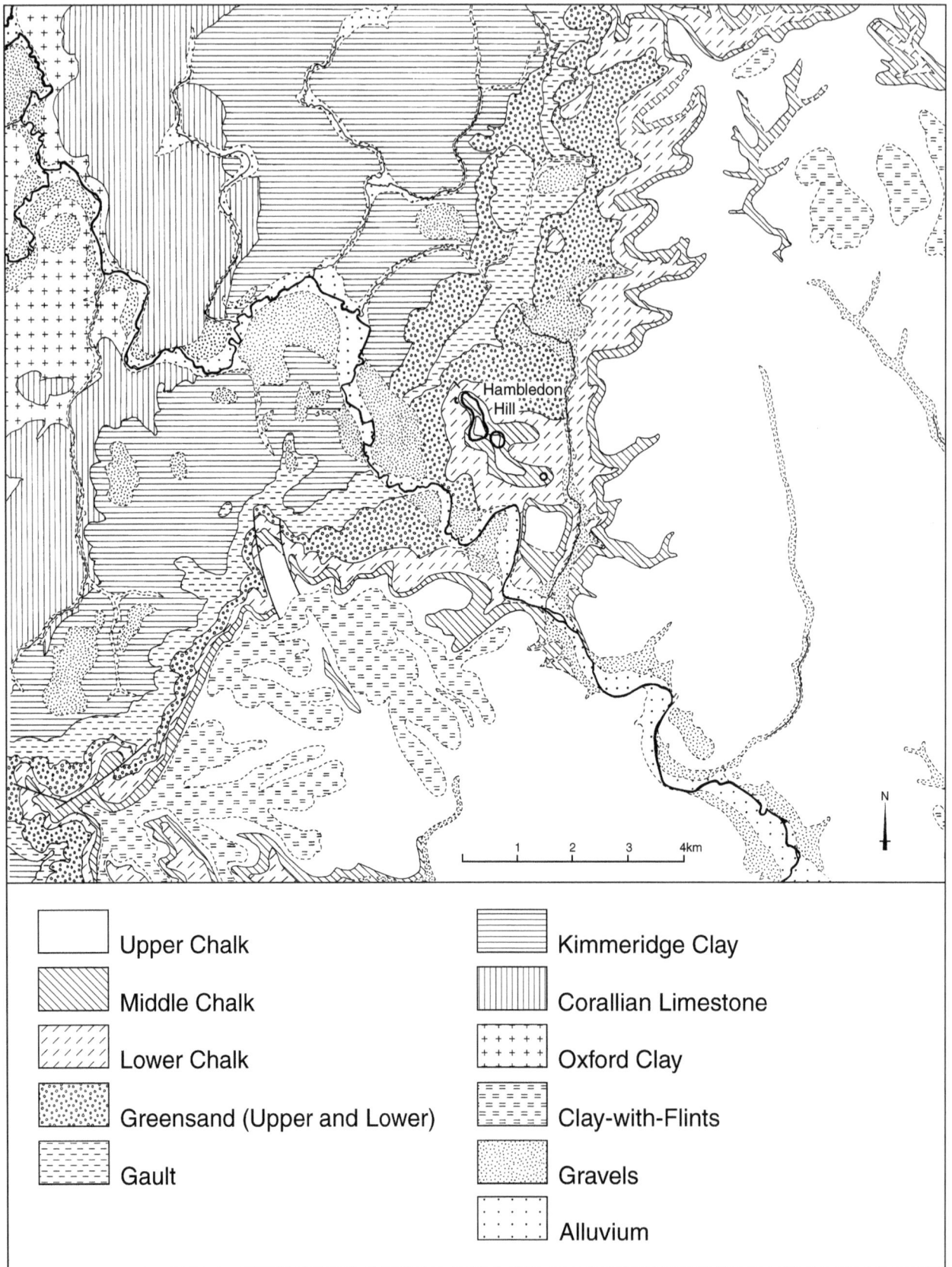

Fig 1. Hambledon Hill. Geology of the surrounding area.

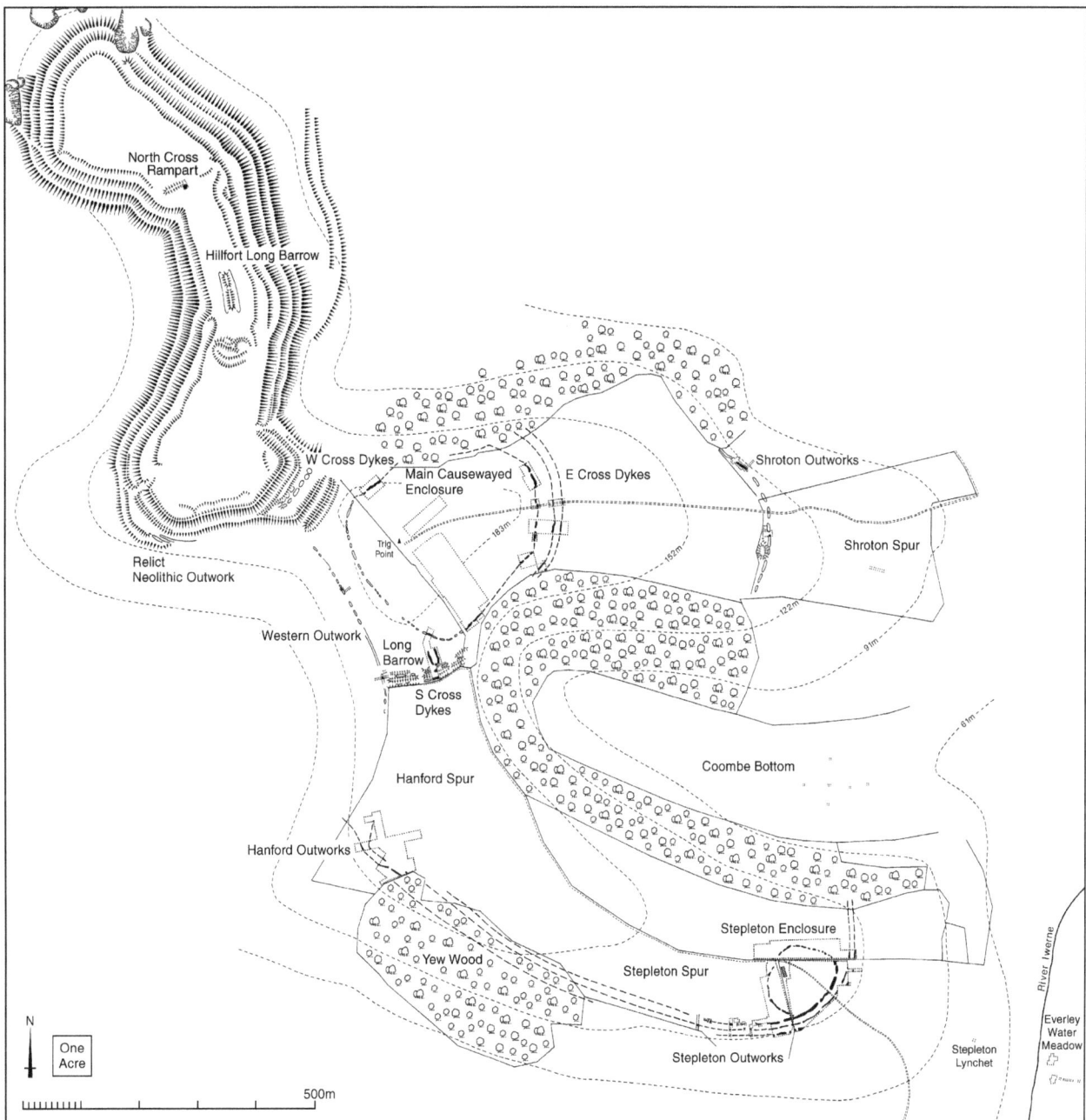

Fig 2. Hambledon Hill. Earthworks and location of 1974–86 excavations.

however, accounts for only a minute amount of the assemblage (Cleal 1991, microfiche M9:A9, M9:C13–C14), while the red pellet fabrics make up a large part of the Hambledon pottery (Figs 4–5). Darvill could find no match among local clays, but thought that the mineralogy and texture of the matrix hinted at a riverine source. If the clay were after all local to the Hambledon, it might be expected to recur in later ceramics, but haematite and unidentified small rounded pellets occur only very rarely in the predominantly flint-, sand- and calcareous-tempered early Iron Age fabrics from the hillfort on the north spur of the hill (Brown forthcoming). Roe (forthcoming) suggests a source in what is now the heathland of south-east Dorset, between Wareham and

Poole, at least 20km from Hambledon, where red clays are interbedded with sandstones (Bristow et al. 1991, 23 – 32). If this is the case, however, it is curious that the same clays do not seem to have been used in the significant Iron Age and Romano-British pottery industry of the same area (Brown 1987; Brown 1991; Davies 1986; Lancely & Morris 1991; Seager Smith 1993; Seager Smith 1997). Given the amount of Neolithic Bowl pottery known from Wessex, the lack of matches for this fabric prompts the reflection that it might even have been made specifically for use at Hambledon.

The third main fabric group is characterised by calcareous inclusions, almost entirely derived from the

13

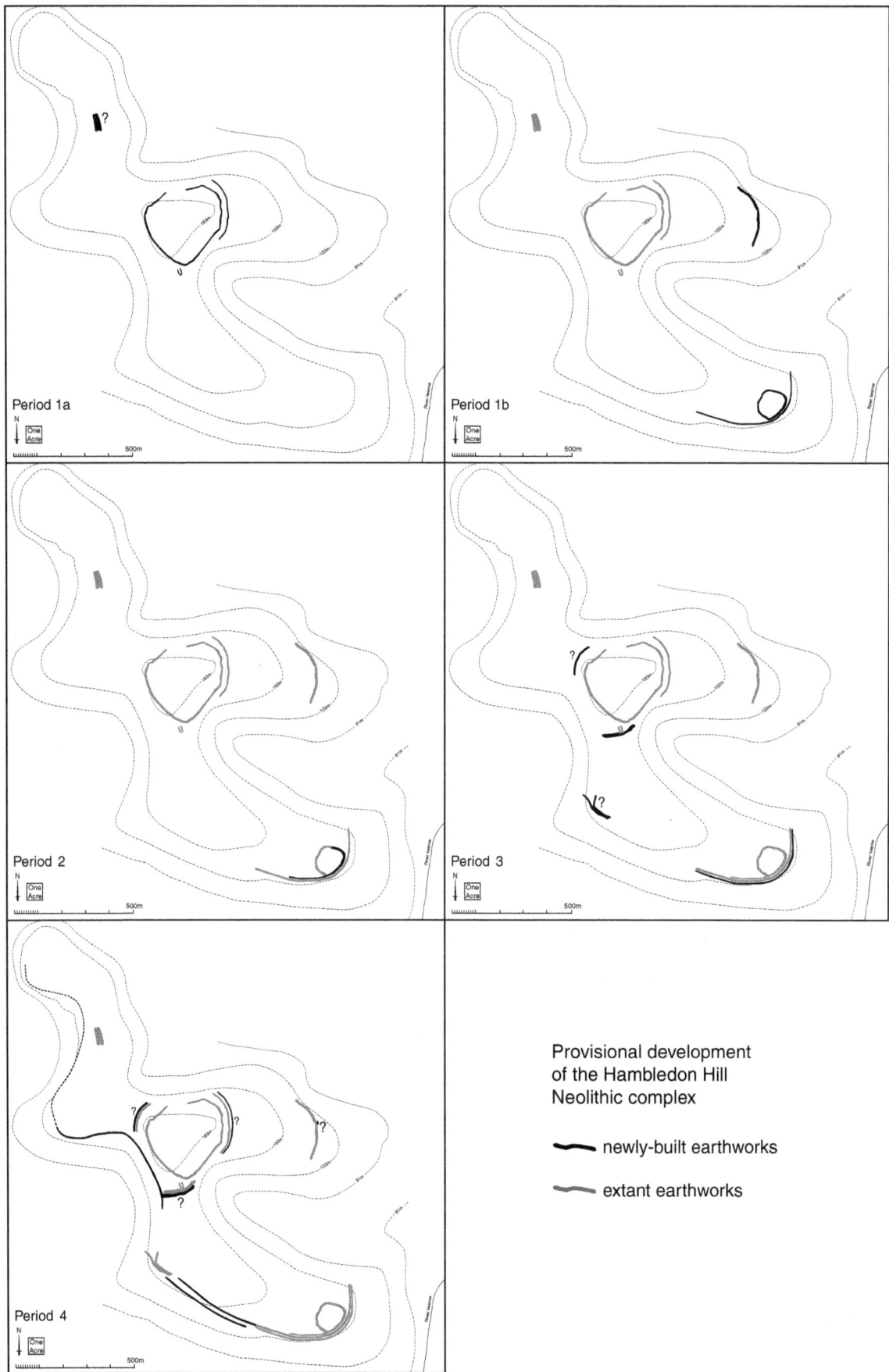

Fig 3. Hambledon Hill. Development of the Neolithic complex.

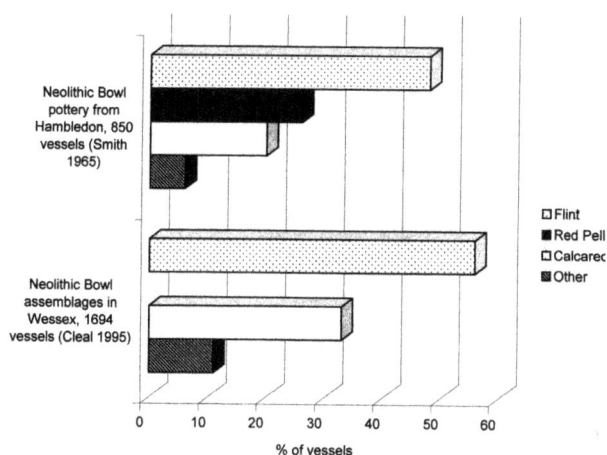

Fig 4. The main fabric groups identified among Neolithic Bowls from Hambledon Hill (Smith forthcoming) and in published assemblages from Wessex (Cleal 1995).

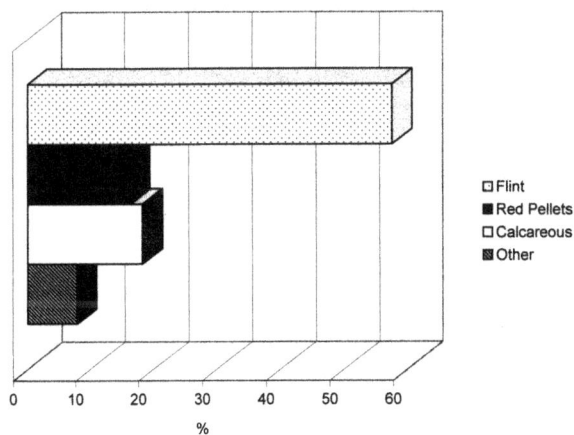

Fig 5. The main fabric groups of Neolithic Bowl pottery from all contexts at Hambledon Hill as percentages of total weight. 'Calcareous' is made up of Jurassic limestone debris consisting mainly of fossil shell (14%), Jurassic limestone debris consisting mainly of ooliths (2%), calcite (1%), and fresh shell with flint (1%); 'other' is made up of sand (4%), Gabbroic inclusions (2%), burnt- or leached-out organic inclusions (1%), and sandstone (0.3%).

Jurassic ridge 25 – 60km to the west and north-west of the hill. Fossil shell is the most frequent of these, with smaller quantities of ooliths. The fabrics are varied, sometimes combining shell and ooliths and incorporating small quantities of other inclusions, among them calcite, flint, rock containing re-crystallised ooliths, and other limestone fragments. These pots were well-made and well-finished. Darvill provides an insight into the practice of potting in this area by showing that adjacent coils of one sherd are in different fabrics (Fig 6). In other words, clays collected from different sites and/or prepared in different ways were both to hand at the location where the pot was made.

Cleal's overview (1995) is a reminder of how much

pottery from the Jurassic ridge was transported into Wessex in the fourth millennium. The widespread dispersal of these wares, their relatively high quality, and the fact that the technological problems of firing fabrics with calcareous inclusions, which are prone to spall or even disintegrate, were successfully overcome (Cleal 1995, 191), would all be compatible with a focus of relatively specialised pottery production along the Jurassic ridge. Darvill suggests (2004) that one of the reasons for the selection of fabrics with Jurassic and other 'soft-rock' inclusions (as well as organic ones) is that pots made from them, while less effective cooking vessels than those in 'hard-rock' fabrics, are suited to the storage of temperature-sensitive liquids like milk, blood, or water, because of the cooling effect of moisture evaporating through their porous walls. This accords with evidence for dairying in the fourth millennium cal. BC (Copley *et al.* 2003; Copley *et al.* forthcoming; Legge forthcoming). It does not, however, account for the frequently high quality of Jurassic wares in Wessex, or with the porosity of even the 'hard rock' fabrics of the period. Comparison of the relatively small number of specific lipid identifications from Hambledon (Copley *et al.* forthcoming) with the fabrics of the sherds on which they were made does not show any correlation between contents and fabric.

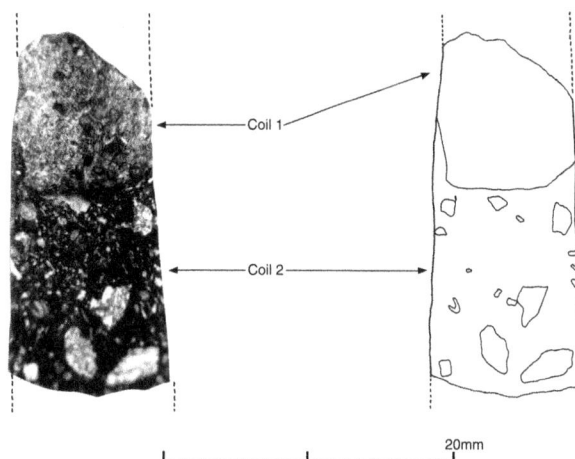

Fig 6. Photomicrograph and interpretative drawing of the polished face of sherd HH74 667 from the main enclosure showing a coil junction and the contrasting fabrics used for each coil (ooliths with some fossil shell and calcite in coil 1 and fossil shell with some limestone in coil 2). By Timothy Darvill.

Substantially represented pots

Most Bowl pottery at Hambledon was highly fragmented by the time it was deposited. Semi-complete vessels, the obvious examples of which are listed in the Appendix at the end of this paper, were the exception. Most of these occurred in the same contexts as small, abraded, unattributable sherds, the reverse of the situation obtaining in the causewayed enclosure at Etton, Cambridgeshire, where artefact deposits were clean of intermixed and redeposited material (Pryor 1998, 353). Two concentrations, both on the central dome of the hill, merit particular consideration.

Fig 7. Hambledon Hill. Flint-tempered cup P58 and group XVI axe (S1) *in situ* in B F14. Scale in centimetres. By Roger Mercer.

The first was in a pit near the crown of the hill, within the main enclosure (Figs 7 & 8; Appendix: 2 – 4), where, exceptionally, almost all the sherds could be attributed to identifiable vessels. After the pit had been open long enough for some 0.20m of fine chalky silt to accumulate on its base, more than half of a small flint-tempered cup and a stone axehead of petrological group XVI from the south-west peninsula were placed in it side-by-side (Fig 7). The cup (Fig 8: P58) must have been incomplete when deposited, since it was protected from the plough by the overlying layer, and since further sherds of it occurred in that layer and probably in a neighbouring natural feature. The cup and axehead were covered by dark soil in which were struck flint, animal bone and two large bowls in Gabbroic fabrics (Fig 8: P1, P2). It is unclear whether these pots higher up in the pit were buried complete, because the top of the feature was ploughed down. Also present were sherds of a lugged, flint-tempered bowl with a decorated rim (Fig 8: P138), a charred, immature human skull fragment, animal bone, charcoal and struck flint. The cup and the two Gabbroic

bowls were in fresh condition and almost all the sherds from the pit were attributable to them or to P138. The gabbroic vessels constitute 60% by weight of the 198 sherds/1573g of gabbroic ware from site, the rest of which were thinly scattered. The deposit brought together objects of different kinds from remote south-western sources and combined them with local ones. It might be seen as reflecting the location of the enclosure on the 'frontier' between the Wessex Chalk and the south-west.

The second concentration of semi-complete pots, in the initial silts of the flanking ditches of the south long barrow, was of otherwise unexceptional vessels, some of which had been used, on the evidence of lipids and of superficial sooty residues (Fig 9; Appendix: 23 – 28). This accords with evidence for food preparation and consumption within the complex, in the form of butchered animal bone, already cleaned grain, and querns and rubbers. The two most complete pots were found at single findspots, and, given their position on or very close to the bottom of the ditch, with no sign of post-depositional disturbance, they must have been incomplete when put there. One (Fig 9: P79) was placed in the east ditch after initial silt had begun to accumulate. The other (Fig 9: P73) was in the west ditch. The sherds of four further, less complete, pots (Fig 9: P38, P51, P105 and an unillustrated vessel, Appendix: 28), all represented in the initial silts of the west ditch, were dispersed, not only within those silts, where parts of two of them were clustered with P73, but through later deposits as well. In two cases (Appendix: 24, 28) the dispersal could not have resulted from displacement by recuts. Furthermore, the most abundant and best-preserved sherds from one of these vessels, retaining fresh sooty residue (those of no. 28 which came from L17), were stratified above less well-preserved sherds of the same pot. These vessels must have been broken before deposition, with handfuls of sherds placed in different parts of the ditch bottoms and other sherds placed elsewhere, to be incorporated into the ditch fills at a later date. In the case of the large, well-preserved sherds with residue the environment in which they were held was a protected one. Nothing is known of the structure of the barrow mound, which was bulldozed in the 1960s. It is tempting to think that these sherds were temporarily in a wooden burial chamber.

The south long barrow was the only earthwork in the central area where pottery, including small, abraded sherds as well as semi-complete pots, was abundant in the initial silts (Fig 11). Conversely, there was only a single fragment of human bone in these initial silts, although the remains of at least five individuals were placed in the mound. This contrasts sharply with the adjacent main enclosure, where the ditch bottoms and initial silts yielded little pottery but often contained human remains. A concentration of semi-complete pots in ditch bottoms where there were almost no human remains and their virtual absence from ditch bottoms where human remains were frequent suggests a

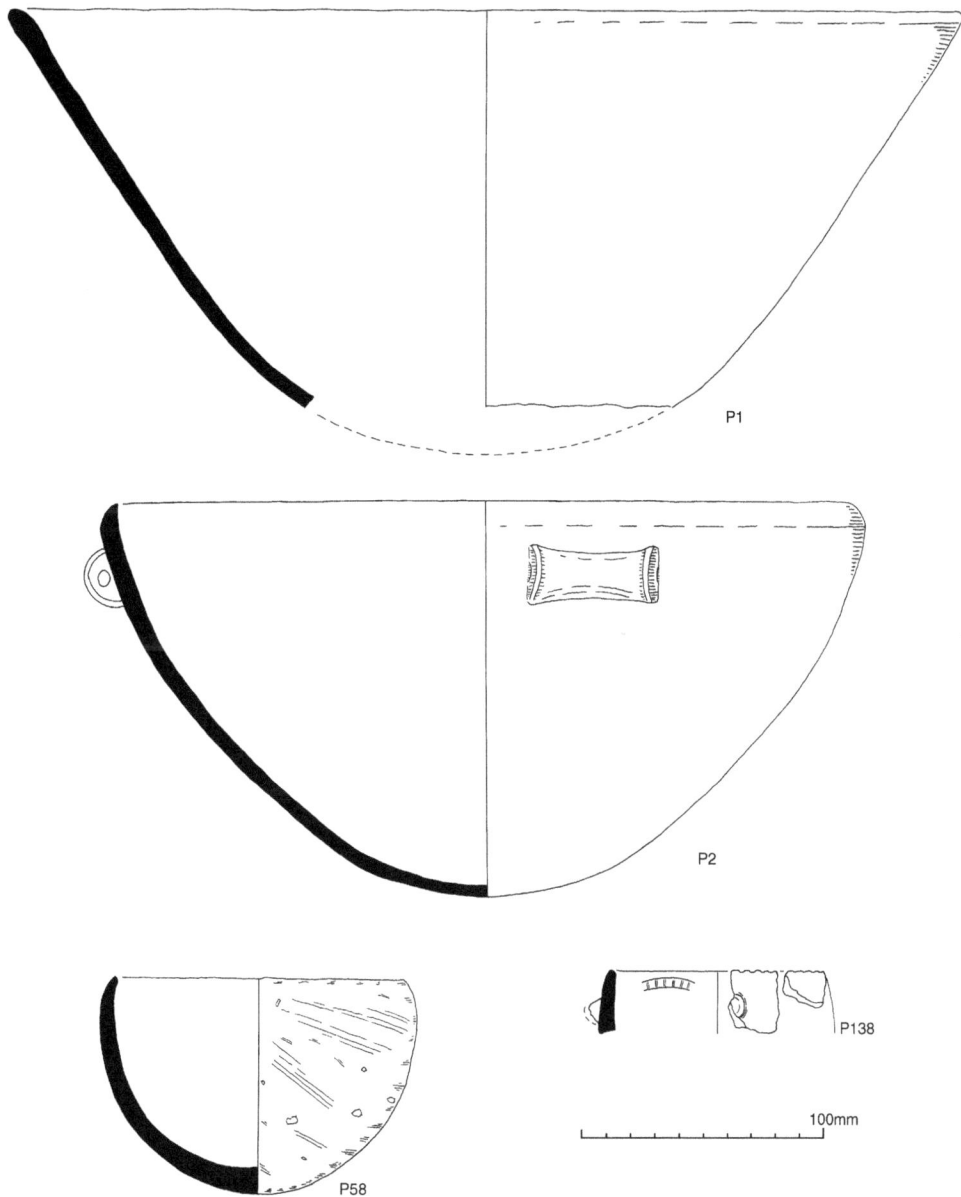

Fig 8. Hambledon Hill. Pots from B F14. By Isobel Smith.

complementarity between the human bones and the pots. Perhaps a recognisable vessel, as distinct from fragmented and abraded sherds, could carry an association with a particular person. Its progressive incorporation into the ditch fills could even echo the treatment of the disarticulated bones of a human skeleton. Elsewhere in the complex, dispersal of substantially represented pots, whether between adjacent ditch segments, between adjacent pits, through a single stratigraphic sequence, or within a single layer, is comparable with the ways in which human bones were buried. In the main enclosure, for example, fragments of a single skull placed 0.50 apart near the base of segment 3 and of another skull similarly spaced near the base of segment 8 echo the disposition of groups of sherds from the same pots set short distances apart (Appendix: 16, 22, 29, 45, 64). In at least one instance, there was an intimate association rather than complementarity, between semi-complete pots, a human femur and a cattle pelvis (Appendix: 65, 66). Recognition of the identity of individual pots, even in a fragmentary state, is clearest in the inner Stepleton outwork. Here, on one side of a massive timber-lined gateway which had burnt down along with a substantial part of the timber-laced rampart in which it was set, sherds of at least four pots were placed in distinct parts of a single cluster on the surface of silts derived from the burning (Appendix: 58 – 61). A deposit made soon after such a catastrophic event may have been laden with significance.

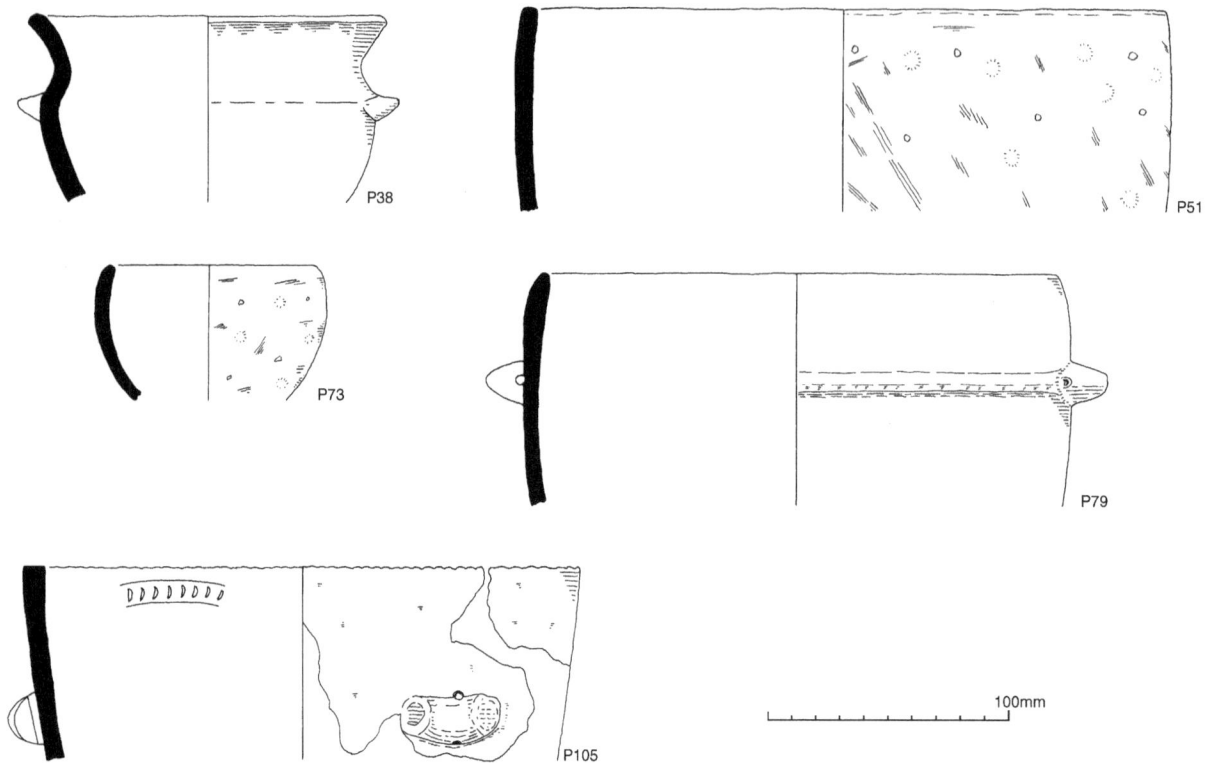

Fig 9. Hambledon Hill. Pots from the initial silts of the south long barrow ditches. By Isobel Smith.

No pot from anywhere in the complex was complete when excavated. In some cases further sherds may remain in unexcavated deposits or an originally complete pot may have been truncated by the plough. Since some incomplete vessels were well-sealed and securely-buried, however, fragmentation seems likely to have been the norm. Zienkiewicz interprets the same circumstance among the pots from Windmill Hill as a reflection of middening prior to deposition (1999, 270). Incompleteness extends to entire assemblage: human and animal skeletons and lithic reduction sequences are equally rarely reconstructable. There were intermediate stages between use and deposition. Missing elements may have been taken elsewhere and/or may have been left to degrade on the surface, where the surviving durable components would have been machined away immediately prior to excavation. Whatever the processes, there is a sense of part-for-whole in the ditch deposits, as in fourth millennium pits. It was appropriate to bury only a part of the pot, the person, the animal or the reduction sequence, and similar interpretations to those offered for pit deposits are feasible, like Thomas' 'means of commemorating particular events . . . by placing such representative residues of such events in the ground, a durable trace of their memory was created (1999, 70).

Semi-complete pots were often put in segment butts, a focus of deposition at other enclosures, especially Etton (Pryor 1998, 357; Appendix: 12, 13, 14, 22, 30, 44, 47, 48, 51, 52, 56, 65, 66, 67, 68). Some of these (Appendix:

17, 29, 58 – 61) were at locations which were certainly or arguably entrances. This corresponds to another aspect of the ditches of the south long barrow. The west ditch of the barrow, in which were most of the semi-complete pots, lies beside an entrance to the main enclosure, giving onto Stepleton-Hanford spur of the hill and forming one end of a route between the two enclosures (Fig 2). The west ditch was far richer in artefacts and food remains than the east ditch and seems to have been a focus for deposition by those passing to and from the central area. Its outer, south butt in particular was marked by a concentration of fragmentary stone implements and a dump of burnt and unburnt animal bone, burnt flint, charcoal and charred hazelnut shells. From this perspective, the fragmented and dispersed but still recognisable pots in the ditch could relate to the preoccupations of the living as much as to commemoration of the dead.

Distributions
Through time
The size and chronology of the Hambledon assemblage, together with the fact that it is well contexted, provide scope for examining vertical and horizontal distributions. The main vertical trends are the same in the ditches of both enclosures. Decoration becomes less infrequent with time (Smith forthcoming table 9.11). The quantity of pottery increases with time (Fig 10), part of a general increase in the amount of cultural material being placed

18

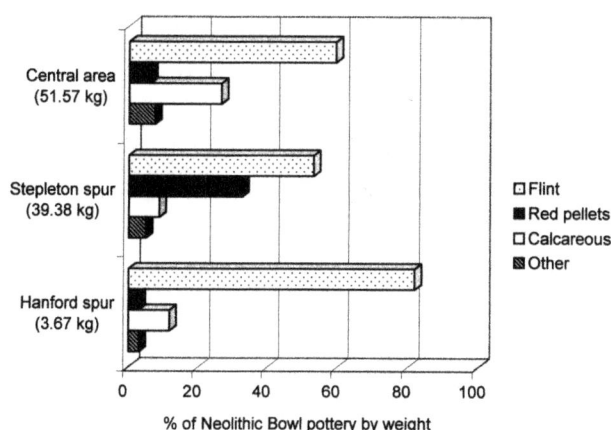

Fig 10. The main fabric groups of Neolithic Bowl pottery from the three main excavated areas on Hambledon Hill as percentages of the total weight from each.

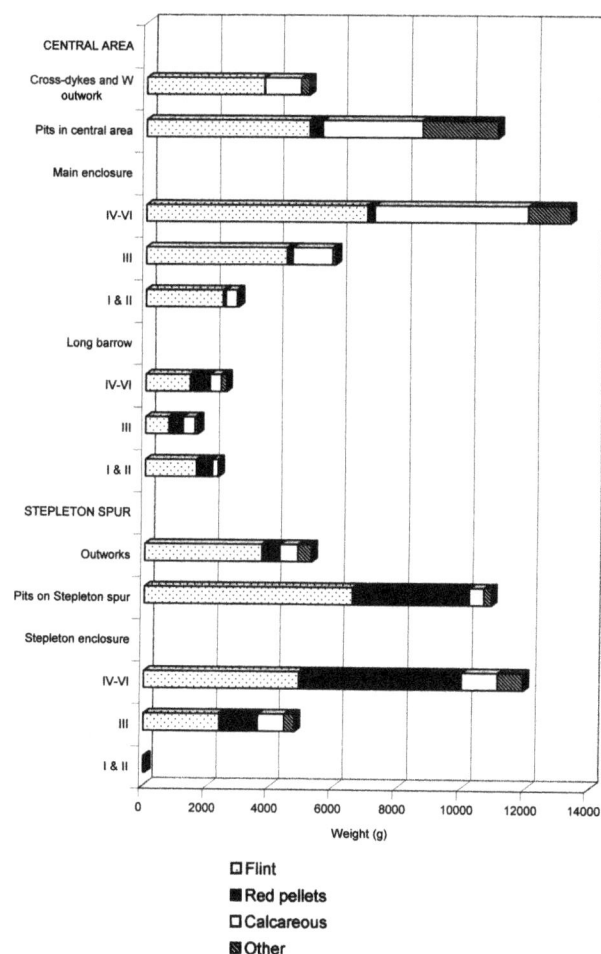

Fig 11. The main fabric groups of Neolithic Bowl pottery from earlier Neolithic contexts only in the central area and on the Stepleton spur at Hambledon Hill, by weight. Only the pottery from earlier Neolithic contexts in each ditch is included because the sometimes large quantities of Bowl pottery from the Bronze Age and later ploughsoils which fill the ditch tops could have derived from other contexts upslope from the ditches. I & II = successive fine silts on or just above the ditch floor, III = predominantly chalk rubble fills overlying I & II, IV–VI = recuts and secondary fills, varying in character from ditch to ditch.

in the ditches. This is a development common to several causewayed enclosures, seen, for example in the 'midden' in the inner ditch at Abingdon, Oxfordshire (Avery 1982, 16–17), successive 'midden' layers in the inner ditch at Maiden Castle (Sharples 1991, 50–51), or the phase 1C recuts at Etton (Pryor 1998, 13 – 51). Finally, non-flint fabrics, present from the first, become more frequent with time (Fig 11). The last two of these invite several interpretations, none of them mutually exclusive. Beliefs and practices would have changed: 310 – 370 years are a long time; people from a progressively larger catchment may have come to the hill; the scale and tempo of exchange may have heightened over the centuries; pottery production at particular locales may have intensified — the sherd illustrated in Fig 6, with its connotations of complex clay procurement, came from this stage of the use of the main enclosure. Any or all of these suggest that a visitor to the hill in the 3400s may have met, however fleeting, more other people from more areas than a visitor to the complex in the 3600s. In both enclosures, the composition of fabrics from the pits was closest to that of the secondary fills and recuts in the ditches (Fig 11: IV – VI). Although it would be rash to conclude that most of the pits might date from this same period, it is noteworthy that the topmost fills of more than half of the pits in the central area were densely packed with flint nodules in the same way as many of the slot-like recuts in the enclosure ditches.

The progressive increase in non-local fabrics seen in the Hambledon sequence may have been only the later, most conspicuous part of a longer process, already under way when the complex began to be built. Cleal (2004b) has identified four assemblages from Wessex and the south-west as definitely or possibly dating to the first quarter of the fourth millennium, before the inception of the Hambledon complex. Morphologically, these are characterised by the absence of decoration, simple, unelaborated rims and predominantly open or neutral forms, with few of the unshouldered, bag-shaped profiles common in the South-Western style (Cleal 2004b, figs 4 – 5). Their fabrics are more internally homogeneous and more consistently local in origin than those from even the early periods at Hambledon and those from other causewayed enclosures.

The main inclusions in the ten or eleven pots found beside the probably short-lived Sweet Track in the Somerset Levels, the construction of which is dated dendrochronologically to 3807 – 3806 BC (Coles & Coles 1990, 218), are quartz and quartz sand, with single instances of calcite and fossil shell (Smith 1976; Kinnes 1979; Coles & Orme 1984), all of which could have been obtained within a few kilometres of the track. The seven pots represented in a pit at Rowden on the South Dorset Ridgeway are mainly tempered with combinations of fossil shell and quartz sand, a couple containing sand alone (Davies et al. 1991, 97 – 98), with none of the flint tempered wares frequent at the Maiden Castle causewayed enclosure 5km away (Cleal 1991, table 54). The authors emphasise how different the Rowden assemblage is from the Maiden Castle one, in its predominance of shouldered forms and absence of lugs. Even closer to Maiden Castle, in the thirteen to fourteen pots represented in pits predating the late fourth/early third millennium Flagstones enclosure in Dorchester the only two inclusions are fossil shell and flint (Cleal 1997, table 98) with none the of the wider variety of inclusions found in Bowl pottery from later contexts at Flagstones or at Maiden Castle itself (Cleal 1991, table 54). Both Rowden and Flagstones were less than 15km from possible sources of fossil shell (Cleal 1991, 173). Farther away from such sources, the 43 – 47 pots represented in the large pit known as the Coneybury anomaly, surrounded on all sides by the Chalk of Salisbury Plain, are overwhelmingly flint- and sand-tempered, with minimal amounts of other materials, of which shell, (present in less than 1% of the sherds) is the only non-local one (Cleal 1990, table 10, fig 32).

All four assemblages could thus have been made entirely or almost entirely from locally available materials, calcareous inclusions being significant only where they could have been obtained within a limited range. None includes any Gabbroic ware, the transport of which into Wessex seems to have begun when causewayed enclosures started to be built (Cleal 2004b, 180). This is in marked contrast to the spectrum of fabrics from Hambledon, Windmill Hill and other causewayed enclosures in Wessex, even when only small samples of pottery are available from them, as at Whitesheet Hill, Wiltshire (Cleal 2004a, table 2). The 1441 sherds from the primary deposit in the Coneybury anomaly contrast sharply with the 230 sherds from the Robin Hood's Ball causewayed enclosure, just 5km away. At Robin Hood's Ball, despite the smaller amount of pottery, Gabbroic wares are present, over 20% of the sherds are in calcareous fabrics, and there is a wide range of miscellaneous inclusions, each identified in only a handful of sherds (Thomas 1964, table 1). The morphological contrast between the Coneybury and Robin Hood's Ball assemblages is as great as that between the Rowden and Maiden Castle ones. The seventeen pots from Robin Hood's Ball illustrated by Thomas (1964, fig 4) are predominantly neutral and closed forms, with none of the widely-splayed rims which occur at Coneybury (Cleal 1990, figs 28 – 31).

The predominance of local fabrics in these groups may be due, wholly or in part, to the different roles of trackways, pits and enclosures, the range of material buried at the last reflecting their role as aggregation sites. But this ignores the certainly earlier date of the Sweet Track assemblage and the probably to possibly earlier dates of the remaining three, as well as the morphological distinctions between the Rowden and Coneybury assemblages and those of nearby enclosures. Non-local fabrics may already have become more common when

the Hambledon complex and other causewayed enclosures began to be built than they had been in the preceding centuries, part of an horizon of rapid change and development which included the diversification of Neolithic Bowl potting traditions (Cleal 2004b, 180) and a progressive intensification of exchange networks.

Across space

Horizontal distinctions at Hambledon are even more marked than vertical ones. Pottery was unevenly distributed between ditches (Table 1). Allowing for the potential unreliability of the figures where only a few metres of ditch were excavated, it was densest in the ditches of the long barrow and of the two causewayed enclosures, and sparse in some of the most massive outworks. This is part of a greater overall intensity of deposition, reworking and recutting in the enclosure and barrow ditches than in the other earthworks.

The main non-flint fabrics vary in frequency between the main excavated areas (Fig 10): calcareous inclusions outnumber red pellets in the central area; red pellets outnumber calcareous inclusions on the Stepleton spur, and both are rare on the Hanford spur. Furthermore, such calcareous fabrics as there are on the Stepleton spur are more often oolithic (1.14kg out of 2.77kg) than those in the central area (0.71kg out of 11.9kg). There are also considerable differences in the fabrics present in different contexts within these two areas. Non-flint fabrics were concentrated in the ditches of the two enclosures and the south long barrow. Other earthworks had higher proportions of flint-tempered pottery (Fig 11). This is not an effect of construction date, because the most artefact-rich levels of the enclosures and long barrow accumulated as the later earthworks were being built.

The long barrow assemblage is exceptional in that it is the only earthwork in the central area with more than a minimal proportion of red pellet fabrics (Fig 10). These were even all but absent from the adjacent inner south cross-dyke, the primary fills of which would have been accumulating while material was being placed in the secondary fills and recuts of the long barrow ditches. The barrow, at the entrance to main enclosure, has a concentration of the fabric prevalent in the smaller enclosure. It is as if the deposition related to the role of the barrow in marking the passage from one enclosure to the other. Correspondingly, such calcareous fabrics as there were in Stepleton enclosure were concentrated in the segments flanking the entrance giving onto the route to and from the central area, although here, as elsewhere on the spur, they were largely oolithic. One of these segments had a flint-packed, slot-like recut, unlike any other on the spur, but similar to those repeatedly made in the segments of the main enclosure. There is a strong suggestion that the deposits relate to movement between the two enclosures and to the different acts which took place in each. It is even possible to envisage individuals

Period	Ditch	Weight (g) of Neolithic Bowl pottery from earlier Neolithic levels	Metres of ditch excavated	Average sectional area (sq m)	Volume of excavated deposit (cu m, rounded)	Weight (g) of Neolithic Bowl pottery per cu m of excavated deposit (rounded)
1A	Main enclosure	26709	155	4.4	682	39
	Inner E cross-dyke	1333	37.48	1.6	60	22
	Long barrow	7056	49.6	3.35	166	43
1B	Shroton spur outwork	458	23.6	8.3	196	2
	Stepleton enclosure	21235	130.2	2.5	326	65
	Middle Stepleton outwork	321	56.2	2.3	129	2
2	Inner Stepleton outwork	5642	119.5	5.65	675	8
3	Inner S cross-dyke	3786	7.5	3.7	28	135
	Outer Stepleton outwork	626	37	3.2	118	5
3?	Inner Hanford spurwork	2754	16.9	2.93	50	55
	Outer Hanford spurwork	469	21.4	2.42	52	9
4	Outer E cross-dyke	941	29.7	2.09	62	15
	Western outwork	302	5	3.75	19	16
4?	Inner Stepleton-Hanford outwork	0	3.4	2.58	9	0
	Outer Stepleton-Hanford outwork	5	8.3	2.58	1	5

Table 1. Hambledon Hill. Frequency of Neolithic Bowl pottery in individual ditches, ordered by period of construction. Based on the work of Roger Mercer and Rachael Seager Smith.
The outer S cross-dyke is excluded because most of its fills were removed by an Iron Age recut.
Figures for the inner S cross-dyke, the western outwork and all the ditches on the Hanford spur may be unrepresentative because only short lengths of each were excavated; this is particularly likely in the case of the inner S cross-dyke because of a dense concentration of pottery in its western butt. A high density for the inner Hanford spurwork is similarly due to a single concentration of pottery in one ditch butt (Appendix: 68).

Main enclosure and central area	Stepleton enclosure and adjacent area
Recutting frequent and complex, with a measure of regularity around enclosure, many pits also recut	Recutting of ditch less frequent and less regular, pits rarely recut at all
Upper, linear recuts ('slots') in enclosure and cross-dyke ditches, and recuts in pits both often packed with unworked flint nodules and fragments	Only one flint-packed recut in an enclosure segment, close to entrance giving onto route to main enclosure.
Human remains placed in ditches from first	Human remains placed in ditches only after some fill had accumulated
Deer bone (as distinct from antler) rare	Deer bone (as distinct from antler) less rare
Articulated animal bone most abundant in final linear recuts ('slots') made in almost fully silted ditch, which were the ditch contexts richest in bone and other cultural material	Articulated animal bone rarer than in main enclosure and virtually absent from final midden-like deposits made in almost fully silted ditch, although these were the ditch contexts richest in bone
Material in 'slots' often placed in discrete piles	Little obvious placement of material in midden-like upper deposits
Antler implements concentrated in pits in interior	Antler implements concentrated in enclosure ditch
Almost no refitting knapping debris	Clusters of refitting knapping debris on ditch floors and higher up sequence
Almost all of the 39 chert artefacts from the site, including 6 leaf arrowheads; also 1 leaf arrowhead of variegated red/white flint	Almost none of the 39 chert artefacts from the site; no chert or coloured flint arrowheads
Hammerstones include beach pebbles	No beach pebbles
Many axeheads and fragments of rocks from remote sources	Almost all axeheads and fragments of flint
Most frequent non-local quern material Old Red Sandstone from Mendips	Most frequent non-local quern material heathstone from between Wareham and Poole, in south-east Dorset
Gabbroic vessels concentrated in pits in interior	Gabbroic ware extremely rare
Most abundant non-flint-tempered pottery well made and finished and derived from limestone ridge to north-west and west	Most abundant non-flint-tempered pottery roughly made and finished and possibly derived from same area as heathstone

Table 2. Some of the differences between the central area and the Stepleton spur (from Healy 2004)

or crowds proceeding from one to the other. The topography ensures that, for most of the gentle ascent from the Stepleton spur to the central dome of the hill, the main enclosure and its surrounding earthworks remain out of sight, bursting into view quite suddenly at a late stage of the approach. In the fourth millennium this effect would have been heightened by the wooded conditions inferred from the molluscan evidence. Its impact on those who knew the significance of the earthworks and knew at least the general nature of what was to take place inside them can only be guessed at.

The ceramic differences between the two enclosures form part of a gamut of distinctions in material culture and depositional practice (Table 2), just as stylistic differences between the pottery from the three circuits of Windmill Hill (Zienciewicz 1999, figs 193 – 5) are woven into a mesh of differentiated activity and deposition (Whittle *et al.* 1999, 344 – 390). The spatial distinctions at both sites, like those between the two sides of the Etton enclosure (Pryor 1998, 363 – 368), surely reflect beliefs, traditions and prescriptions as to what should be done where, by whom, in what circumstances and in what sequence.

Acknowledgements

Thanks are warmly extended to Roger Mercer, for the opportunity to work on the analysis and publication of Hambledon Hill and to publish this paper, to Isobel Smith for her magisterial analysis of the Hambledon pottery, to Timothy Darvill for his petrological analysis and for permission to publish Figure 6, to Rachael Seager Smith for her painstaking recording of a dauntingly large assemblage, without which this paper could not have been written, to Rosamund Cleal for her sustained elucidation of Neolithic pottery in Wessex over the decades and for commenting on this paper, to John Borland and Sylvia Stevenson for Figures 1–3, and to Alex Gibson for his invitation to contribute to this volume.

References

Avery, M., 1982. The Neolithic causewayed enclosure, Abingdon. In Case, H.J., & Whittle, A.W.R. (eds), *Settlement Patterns in the Oxford Region: Excavations at the Abingdon Causewayed Enclosure and Other Sites* (Council for British Archaeology Research Report 44), 10 – 50. London: Council for British Archaeology.

Barrett, J.C., Bradley, R. & Green, M., 1991. *Landscape, Monuments and Society. The Prehistory of Cranborne Chase*. Cambridge: Cambridge University Press.

Bayliss, A., Healy, F., Bronk Ramsey, C., McCormac, F.G. & Mercer, R., forthcoming. Interpreting chronology. In Mercer R. & Healy, F., forthcoming.

Bowden, M., 1984. *General Pitt Rivers: the Father of Scientific Archaeology*. Salisbury: Salisbury and South Wiltshire Museum.

Bristow, C. R., Freshney, E. C. & Penn, I. E., 1991. *Geology of the Country around Bournemouth. British Geological Survey, Memoir for Sheet 329*. London: H.M.S.O.

Brown, L., 1987. The late prehistoric pottery. In Cunliffe, B.W., *Hengistbury Head, Dorset. Volume 1: Prehistoric and Roman Settlement, 3500 BC – AD 500* (OUCA Monograph 13), 207 – 303. Oxford: Oxford University Committee for Archaeology.

Brown, L., 1991. Later prehistoric pottery. In Sharples, N.M., *Maiden Castle. Excavations and Field Survey 1985 – 6* (English Heritage Archaeological Report 19), 185 – 205. London: English Heritage.

Brown, L., forthcoming. Later prehistoric pottery from the hillfort. In Mercer R. & Healy, F., forthcoming.

Cleal, R.M.J., 1990. The prehistoric pottery [from the Coneybury 'anomaly']. In Richards, J., *The Stonehenge Environs Project* (English Heritage Archaeological Report 16), 45 – 57. London: Historic Buildings and Monuments Commission for England.

Cleal, R.M.J., 1991. Earlier prehistoric pottery. In Sharples, N.M., *Maiden Castle. Excavations and Field Survey 1985 – 6* (English Heritage Archaeological Report 19), 171 – 85, microfiche M9:A4–E4. London: English Heritage.

Cleal, R.M.J., 1995. Pottery fabrics in Wessex in the fourth to second millennia BC. In Kinnes, I. & Varndell, G. (Eds), *'Unbaked urns of rudely shape'. Essays on British and Irish pottery for Ian Longworth* (Oxbow Monograph 55), 185 – 94. Oxford: Oxbow Books.

Cleal, R.M.J., 1997. Earlier prehistoric pottery. In Smith, R.J.C., Healy, F., Allen, M.J., Morris, E.L., Barnes, I. & Woodward, P.J., *Excavations along the Route of the Dorchester By-pass, Dorset, 1986–8* (Wessex Archaeological Report 11), 86 – 102. Salisbury: Wessex Archaeology.

Cleal, R.M.J., 2004a. Pottery. In Rawlings, M., Allen, M.J. & Healy, F., Investigation of the Whitesheet Down environs 1989 – 90: Neolithic causewayed enclosure and Iron Age settlement. *Wiltshire Studies* 97, 155 – 60.

Cleal, R.M.J., 2004b. The dating and diversity of the earliest ceramics of Wessex and South-west England. In Cleal, R. & Pollard, J. (eds), *Monuments and Material Culture. Papers in Honour of an Avebury Archaeologist: Isobel Smith*, 164 – 192. East Knoyle: Hobnob Press.

Coles, J.M., & Orme, B.J., 1984. Ten excavations along the Sweet Track (3200 bc). *Somerset Levels Papers* 10, 5 – 45.

Coles, J. M. & Coles, B. J., 1990. Part II: the Sweet Track date. In Hillam, J., Groves, C.M., Brown, D.M., Baillie, M.G.L., Coles, J.M. and Coles, B. J., Dendrochronology of the English Neolithic, *Antiquity* 64, 216 – 20.

Copley, M.S., Berstan, R., Dudd, S.N., Docherty, G., Mukherjee, A.J., Straker, V., Payne, S. & Evershed,

R. P., 2003. Direct chemical evidence for widespread dairying in prehistoric Britain. *Proceedings of the National Academy of Science* 100(4), 1524 – 9.

Copley, M., Berstan, R., Stott, A. & Evershed, R., forthcoming. Organic residue analysis of pottery vessels: determination of vessel use and radiocarbon dates. In Mercer R. & Healy, F., forthcoming.

Darvill ,T.C., 1983. *The Neolithic of Wales and the Mid-West of England: a Systemic Analysis of Social Change through the Application of Action Theory.* Unpublished Ph.D. thesis, University of Southampton.

Darvill, T., 2004. Soft rock and organic tempering in British Neolithic pottery. In Cleal, R. & Pollard, J. (eds), *Monuments and Material Culture. Papers in Honour of an Avebury Archaeologist: Isobel Smith*, 193 – 206. East Knoyle: Hobnob Press.

Darvill, T.C., forthcoming. Petrological analysis of Neolithic pottery fabrics. In Mercer, R. & Healy, F., forthcoming.

Davies, S.M., 1986. The coarse pottery [from Rope Lake Hole]. In Sunter, N. & Woodward, P.J. (eds), *Romano-British Industries in Purbeck* (Dorset Natural History and Archaeological Society Monograph 6), 150 – 7. Dorchester: Dorset Natural History and Archaeological Society.

Davies, S.M., Woodward, P.J. & Ellison, A.B., 1991. The pottery, in Woodward, P.J., *The South Dorset Ridgeway: Survey and Excavations 1977 – 84* (Dorset Natural History and Archaeological Society Monograph 8), 96 – 101. Dorchester: Dorset Natural History and Archaeological Society.

Green, M., 2000. *A Landscape Revealed: 10,000 Years on a Chalkland Farm.* Stroud: Tempus.

Healy, F., 2004. Hambledon Hill and its implications. In Cleal, R. & Pollard, J. (eds), *Monuments and Material Culture. Papers in Honour of an Avebury Archaeologist: Isobel Smith.* East Knoyle: Hobnob Press, 15 – 38.

Kinnes, I.A., 1979. Description of the Neolithic bowl, in Coles, J.M. & Orme, B.J., The Sweet Track: Drove site. *Somerset Levels Papers* 5, 52 – 54, fig. 39.

Lancely, J. & Morris, E.L., 1991. Iron Age and Roman pottery. In Cox, P.W. & Hearne, C.M., *Redeemed from the Heath: the Archaeology of the Wytch Farm Oilfield (1987 – 90)* (Dorset Natural History and Archaeological Society Monograph 9), 180 – 97. Dorchester: Dorset Natural History and Archaeological Society.

Legge, A.J., forthcoming. Livestock and Neolithic society at Hambledon Hill. In Mercer, R. & Healy, F., forthcoming.

Mercer R. & Healy, F., forthcoming. *Hambledon Hill, Dorset, England. Excavation and Survey of a Neolithic Monument Complex and its Surrounding Landscape* (English Heritage Archaeological Report). Swindon: English Heritage.

Morris, E.L. & Woodward, A., 2003. Ceramic petrology and prehistoric pottery in the UK. *Proceedings of the*

Prehistoric Society 69, 279 – 303.

Pryor, F., 1998. *Etton: Excavations at a Neolithic Causewayed Enclosure near Maxey, Cambridgeshire, 1982 – 8* (English Heritage Archaeological Report 18). London: English Heritage.

Roe, F.E.S., forthcoming. Worked stone other than axes. In Mercer, R. & Healy, F., forthcoming.

Seager Smith, R., 1997. Late Iron Age and Roman pottery. In Smith, R.J.C., Healy, F., Allen, M.J., Morris, E.L., Barnes, I. & Woodward, P.J., *Excavations along the Route of the Dorchester By-pass, Dorset, 1986–8* (Wessex Archaeological Report 11), 102 – 118. Salisbury: Wessex Archaeology.

Seager Smith, R, 1993. The pottery. In Smith, R.J.C., *Excavations at County Hall, Colliton Park, Dorchester, Dorset, 1988* (Wessex Archaeological Report 4), 42 – 63. Salisbury: Wessex Archaeology.

Sharples, N.M., 1991. *Maiden Castle. Excavations and Field Survey 1985 – 6* (English Heritage Archaeological Report 19). London: English Heritage.

Smith, I.F., 1965. *Windmill Hill and Avebury: Excavations by Alexander Keiller, 1925 – 1939.* Oxford: Clarendon Press.

Smith, I.F., 1976. The pottery. In Coles, J.M., & Orme, B.J., The Sweet Track: railway site. *Somerset Levels Papers* 2, 63 – 64.

Smith, I.F., forthcoming. The pottery from the hilltop excavations of 1974 – 82. In Mercer R. & Healy, F., forthcoming.

Thomas, J., 1999. *Understanding the Neolithic.* London and New York: Routledge.

Thomas, N., 1964. The Neolithic causewayed camp at Robin Hood's Ball, Shrewton, *Wiltshire Archaeological and Natural History Magazine* 59, 1 – 27.

Whittle, A., Pollard, J. & Grigson, C. 1999. *The Harmony of Symbols: the Windmill Hill Causewayed Enclosure, Wiltshire* (Cardiff Studies in Archaeology). Oxford: Oxbow Books.

Zienkiewicz, L., 1999. Pottery. Part 1: early Neolithic including Ebbsfleet. In Whittle, A., Pollard, J. & Grigson, C., 1999, 258 – 92.

APPENDIX. SUBSTANTIALLY REPRESENTED POTS AND THEIR CONTEXTS

Based on the work of Isobel Smith and Rachael Seager Smith

Drawing numbers, prefixed by 'P', follow serial numbers in brackets

* = pot sampled for lipids

A find number may encompass sherds of more than one vessel

In the 'Abrasion' column 1 = fresh, 2 = abraded, 3 = markedly abraded

In the 'Possibly truncated' column 'Y' = pot could have been subject to post-depositional truncation by ploughing-down of tops of shallowly buried deposits

Serial no.	Find number(s)	Context (L = layer)	Sherds	Weight (g)	Abrasion	Mean sherd weight (g)	Approx. amount of rim in all contexts	Fabric group	Description	Possibly truncated
	PITS IN CENTRAL AREA									
1	HH74 1209, 1210, 1211, 1212	A F105	123	341	2	3	<10%	Flint	Open uncarinated bowl with narrow ring lug and simple flat rim	Y
2 (P1)*	HH75 400, 401, 557	B F14 L3 and L3? In large fragments at most 0.70 m apart, in W half of pit.	10	574	1	57	35%	Gabbroic	Open, uncarinated bowl with simple rounded rim, 400 mm in diameter. Trace of unidentified lipids	Y
3 (P2)*	HH75 402–406, 500, 609, 624	B F14 L3 In smaller fragments than P1, dispersed over 1.20 m, mainly in E half of pit.	30	352	1	12	50%	Gabbroic	Open, uncarinated bowl with simple internally bevelled rim 310 mm in diameter and trumpet lug	Y
4 (P58)	HH75 253, 321, 551, 610	B F14 interface of L3 and L4 Single large fragment weighing 158 g on surface of silt in base of pit, remainder in overlying layer	39	179	1	5	75%	Flint	Neutral, uncarinated cup with simple rounded rim 115 mm in diameter	Y
4?	HH75 504	B F12. Top of probable solution pipe, adjacent to B F14	5	21	2	4				
5 (P8/P9)	HH75 273, 274, 276	C F3 L1	44	89	1 and 2	2	<10%	Gabbroic	Bowl with out-turned rim	Y

Serial no.	Find number(s)	Context (L = layer)	Sherds	Weight (g)	Abrasion	Mean sherd weight (g)	Approx. amount of rim in all contexts	Fabric group	Description	Possibly truncated
6	HH77 1143	N F1 L3	55	120	3	2	7%	Flint	Bowl with elongated solid oval lug and simple flat rim 260 mm in diameter	Y
7	HH77 1423, 1825, 2094	N F7i/ii L3+L4	90	186	3	2		Fossil shell	Plain body sherds possibly from a single vessel	Y
8 (P25)	HH77 826, 1344, 1424, 1494	N F23 L3, L2	254	342	3	2		Fossil shell	Closed bowl with trumpet lug	Y
9 (P63) *	HH77 1700, 2089	N F42, most sherds at interface of L3 and L4, 'smashed across the bottom' of L3	90	294	2	3	15%	Flint	Neutral uncarinated bowl with simple flat rim 220 mm in diameter Mixed animal fat	N
10* (P11)	HH7 632	N F17, L2, adjacent to N F82	10	50	2	5		Calcite	Open uncarinated bowl with simple rounded rim 180 mm in diameter and solid bilobate lug Trace of unidentified lipids	Y
	HH77 1739, 1952, 2128, 2184, 2247	N F82 L5, L4, L3, adjacent to N F17	81	476	2	6				
	MAIN ENCLOSURE									
11	HH77 468, 502, 550, 595	Segment 1, F5. In 1 of successive slots cut along largely silted ditch	76	220	3	3		Fossil shell with recrystallised ooliths	Bowl with simple pointed rim, elongated solid oval lug and wiped surface.	N
12	HH74 838	Segment 2 L9/L8 interface. On surface of 'sausage' of soil placed along centre of segment floor. Sherds clustered together near segment butt	52	224	1	4	10%	Flint	Closed bowl with simple rounded rim 200 mm in diameter and solid oval lug	N
13 (P66)	HH74 763	Segment 3 AII L5. In second of two slots cut along largely silted segment. Found together 3 m from the NE butt; on opposite side of causeway to other sherds	35	306	2	9	40%	Fossil shell	Open uncarinated bowl with simple flat rim 210 mm in diameter and solid oval lug	Y

Serial no.	Find number(s)	Context (L = layer)	Sherds	Weight (g)	Abrasion	Mean sherd weight (g)	Approx. amount of rim in all contexts	Fabric group	Description	Possibly truncated
	HH74 648	Segment 4 AII L5. In second of two slots cut along largely silted segment, on opposite side of causeway to other sherds	2	106	2	53				
14	HH76 1657	Segment 6.1 L7. Silt within main rubble fill of segment. Sherds found together near SW butt	20	343	1	17	15%	Flint	Open uncarinated bowl with simple rounded rim 280 mm in diameter and wiped surface	N
15	HH76 864	Segment 6.1 L6. Main chalk rubble fill of segment, joining sherds from L5/L5A	1	16	3	16	<25%	Red pellets	Open, uncarinated bowl with simple flat rim 120 mm in diamctcr	N (L6, L8), Y (L5A, L7)
	HH76 969, 2663	Segment 6.1 L5A. Slot cut along largely silted segment. Sherds joining each other and sherd from L6	3	52	3	17				
	HH76 2639, 2653, 2654	Segment 7 L8. Hollow cut into initial silt. All found together	37	76	3	2				
15?	HH76 2611	Segment 7 L7. Slot cut along largely silted segment	1	22	3	22				
16 (P37)	HH75 1846, 1892, 2013	Segment 8 Site F L7. Near top of main rubble fill of segment. At 3 findspots within 0.40 m of each other	77	270	2 and 3	4	22%	Flint	Open uncarinated bowl with out-turned, internally bevelled rim 160 mm in diameter and indeterminate lug Dairy and ?ruminant fat	N
17* (P57)	HH76 900	Segment 9 surface of L9. Found together on surface of initial silt at inner side of S butt, beside causeway giving onto Shroton spur	62	582	1	9	44%	Flint	Open uncarinated bowl with simple flat rim 220 mm in diameter Trace of unidentified lipids	N

Serial no.	Find number(s)	Context (L = layer)	Sherds	Weight (g)	Abrasion	Mean sherd weight (g)	Approx. amount of rim in all contexts	Fabric group	Description	Possibly truncated
	HH75 852, 853, 1169	Segment 9, L7. In rubble fill of ditch, overlying L9. At two findspots at inner edge of S butt, within 1m, horizontally, of each other and of sherds of same pot on surface of L9.	192	912	1 and 3	5				
18* (P82)	HH75 723, 726, 727, 728, 729, 734, 740, 755, 902, 903, 905	Segment 9, L7. Chalk rubble fill of ditch	20	536	1 and 2	32	<50%	Flint	Open uncarinated bowl with slightly T-shaped rim 200 mm in diameter and elongated solid oval lug	N (L7, L5), Y (L6)
	HH75 720	Segment 9 L5. Secondary silts above chalk rubble	1	18	2	18			Trace of free fatty acids	
	HH75 657	Segment 9 L6. Slot cut along largely silted segment	3	68	2	23				
19	HH75 1979	Segment 11 L11. 'Sausage' of soil placed on initial silt along centre of ditch floor. Found scattered	85	309	3	4	<5%	Flint	Bowl with simple flat rim	N
20* (P31)	HH76 3000	Segment 17 L10. Recut truncating initial silt	14	53	3	4	<28%	Fossil shell	Neutral shouldered bowl with bead rim 140 mm in diameter and elongated solid oval lug	N
	HH76 2883	Segment 17 L9. Silts overlying rubble fills	4	30	2	8			Traces of free fatty acids and ketones	
	HH76 2003	Segment 17 L8. Silt between successive slots cut into largely silted segment	7	96	1	14				
21	HH76 2877, 2924, 2930	Segment 17 L9A. Charcoal-rich deposit overlying rubble fills	37	216	2	6	<5%	Organic	Open, uncarinated bowl with solid oval lug and simple rounded rim and internal wiping	
	OUTER E CROSS-DYKE									

Serial no.	Find number(s)	Context (L = layer)	Sherds	Weight (g)	Abrasion	Mean sherd weight (g)	Approx. amount of rim in all contexts	Fabric group	Description	Possibly truncated
22	HH75 1378, 1549	Segment 5 L4B. Slot cut along largely filled segment. Sherds from 2 findspots *c* 0.20 m apart in S butt	32	179	2	6		Fossil shell	Joining body sherds	
	SOUTH LONG BARROW									
23* (P38)	HH77 2303	LB2, SV, L26. Initial silt, *c* 2 m from sherds in L27	15	60	2	4	<5 %	Flint	Open shouldered bowl with simple rounded rim 160 mm in diameter and solid oval lug	N (L26, L27), Y (L22)
	HH77 1298	LB2, SII, L27. Initial silt, *c* 2 m from sherds in L26	27	36	3	1			Dairy fat	
	HH77 1588, 1589, 1590, 1591,1594	LB2, SII, L23/L22 interface and L22 Displaced from initial silt into recut	42	100	2 and 3	2				
24* (P51)	HH77 2206, 2207, 2295	LB3, SIII, L34. Initial silt of SE butt of W ditch of long barrow. Clustered with P73 and sherds of unillustrated vessel in red pellet fabric	6	149	1 and 2	24	21%	Flint	Neutral uncarinated bowl with simple squared rim 250 mm in diameter Trace of unidentified lipids	N
	HH77 1922	LB3, SIII, F6, L41. 5 m away horizontally from those in L34 and in fill of recut which did not extend into L34	12	125	2	10				
25 (P73)	HH77 2207	LB3, SIII, L34. Initial silt of SE butt of W long barrow ditch	23	105	1	5	80%	Red pellets	Hemispherical cup with simple rounded rim 80 mm in diameter	N
26* (P79)	HH77 1924	LB5, L17. Initial silt of E ditch of long barrow, at single findspot	354	1016	2	3	50%	Flint	Neutral, uncarinated, bowl with simple rounded rim 200 mm in diameter with applied cordon and horizontally perforated lug Ruminant fat?	N

Serial no.	Find number(s)	Context (L = layer)	Sherds	Weight (g)	Abrasion	Mean sherd weight (g)	Approx. amount of rim in all contexts	Fabric group	Description	Possibly truncated
27 (P105)	HH77 2076, 2158	LB2, SV, L26. Initial silt of N end of W ditch of long barrow. HH77 2076 in N butt, HH77 2158 *c* 8 m farther S	27	90	2	3	38%	Fresh shell with flint	Open uncarinated bowl with horizontal tubular lug and simple flat rim 240 mm in diameter with fingernail impressions around the rim top	N
	HH77 905	LB4, F4. Recut in N butt of E ditch of long barrow, possibly derived from L16	16	148	2	9				
	HH77 1216	LB4, L16. Primary fill of N butt of E ditch of long barrow	6	4	3	1				
28	HH77 2206, 2297	LB3, SIII, L34. Initial silt of S butt of W long barrow ditch. Clustered with P73 and sherds of P51 and with stone implements, 1–4 m away from sherds in overlying layers.	15	175	2	12	40%	Red pellets	Open uncarinated bowl with in-turned rim *c* 160 mm in diameter, smoothed exterior and wiped interior	N
	HH77 1527, 1530	LB3, SII, L35. Silt derived from Clay-with-Flints in W ditch of long barrow, overlying initial silt	16	92	3	6				
	HH77 2208	LB3, SIV, L19. Chalk rubble fill of W long barrow ditch, overlying initial silts	17	63	2	4				
	HH77 2271, 2287, 2292	LB3, SIV, L17. Deposit of burnt material in S butt of W long barrow ditch. Sherds unlikely to have been displaced from earlier layers because L17 dumped rather than placed in a cut	62	548	1	9				

Serial no.	Find number(s)	Context (L = layer)	Sherds	Weight (g)	Abrasion	Mean sherd weight (g)	Approx. amount of rim in all contexts	Fabric group	Description	Possibly truncated
28?	HH77 1908	LB3, SIV, L40. Initial silt of W long barrow ditch	6	21	2	4				
	HH77 1808	LB3, SII, L38. Silt derived from Clay-with-Flints in W ditch of long barrow, overlying initial silts	1	13	3	13				
	HH77 1526, 2080, 2083	LB3, SII, L35. Silt derived from Clay-with-Flints in W ditch of long barrow, overlying initial silt	33	115		33				
	INNER S CROSS-DYKE									
29	HH77 737	Site P2 (segment 1) SXD1 L12. Found together in initial silts in NW corner of ditch butt beside causeway leading to W ditch of long barrow	136	271	3	2	27%	Flint	Neutral uncarinated bowl with simple rounded rim 220 mm in diameter and solid oval lug	N
	HH77 738	Site P2 (segment 1) SXD1 L11. Found together, also in initial silts, c 1.30 m away from HH77 737, near centre of butt	15	92	2	6				
30* (P46)	WOWK82 29, 34, 35, 37, 39, 115, 121	WOWK area 4 (segment 2), L7. Fill of slot-like recut in W butt of earthwork. From 7 findspots within 1 m of each other.	21	689	2	33	11%	Flint	Neutral, uncarinated bowl with slightly T-shaped rim 260 mm in diameter. Trace of unidentified lipids.	Y
	SHROTON SPUR OUTWORK									

Serial no.	Find number(s)	Context (L = layer)	Sherds	Weight (g)	Abrasion	Mean sherd weight (g)	Approx. amount of rim in all contexts	Fabric group	Description	Possibly truncated
31	HH76 1225	Site K/L L7. Chalk rubble fill of outwork ditch, found as single fragment	16	56	2	56	11%	Sand	Roughly made open, uncarinated cup 40 mm high with simple rounded rim 65 mm in diameter and slightly flattened base	N
	PITS ON STEPLETON SPUR									
32 (P62)	ST78 1157, 1188, 1189, 1192, 1193, 1194	Pit 1A F110 L2. The only pottery from pit, scattered through fill rich in charred cereal	11	40	2	4	<16%	Red pellets	Cup with simple rounded rim 140 mm in diameter and fragmentary lug	Y
33* (P13)	ST79 2223	Pit 2A F134	3	149	2	50	11%	Red pellets	Open, uncarinated bowl with horizontal tubular lug and simple rounded rim 280 mm in diameter Dairy and ruminant fats	Y
34	ST79 2063, 2065, 2066, 2225, 2410	Pit 2A F134	93	390	2 and 3	4		Red pellets	Body sherds from a single pot with finger-smeared interior	Y
35* (P74)	ST79 1582, 1659, 2086, 2703, 2704, 2716	Pit 2A F159 L1, L2. Possibly same vessel as body sherds from 2A F7 28 m away	57	464	2	8	<44%	Flint	Neutral uncarinated vessel with bead rim 250 mm in diameter and vertically perforated triangular lug Dairy fats	Y
35?	ST79 1115, 1556, 1493, 1494	Pit 2A F7, perhaps same pot as P74 from 2A F159 28 m away from 2A F159	54	190	2 and 3	4		Flint	Body sherds, all probably from same vessel	Y
36* (P61)	ST79 2564, 2612	2A F201	7	175	2 and 3	25	<30%	Red pellets	Neutral uncarinated bowl with simple rounded rim 180 mm in diameter, and internal wiping Ruminant and dairy fats	Y

Serial no.	Find number(s)	Context (L = layer)	Sherds	Weight (g)	Abrasion	Mean sherd weight (g)	Approx. amount of rim in all contexts	Fabric group	Description	Possibly truncated
37* (P77)	ST79 1993, 2001, 2015, 2035, 2055	2A F268 Rim sherds seemed to have been smashed against wall of pit. Adjacent to F269	109	445	3	4	<15%	Flint	Closed bowl with bead rim Trace of unidentified lipids	Y
	ST79 2509	2A F269 L1. Adjacent to F268	21	40	3	2				
38	73 finds, numbers between ST81 1404 and 2158	4B F129	406	575	2 and 3	1	<10%	Red pellets	Neutral uncarinated bowl with simple rounded rim 200 mm in diameter and a solid oval lug	Y
39	ST81 1521, 1549, 1883, 2084, 2160	4B F129	19	49	2 and 3	2	18%	Sand	Neutral uncarinated cup with simple internally bevelled rim 80 mm in diameter	Y
40	ST81 1379–80, 1387, 1498, 1501, 1608–9, 1632, 2140, 3046, 3052, 3058	4B F130	88	263	2 and 3	3	<10%	Red pellets	Open uncarinated bowl with T-shaped rim	Y
41	ST81 3092, 3108–11, 3113–15, 3123, 3155–58, 3163–64, 3171–73	4B F712 L2, L1. Fills covering articulated burial of young adult male. Most sherds in L1, larger, better preserved, joining sherds, some of them vertical in the fill, clustered in 2 groups c 0.40 m apart	up to 59	up to 389	2 and 3 (mainly 3)	7	<10%	Flint	Open uncarinated bowl with simple rounded rim	Y
42 (P59)	ST82 96	ST82 F39. Apparently placed whole on top of charred grain deposit in pit outside Stepleton enclosure	69	185	2	3	70%	Flint	Neutral uncarinated cup with simple rounded rim 100 mm in diameter	Y

Serial no.	Find number(s)	Context (L = layer)	Sherds	Weight (g)	Abrasion	Mean sherd weight (g)	Approx. amount of rim in all contexts	Fabric group	Description	Possibly truncated
43* (P16)	ST82 69, 70, 80, 82, 87, 96, 98, 101	ST82 F39. Scattered in pit containing charred grain deposit outside Stepleton enclosure	24	133	2 and 3	6	<25%	Flint	Open, uncarinated bowl, with in-turned rim 210 mm in diameter and vertically perforated lug Dairy fats Some sherds also have sooty internal residue, one with calcareous external concretion	Y
	STEPLETON ENCLOSURE									
44* (P36)	ST81 375, 692, 763, 795, 870	Segment 7, L2. Upper, artefact-rich fill of segment. Scattered in area 1.50 m x 1 m in N butt.	7	59	2 and 3	8	<5%	Sand	Open carinated bowl with out-turned rim Trace of free fatty acids	Y
	ST81 349	Segment 8 L2. Upper, artefact-rich fill of segment adjacent to segment 7	1	14	2	14					Y
45	ST81 1228, 1233	Segment 7, L2. Upper, artefact-rich fill of segment. Sherds found in 2 groups 0.40 m apart	38	177	3	5		Flint	Plain body sherds with internal sooty residue	Y
46	ST81 627	Segment 8, L2. Upper, artefact-rich fill of segment. At single findspot	18	72	2 and 3	4	<5%	Flint	Neutral bowl with simple rounded rim and solid oval lug	Y
47	ST81 640, 643, 649, 661	Segment 12 L3A. Secondary fill. All in SW butt	102	384	2 and 3, mainly 3	4	<20%	Red pellets	Bowl with in-turned rim and solid oval lug	N
48	ST81 733	Segment 12, L2. Upper, artefact-rich fill of segment, mainly in SW butt	41	131	3	3		Red pellets	Bowl with in-turned rim	Y

Serial no.	Find number(s)	Context (L = layer)	Sherds	Weight (g)	Abrasion	Mean sherd weight (g)	Approx. amount of rim in all contexts	Fabric group	Description	Possibly truncated
49*	ST81 938	Segment 14, L3B. Upper chalk rubble fill	70	301	2	4	<5%	Red pellets	Bowl with expanded rim and solid oval lug Ruminant and dairy fat from this vessel or no. 51	N
50*	ST81 938	Segment 14, L3B. Upper chalk rubble fill	18	70	3	4	11%	Flint	Neutral bowl with beaded rim 160 mm in diameter and indeterminate lug Ruminant and dairy fat from this vessel or no. 50	N
51* (P144)	ST81 518, 944, 966	Segment 14, L2. Upper, artefact-rich fill of segment, almost all in E butt	164	757	3	5	<15%	Red pellets	Bowl with in-turned rim and hollow internal bevel and solid oval Trace of unidentified lipids	Y
52*	ST81 96, 179, 236, 257, 735	Segment 15, L3B. Upper chalk rubble fill, found close together in E butt	17	375	2	22	11%	Flint	Joining sherds from an open uncarinated lugged bowl with a simple rounded rim 320 mm in diameter Ruminant fat	N
53	ST81 1087	Segment 15, L3B. Upper chalk rubble fill	22	78	3	4	10%	Ooliths	Bowl with simple rounded rim180 mm in diameter and indeterminate lug	N
54	ST81 2205, 2225, 2226, ?1881	Segment 16, L3B. Upper chalk rubble fill	55	113	2	2	25%	Flint	Open uncarinated bowl with simple rounded rim 180 mm in diameter and internal wiping	N
55* (P33)	2200, 2369	Segment 16, L3B, L3D. Upper chalk rubble fills	8	76	2	10	10%	Flint	Neutral carinated bowl with out-turned rim 240 mm in diameter with sooty external residue Trace of unidentified lipids	N

Serial no.	Find number(s)	Context (L = layer)	Sherds	Weight (g)	Abrasion	Mean sherd weight (g)	Approx. amount of rim in all contexts	Fabric group	Description	Possibly truncated
56 (P53)	ST81 2244, 2249	Segment 17, L3C. Localised deposit of dark brown silt loam with chalk rubble and charcoal in chalk rubble fill in SE butt	15	133	2 and 3	9	15%	Fresh shell with flint	Neutral uncarinated bowl with bead rim 280 mm in diameter and external smoothing	N
57*	ST81 2241	Segment 17, L3B. Upper chalk rubble fill, found together	9	124	1	14	16%	Red pellets	Open uncarinated bowl with simple rounded rim 220 mm in diameter Ruminant fat	N
	INNER STEPLETON OUTWORK									
58* (P47)	ST80 1322, 1337, 1480, ?1328	Segment 4.2, L4A. On surface of grey, ashy silt with charcoal and chalk lumps covering ditch floor in E butt beside burnt-down timber gateway. Sherds of each vessel separate within single cluster	21	134	2	6	23%	Fossil shell	Open uncarinated cup with simple rounded rim 80 mm in diameter and wiped interior Dairy fat	N
59	ST80 1157, 1158, 1159	As 58	81	413	2 and 3	5	<30%	Flint	Closed uncarinated bowl with a beaded rim 210 mm in diameter and an unperforated trumpet lug	N
60	ST80 1186, 1363	As 58	24	143	2 and 3	6		Flint	Plain body sherds from single vessel	N
61	ST80 1393, 1407	As 58	17	143	2 and 3	8		Flint	Plain body sherds with wiped exteriors from single vessel	N
62	ST80 1435, 2454	Segment 5 L4A, U1–U2. At two separate findspots in grey silts with charcoal and chalk lumps on ditch floor in W butt	12	75	2	8		Flint	Plain body sherds from single vessel	N

Serial no.	Find number(s)	Context (L = layer)	Sherds	Weight (g)	Abrasion	Mean sherd weight (g)	Approx. amount of rim in all contexts	Fabric group	Description	Possibly truncated
63	ST79 2697, 2700	Segment 5 L4, C13. Chalk rubble fill	7	71	2	6	10%	Flint	Neutral bowl with a T-shaped rim 200 mm in diameter	N
64* (P85)	ST79 1567, 1684, 1685	Segment 6, L4A, C1. From 3 findspots in layer with burnt clay and charred timbers overlying ditch floor and skin of initial silt in centre of segment.	48	181	1, 2 and 3	4	<17%	Flint	Neutral uncarinated bowl with flattened out-turned rim 220 mm in diameter Trace of unidentified lipids	N
65 (P60)	ST79 1015	Segment 6, L6, C3. At single findspot in silt covering ditch floor, in SW butt immediately above human femur and cattle pelvis fragments placed in natural fissure in chalk	22	68	2	3	<58%	Red pellets	Hemispherical cup with simple flat rim 90 mm in diameter	N
	ST79 1016, 1018, 1019	Segment 6, L4, C3. At single findspot in base of chalk rubble fills, with sherds of P68, immediately overlying fragments of same pot in L6	50	89	2	2				
66* (P68)	ST79 1016, 1017, 1018, 1019	Segment 6, L4, C3. At single findspot in base of chalk rubble fills, with sherds of P60, immediately overlying fragments of P60 in L6	121	391	2	3	<16%	Flint	Neutral uncarinated bowl with out-turned rim 240 mm in diameter and solid lug Traces of free fatty acids, monoacylglycerols, n-alkalines, n-alcohols	N
	OUTER STEPLETON OUTWORK									

Serial no.	Find number(s)	Context (L = layer)	Sherds	Weight (g)	Abrasion	Mean sherd weight (g)	Approx. amount of rim in all contexts	Fabric group	Description	Possibly truncated
67	ST80 1902, 1925, 1927, 1931, 1933, 1936, 1955, 2192, 2297, 2301, 2389, 2317	Segment 4, L4A, U5. Chalk rubble fill in E butt	45	112	3	2	<5 %	Flint	Bowl with simple pointed rim	N
	INNER HANFORD OUTWORK									
68* (P71)	HN82 309, 310, 311	Segment 3, L4, U1. Chalk rubble fill in segment butt, near edge of L3C	106	408	2	4	50%	Flint	Neutral uncarinated bowl with simple rounded rim 290 mm in diameter and elongated oval lug Traces of unidentified lipids	N

CHAPTER 3

Exchange & Art:
Ceramics and Society in the Early Chalcolithic of Central Anatolia

Jonathan Last & Catriona Gibson

Introduction

Ever since the emergence of archaeology as a scientific discipline in the 19th century, it has been recognised that artefact styles and their changes over time can be used to create typologies and chronologies. However, these practical applications for relative dating, well-understood by pioneering fieldworkers like Pitt-Rivers and Petrie (see Lucas 2001), have overshadowed consideration of why objects like pots are decorated in the first place and how that decoration can be interpreted. For typological purposes it is assumed that styles either just change in a random (but measurable) way or show sudden ruptures marking an invasion or acculturation. There has been relatively little consideration of the agency of potters, or the relationship between potters and their products in different social contexts. Hence we end up with pottery defining cultures and social groups in prehistory (Beakers, for instance) rather than the other way around. In this paper we wish to look at the emergence of decorated pottery as part of a suite of social and economic changes occurring around the turn of the 6th millennium cal BC on the Konya Plain in south-central Anatolia, and try to address some aspects of that deceptively simple-looking question: why decorate pots?

Style and Decoration

As John Barrett has reflected, following Gordon Childe, if potters were simply left to their own devices they might be expected to create 'an overwhelming variety' of forms and decoration (as those working in a fine arts context do today), but 'such variety is precisely what the archaeologist does not find' (Barrett 1991, 201-2). Yet the properties of clay offer virtually no physical constraints on what potters might produce, so the observed uniformity must 'lie at the level of the social and not at the level of an individual motivation which could transcend the social' (ibid.). Therefore the classifications underlying our typologies are not value-free - they demand an attention to social theory.

In relation to ceramic styles, it can be argued that such attention has so far been inadequate. For the culture-history school of archaeologists, if such issues were addressed at all, style reflected cultural norms that pre-existed human action and to some extent determined it (Barrett, ibid.) With the emergence of processual archaeology these norms became more explicit - environment, social structure, etc. This led to style first being considered somewhat irrelevant to the business of explaining the function of material culture, and then being subsumed into those functional explanations, for example as a means of creating or maintaining group boundaries (Lucas 2001, 87).

Recent processual approaches to pottery have generally focussed on technology rather than style, as in a number of papers by Michael Schiffer and James Skibo. In a discussion of cooking pots as female technology, they critique approaches which treat pottery decoration as artistic expression, arguing that we need to consider 'pots as tools' (Skibo & Schiffer 1995). However, in stressing the impressive and generally undervalued technological achievements embodied in the 'humble clay pot', decoration is marginalised, with the implication that it is secondary and inefficient: 'In traditions in which the socio-functions of ceramics become paramount, one finds enormous expenditure of manufacturing effort to enhance visual impact' (Schiffer & Skibo 1987). Such approaches seem to be related to the common assumption that 'fancy' means 'non-utilitarian' (Arnold 1999, 164).

In contrast, the broadly post-processual approach within British 'social archaeology' has recognised the significance of pottery decoration and its active role in society, although it is still primarily discussed in terms of group identity and ethnicity. Moreover, this approach has largely concentrated on how pots were used and consumed in strategies that may, for instance, emphasise or deny social divisions (Lucas 2001, 88). A good example in a Near Eastern context is Orrelle's and Gopher's (2000, 302) suggestion that pottery vessels of the Yarmukian culture in the southern Levant 'acted as a kind of blueprint onto which the norms and beliefs of society were displayed' and the motifs specifically 'stand as symbols for a social system governing rules of access to women' (ibid., 299). However, production and the role of the potter are notably under-theorised - it seems unlikely that potters consciously work with such strategies in mind, so how do their products come to play these roles? In the key text on British prehistoric ceramics, Gibson and Woods (1997, 6) note that pots may be 'convenient vehicles for display', they may 'communicate cultural affiliation or even the status of the individual within his or her society' but 'this ... aspect of the study of ceramics has not yet received sufficient attention'.

The issue has recently been addressed in a British context by several papers in a volume edited by Woodward and

Hill (2002), but when it comes to the question of 'why decorate ... pots' (Hill 2002, 80) most authors raise issues and methods for future research (*e.g.* Morris 2002, 58), rather than developing the social theory called for by Barrett (1991). The most substantial reflection on these issues, by Boast, notes how the archaeological urge to classify has hindered understanding of the 'various significations ... built into the productive process as an anticipation of programmes of action' (Boast 2002, 105). The failure of typology to 'decode the underlying "rules"' of Beaker decoration (*ibid.*, 101) underlines the critique of the 'type fossil' approach to pottery. For Boast it requires nothing less than 'a radical reconsideration of how we examine pots' (*ibid.*, 105).

Ultimately the task is one of articulating the role of pottery within society with the potter's thoughts, beliefs and motor actions, which go into the production of any given pot. This is of course the classic problem of structure and agency, perhaps best resolved in the context of small-scale societies by Pierre Bourdieu's (1990) concept of the *habitus*, essentially those dispositions and sensibilities that people acquire in the course of their socialisation and interactions with others and with the world around them. Crucially the *habitus* does not take the form of a mental structure or cultural model - it exists only when instantiated in skilled practice, as Ingold (2000, 162) makes clear. Thus understanding the significance of pottery decoration requires attention to the practice of making pots.

Talking to Potters

Barrett's (1991) paper represents a rare attempt to consider the role of the potter in an interpretive framework. However, his main interest is to present a critique of under-theorised typologies and classifications, so the creation of categories receives more attention than the significance of decoration: Barrett (1991, 206-7) simply suggests that because decoration is 'in part structured by the existing surface zones upon which that decoration could have been applied' it does not have a primary role in creating particular vessel categories. This may not be the view of potters themselves, however. For instance, Rye (1981), writing from the viewpoint of a potter rather than an archaeologist, notes that 'to the potter, form is not clearly separable from decoration; each influences the other'. Moreover in ethnographic contexts potters may often downplay their own creative role, stressing instead the agency of the pot: 'It is not the potter, but the clay dictating how it will be used and shaped, what beauty it holds to be revealed by the potter' (Bernstein & Brody 2002, 9). We might interpret this transference of the creative role as a reflection of the non-verbal nature of the *habitus*, which limits potters' ability to explain their motivations in words.

A rare anthropological case study of pottery decoration sheds a little more light on how potters in small-scale societies understand their own activity. According to the mainly female Pueblo potters in the American south-west interviewed by Ruth Bunzel in the 1920s, all potters have a whole design in their head before they start painting, indeed many dream about those designs (Bunzel 1929). They emphasise the originality of their own work, saying 'We paint our thoughts'. But there is discrepancy between theory and practice: the potters deny repeating designs but in practice they do repeat them. Bunzel describes their 'pervading unanalytical attitude' and how they are surprised when confronted with examples of their repetition. On the other hand they happily analyse the work of others, with designs from different Pueblos viewed with curiosity or even amusement. It is differences in the innate sense of which designs do and do not work aesthetically that seem to distinguish one site from another.

These statements offer further clues to understanding the agency of potters, and the role of the *habitus* in constraining experimentation through an aesthetic sense that is not verbalised but exists only in the act of potting. Bunzel's own interpretations, however, are clearly influenced by the psychological approach of Boas (see Ingold 2000, 159). She refers to 'the mysterious phenomenon of style' that limits potters' freedom of expression but sees stylistic persistence and change in terms of individual abilities: the lack of a creative faculty, reflected in the persistence of stereotypes, is contrasted with those creative potters who can cause new styles to emerge, especially when 'general cultural instability works upon the mind of a sensitive individual'.

The bulk of the Pueblo pottery described by Bunzel has geometric decoration, with elaborate designs composed of simple motifs: steps and spirals are most important, triangles are used as fillers. In terms of meaning, there is an absence of fixed symbolism but informants tend to clothe their designs with subjective significance. This also varies between Pueblos: all designs have meanings and associated stories for the Zuni (though these can vary contextually), while Hopi designs are just pictures of material objects and at Acoma there is apparently no trace of symbolism: 'We have only three names for designs: red, black and striped'. Moreover, the meanings explained to Bunzel varied between potters as well as between Pueblos, for example, the subtly different explanations of motifs by three San Ildefonso potters (Bunzel 1929, 71) (Fig 1). Thus meaning, in the discursive sense, seems a less intrinsic aspect of decoration than how well it works, in an aesthetic sense.

Theorising pottery decoration therefore appears as a complex task - individual potters do exhibit varying degrees of creativity and skill, as the Boasian model has it, and varying abilities to express their creativity verbally. But their skills are the product of a learning process or apprenticeship which creates the practical dispositions and aesthetic sense that can be glossed as the

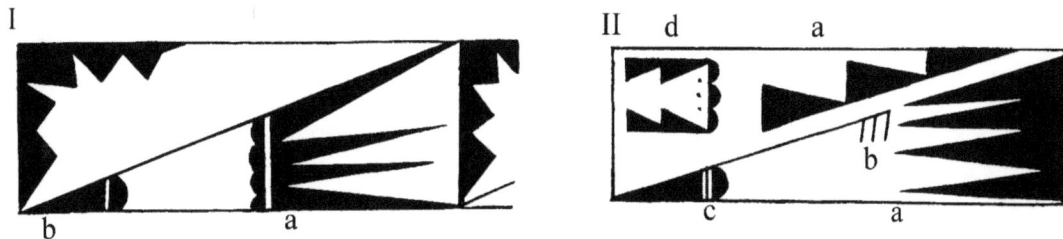

	Julian	Abel	Juan
I	a. Leaf b. Cloud	Clouds and rain going in two directions	Fog standing
II	a. A bird b. Another bird c. Cloud d. Clouds and hailstones	Clouds and rain going in two ways	Yellow fog

Fig 1. San Ildefonso designs and their meanings according to three potters
(after Bunzel 1929, Appendix 3)

habitus. Since that process relates to the potter's socialisation, it ensures that the activity of potting is also a social act. However, the potter's skill is only part of the story, for the subsequent owners of a pot have their own dispositions and creativity which emerge in the use and consumption of the object, some of which we observe archaeologically. The case-study that follows attempts to explore just a few possible threads within this complex pattern.

Çatalhöyük West

The Neolithic site of Çatalhöyük on the Konya Plain in south-central Anatolia (Fig 2) is well-known for many reasons, not least its decoration - not on pots in this case but on architecture, in the form of wall-paintings and mouldings. Numerous interpretations of this 'art' have been put forward since James Mellaart's initial discussions of the 1960s (Mellaart 1967), and new ones continue to appear (*e.g.* Lewis-Williams 2004). Some of this discussion focusses on change over time (*e.g.* During 2001), including the observation that decoration of houses declines or disappears in the upper levels of the site, prior to its abandonment around the last two centuries of the 7th millennium cal BC (see Cessford, forthcoming). At the same time the pottery, which was previously characterised by simple forms and dark burnished surfaces (Last, forthcoming), shows a trend to slightly more complex and varied vessel shapes and the appearance of red slips, though decoration proper remains extremely rare. Assessing the significance of these developments requires an understanding of what comes next. However, 6th millennium activity at Çatalhöyük and, more broadly, on the Konya Plain remains poorly understood.

There is, however, considerable evidence waiting to be uncovered, just across a former course of the Çarsamba river from Neolithic Çatalhöyük (Fig. 3). The 'other' Çatalhöyük (termed the West Mound) covers an area of *c* 8 ha, compared to 13 ha for the Neolithic East Mound, and is assigned to the Early Chalcolithic period (though the utility of that label can be questioned). The site was briefly examined by James Mellaart in 1962 but little was found except for a large assemblage of decorated pottery that bore comparison with other Anatolian sites like Canhasan, Hacılar and Mersin (Mellaart 1965). Recent work by the authors, funded by the British Institute of Archaeology at Ankara and The Wainwright Fund, together with a programme of radiocarbon dating led by Craig Cessford, and the results of the Konya Plain Survey (Baird 2002), have greatly expanded our knowledge of the context in which this pottery was made and used. The upper levels of Çatalhöyük West can now be dated to *c* 6000-5800 cal BC; extrapolating from the depth of buried stratigraphy, it appears that occupation of the site may well overlap with that of the East Mound and that there is a direct connection between the two mounds. At the same time we can see that the developments in ceramics, including the emergence of painted decoration, were part of a whole suite of social and material changes taking place around the turn of the 6th millennium cal BC; it is elements of this story that we wish to outline here.

The West Mound pottery differs from that of the Neolithic period in almost every respect: as well as the appearance of decoration and an order-of-magnitude increase in the quantities in use, the range of vessel forms and sizes is also vastly greater (though some basic forms do show elements of continuity between East and West).

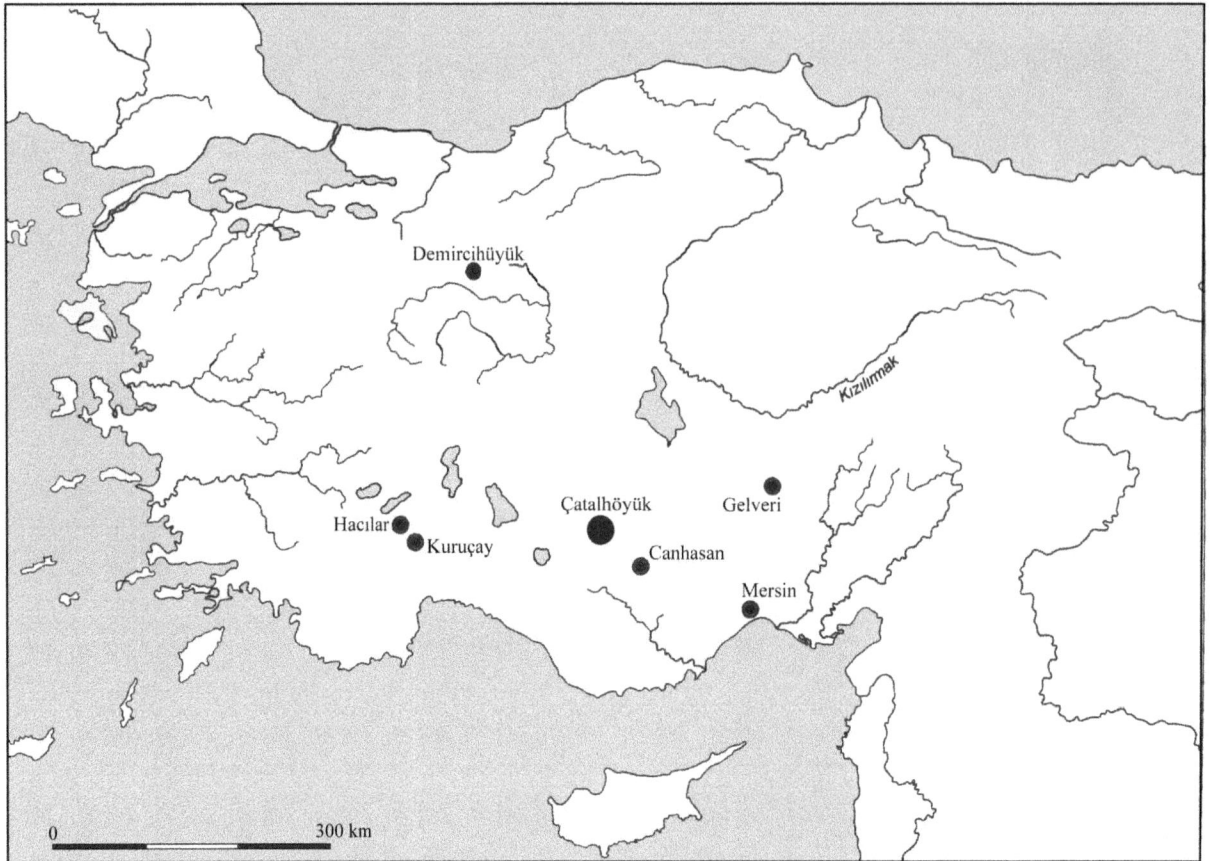

Fig 2. Location map of Çatalhöyük and other sites mentioned in the text

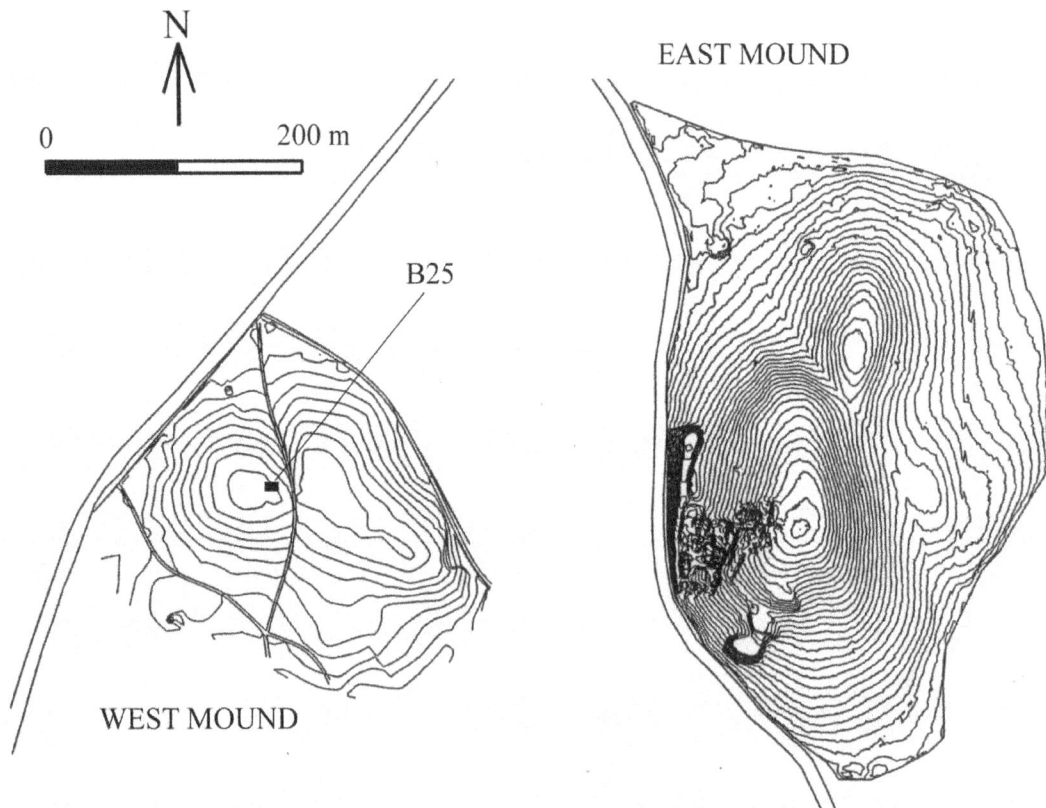

Fig 3. Çatalhöyük site plan

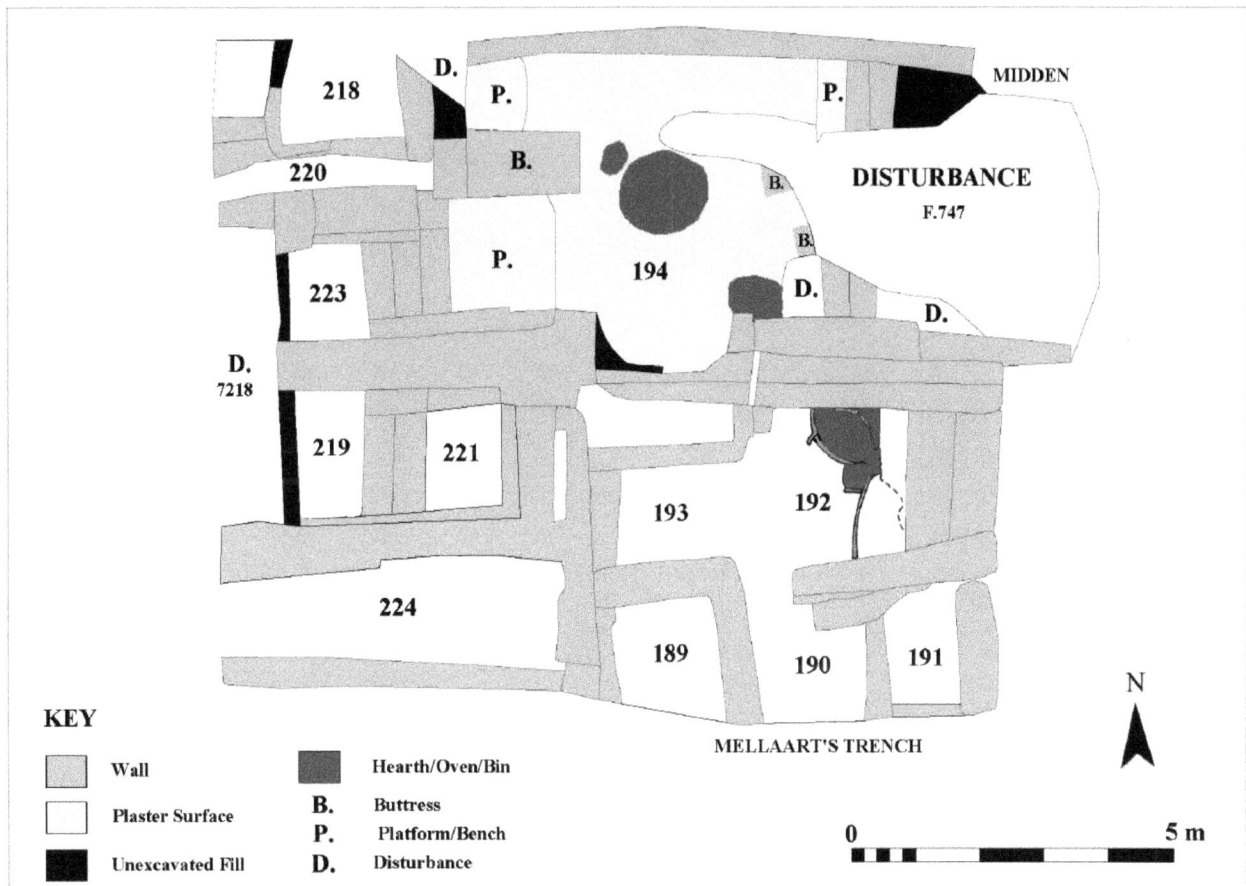

Fig 4. Building 25 plan

This much was clear from Mellaart's work in the 1960s; but now we can suggest that the built environment in which the pottery was used was very different as well.

The buildings on the East Mound, with their bucrania and murals, tend to be fairly small, self-contained, two-roomed structures with a main living area containing hearth, oven and platforms or benches, and some form of annex or store-room adjacent. That excavated on the West Mound (called Building 25) has similar mudbrick and plaster construction methods but shows a fundamental change in architecture (Fig. 4). Instead of the two-roomed Neolithic house we see a relatively large central space, elaborated with plaster floors and benches, surrounded by a large number of small cell-like rooms, the thickness of the walls possibly indicating the presence of a second storey. Despite this architectural complexity, however, the house lacks the paintings, mouldings and internal burials that characterise the Neolithic buildings.

Contemporary with these changes in architecture, we also see developments at a landscape scale, notably the appearance of a number of sites with similar pottery across the Konya Plain - in contrast to the Neolithic when Çatalhöyük East seems to have been the only settlement

of any size. There are developments in economic practices too: the faunal remains from the West Mound suggest an increased focus on sheep herding compared to the East Mound, while the wild cattle that were the focus of Neolithic ritual and art disappear (Sheelagh Frame, pers.comm.).

The changes occurring around 6000 cal BC therefore go far beyond pottery decoration. Yet there is reason to believe that was a significant part of the mosaic. Whatever the merits of the various arguments about shrines, shamans and goddesses rehearsed for Çatalhöyük, there is general agreement that the Neolithic house and its symbolic elaboration through paintings, mouldings and burials was crucial in the creation of community: decoration is always foregrounded. But, as mentioned, we know little about why these practices came to an end. Is it simply a coincidence that the apparent decline of architectural symbols on the West Mound coincides with the appearance in large quantities of well-made painted pottery? The fact that pottery was not decorated in the Neolithic makes this development all the more interesting - why did the locus of decoration shift from walls to pots?

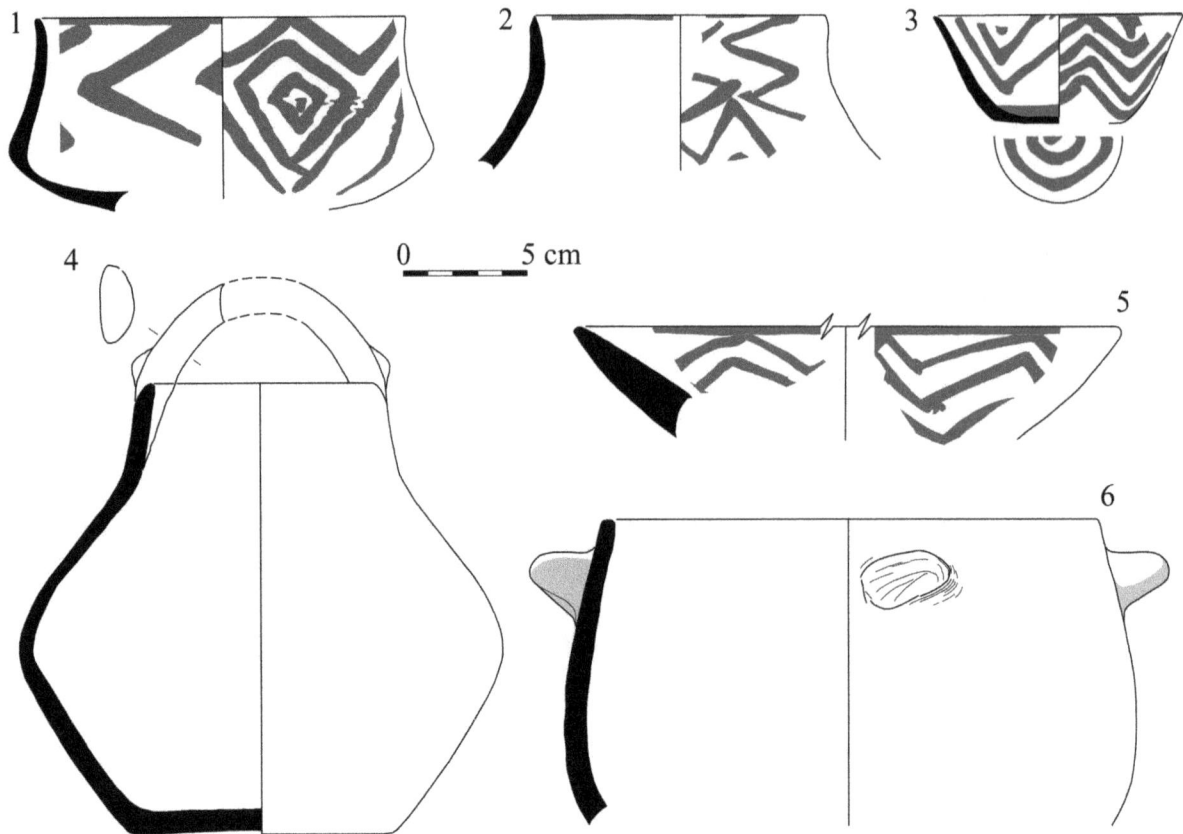

Fig 5. Selected West Mound pottery: 1- S-profiled bowl; 2 - necked jar; 3 - small bowl;
4 - basket-handled jar; 5 - dish; 6 - lugged holemouth

West Mound Pottery

Full publication of the pottery assemblage is forthcoming, and only a few pieces are illustrated here (Figs 5, 6). Many similar vessels to those uncovered during the present work are illustrated by Mellaart (1965).

The role of decoration on the West Mound pottery cannot be understood without first considering the range of forms produced. Key features include the great range of sizes, from miniature pots a few centimetres high (Fig 5.3) to jars holding several litres (Fig 5.6). The range is particularly striking compared to the Neolithic where there is comparatively little variation in size (Last, forthcoming). Shapes range from relatively simple forms like hemispherical bowls and holemouth jars to more complex types like necked jars (Figs 5.2, 6.1), sometimes with basket handles (Fig 5.4), and rarer forms including square pots and platters or dishes (Fig 5.5). The most common form, however, accounting for perhaps one-third of identifiable types in most contexts, is the carinated or S-profiled bowl (Fig 5.1). Interestingly, it is this basic type which, in an undecorated form, has its origins in the late Neolithic of the East Mound.

This typological elaboration implies a much greater range of roles and functions for pottery in the 6th millennium, from storage (solids and liquids) to food preparation and serving. There is little attention to 'non-functional' formal elements, such as the elaboration of rims and bases; both are generally simple, though occasionally anti-splash rims or lid-seats are found, and ring bases are not uncommon. There is more variety in terms of handles, which include loop and basket forms as well as a wide range of lug types. However, particular types seem to be restricted to particular vessel forms: for example, crescent lugs are restricted to unpainted holemouth jars. Most of the handles are found on the larger jars but a few small bowls have perforated lugs placed at the rim, while many of the S-profiled bowls have small 'vestigial' knobs or lugs, though these are primarily a decorative feature. As with vessel forms, the range of handles goes well beyond what is seen in the Neolithic, though a few types, such as basket handles, are occasionally found in the upper levels of the East Mound. The greater emphasis on lugs and handles in the West Mound assemblage suggests that pots were increasingly meant to be picked up, moved and displayed.

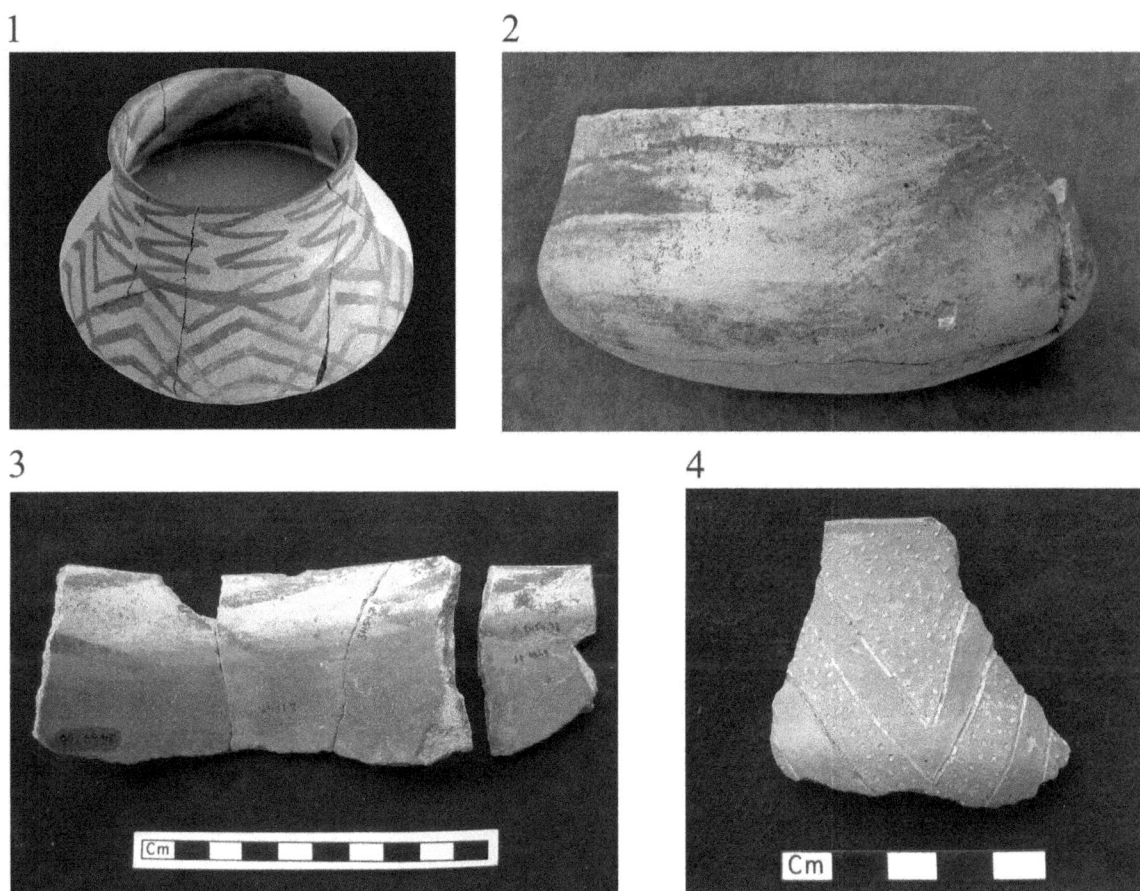

Fig 6. Surface treatments: 1 - fine painted jar rim; 2 - wash-painted bowl; 3 - overslip on interior of bowl;
4 - bowl rim with incised and infilled decoration

Although the West Mound pottery decoration is bold and striking, a key feature is its uniformity and lack of variation, both in general and specific terms. The majority comprises red or brown painted straight-line geometric motifs, applied over a cream or yellowish-buff slip, which is subsequently burnished. Moreover the potters generally adhered to a strong prescription as to how particular types of pottery should be decorated, reinforcing the form categories described above. Particular motifs seem to be reserved for specific vessel shapes, but the range of those motifs is relatively limited. For example, vertical zigzags appear both on the necks of jars and the interiors of carinated bowls (Figs 5.1-2, 6.1), while horizontal stripes are restricted to the necks of jars, and basket handles are invariably painted with chevrons. Even the occasional more complex motifs have their place, such as the dot-filled stars found on some bases.

The decoration particularly serves to emphasise the different zones of the pot, for instance there is always a division between jar necks and bodies (Fig 6.1), while on the interiors of S-profiled bowls the division between wall and base is usually marked. Decoration is also used to accentuate some formal elements such as lugs and handles, while the 'vestigial' lugs mentioned above seem to find their principal purpose as part of the decorative scheme, guiding the application of the zig-zag motifs.

Overall, it appears that about 50% of sherds have painted decoration, although the proportion of decorated *vessels* must be higher as many small, plain sherds may well have come from painted pots. Moreover, the 'undecorated' group also includes a large number of painted vessels, though these have an all-over paint or wash, streakily applied, rather than actual motif designs (Fig 6.2). The division between the pots with painted motifs and with 'all-over-wash' may sometimes (literally) be blurred: despite the strict nature of the design rules, the application of the decoration often appears to have been quite hurried, while the pots were frequently burnished before the paint had dried, causing a smearing effect on vessels of all type. This is so common that it must be deliberate, implying a glossy finish was just as important as a clear definition of the motifs. This may be a further area of continuity from Neolithic ceramics, among which burnishing is the most common surface treatment.

Similarly, the functional performance of pots may sometimes have been of greater consideration than visual appearance. The potters generally used calcareous clays that fire pink or orange (again different from those found in the Neolithic), the larger inclusions sometimes leading to surface spalling. Despite the damage caused to some painted surfaces, these clays were presumably selected because of their properties during manufacture, firing or use.

Another interesting feature in a number of cases is the application of a second layer of paint or slip over part of a pot. In some cases this was done to repair a crack or blemish, though presumably the effect would have been primarily visual rather than genuinely strengthening an area of weakness; mendholes, however, seem comparatively rare. In other cases it seems that the reslipping was carried out to deliberately cover over or repaint areas of decoration (Fig 6.3). As Mellaart (1975, 120) noted, 'this is a practice that reminds one of wall paintings, where one painted layer of plaster covers another'. It also suggests the significance of individual vessels during their use-lives, such that it was chosen to rework them rather than acquire a new pot.

Judging by the degree of wear seen on bases and occasionally rims, most pots were well-used and would have had a lengthy life. When they did finally break, the presence of numerous pot discs and modified potsherds ground into various forms indicates that some fragments were curated and took on new roles.

Following manufacture and use, the third activity that shows the significance of decorated pots at Çatalhöyük West is discard. On the East Mound there seems to be a basic division between building fills, with few potsherds or bulky items of rubbish, and extra-mural 'middens', where most of the sherds and other materials were found. There are a few cases of whole pots left within buildings on abandonment, but little sign of special treatment of broken pottery; other types of artefact show very similar patterning. On the West Mound, however, the complexity of the small spaces making up B25 is mirrored by the various types of pottery deposit found within them, each with sherds in very different conditions. Three main categories can be noted:

(a) generalized building fill with moderate densities of relatively small and abraded sherds, which is typical of the central space of B25 (Sp. 194 - Fig 4).
(b) dumps comprising mainly large sherds of pottery but also some other objects. These dumps occur in a number of the small spaces of B25 and may represent broken objects 'stored' for possible re-use, especially if we see these small rooms as cellars. The sherds generally show a mixture of fresh and abraded conditions, suggesting they may have been collected from various contexts.
(c) special or placed deposits of pottery, which can be discussed further below.

As on the East Mound, there are occasional examples of individual pots left in buildings. In the case of B25 this primarily comprised a large basket-handled jar, which was the only complete artefact left in Sp. 192 (actually in the doorway between 192 and 190), a room containing probable storage bins (Fig 4). Beyond this type of deposit, however, we also find spreads or clusters of sherds, which in B25 mainly came from the upper layers of building fill, not directly associated with surfaces. They may represent closure deposits and can be distinguished from the dumps within the small spaces by the objects represented within them. One example comprised a discrete but scattered group of freshly broken sherds deriving from finely made and decorated vessels (e.g. Fig 6.1). Another was composed of a group of miniature ceramic objects that resembled the larger potstands occasionally found on the site, associated with some pottery. The symbolic use of potstand-like forms, discussed elsewhere (Last 2000), further emphasises the importance of pottery and its various functions on the West Mound.

The analysis from which the summary above is derived shows an increasing diversity and complexity in the manufacture, use and deposition of pottery at Çatalhöyük West, compared to the Neolithic East Mound. Decoration is only part of the story but its role in defining and dividing space at different scales seems to be a key aspect of the observed developments. Painting, though often quickly applied and smeared, was nevertheless vital to mark out particular (functional) categories of pot, to define different parts of the pot (perhaps reinforcing points of symbolic or physical weakness) and to create a gridded, geometric space within those zones. Rather than the surface of the pot serving as a blank field on which decoration could be applied as a secondary action, form and decoration reinforce one another to create clearly defined categories of vessel. In a similar way, it may be that the 'reslipping' observed in some cases reflects a change in decoration relating to a change in the use of the vessel. And at a larger scale the deposition of pottery seems to have been linked to the different categories and divisions of space seen within the West Mound buildings.

Pottery Beyond the House

However, the significance of pottery decoration at Çatalhöyük also relates to developments at a larger spatial scale. When we look at why pots, rather than houses, were being decorated in the 6th millennium, a key point may be changing settlement patterns. The Konya Plain Survey (Baird 2002) has established that there was a significant increase in settlement numbers at this time: surface collection has found pottery very similar to the West Mound style at up to sixteen neighbouring sites, the majority located to the north and east of Çatalhöyük.

Most of the Konya Plain assemblages demonstrate broad similarities with the West Mound in terms of vessel form, method of decoration and motif types (Gibson, in prep.). However, within this general homogeneity it is possible to identify subtle variations in the percentage of decoration and the presence of particular motif types. For example at Bozlan and Musluk, situated 11 km and 20 km south-east of Çatalhöyük respectively, over 60% of the assemblages were decorated, while at Çinili, located 13 km to the north-east, this number was only 30%. At all the sites the predominant motif is, like the West Mound, the horizontal zigzag, although the variety and complexity of decoration varies markedly. The use of complex combinations of motifs on the same vessel was only noted at four sites, while at several others, including Dedeli, only 3 km to the south of Çatalhöyük, painted decoration appears to be restricted to just a few motifs, such as horizontal zigzags and simple painted rim bands. Furthermore, a number of sites display features that are rare at Çatalhöyük, such as curvilinear motifs and infilled decoration (including checkerboard designs), which were noted at Musluk, and dot-filled motifs, which were present at Bozlan.

One aspect of the development of decorated pottery may therefore relate to the portable and exchangeable nature of ceramics. Rather than the architectural decoration of Çatalhöyük East, which implies a concern with establishing relationships at the level of the household, the distribution of West Mound-type pottery across the Plain may reflect an interest in maintaining relationships between these neighbouring settlements, some of which could even represent the dispersed descendants of the larger population of Neolithic Çatalhöyük.

Beyond the Konya Plain, some pots were moving greater distances. This is clear from the occurrence of very different styles and fabrics of pottery in small quantities at Çatalhöyük. These probable imports are primarily dark-faced and vegetable-tempered, which is very rare among the Çatalhöyük West ware. Rather than painted motifs, they are decorated with a variety of incised, grooved or impressed motifs, sometimes with a white infill (Fig 6.4). The inclusion of such styles among the deposit of fine vessels mentioned above shows their significance.

Similar pottery is also found at sites as far afield as Demircihüyük in north-west Anatolia, Canhasan on the southern edge of the Konya Plain, and Mersin on the south coast (Fig 2), but only as small components of assemblages primarily of different type. One site where this style predominates, however, is an undated settlement in Cappadocia, some 200 km east of Çatalhöyük, called Gelveri (Esin 1993) (Fig 2). The Gelveri pottery comprises curvilinear or, less frequently, rectilinear designs of parallel grooves or bands filled with impressions. The link between Cappadocia and areas to the west and south may reflect long-standing connections principally marked by the acquisition of obsidian. However, the incised assemblage from Çatalhöyük differs from Gelveri in the proportions of rectilinear and curvilinear designs, and the presence of other styles (such as a group with small V-shaped incised and infilled

designs on a raised cordon, reminiscent of stitched leather seams) suggests a range of trans-regional connections more complex than the obsidian trade.

Such links may even provide a clue to the development of decorated pottery at Çatalhöyük in the first place. Although the rise of painted pots appears to coincide with a decline in painting on walls, there is little direct connection in the nature of the decoration. The East Mound wall paintings do include geometric motifs but they are generally more varied and complex than the linear and stereotypical pottery motifs of the West Mound. And the famous representational art of the Neolithic - animals, ritual scenes, even a landscape - are not repeated amongst these ceramics (though human figures are found occasionally in the succeeding 'Early Chalcolithic II'). The 'missing link' may lie to the west, in the Lake district around Burdur, where at sites like Hacılar (Mellaart 1970) and Kuruçay (Duru 1994), a 'fantastic' style of pottery decoration, geometrically based but with some similarities to the complex motifs of the wall-paintings, may be contemporary with the later levels of Çatalhöyük East (Schoop 2002) (Fig 2).

Perhaps the idea of painted pottery came from the Lake district and was reworked on the Konya Plain as part of a developing concern with dividing and categorising space at a variety of scales. Certainly the range of variation and innovation in the Hacılar pottery is not matched at Çatalhöyük, and even though geometric pottery more akin to the West Mound style seems to have replaced the 'fantastic style' at the Lake district settlements (Hacılar I), it remains considerably more elaborate and varied (cf. Mellaart 1970, fig. 117). For Mellaart (1970, 147), echoing Boas and Bunzel, the Hacılar style is the sort of 'great art' that 'is produced only by individual genius'. But however we understand individual creativity, it must be grounded in a theory of agency. Even the Hacılar pots were not art objects in the modern sense and the intentions of their makers cannot clearly be separated from those of their users: what we see at these sites is the deployment of different styles of decorated pottery in a variety of contexts, reflecting and reinforcing certain concerns and principles of social life.

Conclusions

At one level the shift in the focus of decoration from walls to pots at Çatalhöyük can be related to other developments on the Konya Plain around 6000 cal BC. Houses were conceptualised less as symbolic foci than as a series of discrete spaces with particular functions. A similar concern with categorisation and function is visible in material culture, especially pottery. At the same time pottery takes on a series of symbolic roles shown in depositional patterns and features like reslipping. These changes in the way material culture was deployed at the level of the household can be linked to changes in patterns of settlement and exchange.

Rather than one large settlement, a series of small or medium sized sites across the Konya Plain used material culture decoration, especially pottery, to establish relationships with one another and with more distant sites.

Decoration was not restricted only to pottery - a so far unique find from B25 was a bichrome painted plaster basin, its motifs recalling the pottery but exceeding it in complexity. However pottery, being so common, served a crucial purpose within these developments, its relatively simple and uniform decoration clearly playing a role in this reworking of social relations between households and settlements. In trying to understand the relationship between pottery decoration and residential mobility in Mesoamerica, Arnold (1999, 167) suggests that assemblages which appear to be 'over-elaborated' reflect situations where pottery may 'perform within a wide range of social contexts'. In other words, no harm is done if an elaborate container is used in an everyday situation, but the same may not be true if an undecorated container is used in an important social context. In mobile situations pottery may have been made in anticipation of such important contexts arising, even if any given pot was never actually used as such. The Konya Plain may not have been residentially mobile in the 6th millennium but personal mobility in the context of exchange networks, etc, might have been important. The decorated pottery may therefore reflect a readiness to engage in hospitality and networking beyond the household or immediate kin; a similar connection between exchange and hospitality has been suggested by Pickup (2004) as an explanation of decoration in Halaf ceramics at roughly the same period further east. Interestingly, there is a marked Halaf influence in the decoration of the succeeding 'Early Chalcolithic II' pottery styles on the West Mound (Mellaart 1965).

Ultimately the key to understanding will be in marrying the small-scale, such as design rules and symbolism of pots, to the large-scale, such as changing settlement patterns. In this respect it must be noted that the interpretive suggestions made in this paper are based on the excavation of just one house. We hope that work on the West Mound can be resumed and trust that new finds will add to and supersede much of this discussion.

At another level, however, we still have to situate the actions and motivations of potters into this broad interpretive framework, and return to the issues raised at the start of this paper. We have tried to show how aspects of making pots provide clues to the significance of their decoration. But further work can still be done, for instance looking at the sequences in which painted lines were applied and motifs built up.

We have also eschewed attempts to find meaning in these designs or other aspects of pottery, but rather focussed on links between the organisation of space at a variety of scales. As for the Pueblo potters, there was a clear sense of 'what worked' in terms of decoration; this seems to have generally been shared between sites on the Konya Plain though, as with individual Pueblos, there may be some aspects that served to distinguish them. The repetition of simple design elements may indicate that, again like some Pueblos, pottery decoration worked in an aesthetic sense rather than in terms of specific discursive meanings. Rather than a very specific set of symbolic concerns concerning e.g. the value and control of women, as suggested by Orrelle and Gopher (2000) for the 6th millennium BC Yarmukian pottery of the southern Levant, the value of the West Mound pottery to an expansive society may have lain in the way it permitted multiple readings.

The lack of variation in the West Mound pottery does not reflect the absence of a 'creative faculty' in Bunzel's (or Mellaart's) sense, rather that individual creativity was not appropriate in a situation where managing or mediating links between households and settlements mattered more. But this serves to distinguish the West Mound pottery from the East Mound wall paintings, where creativity does seem to have been nurtured. Perhaps we need to stop seeing pots individually, as objects in their own right, as our classificatory approaches demand, and consider them as fragments of a social project, pursued both by their makers and their users, partial materialisations of a way of thinking about the world that suited the demands of a networked, outward-looking Early Chalcolithic society.

So can these pots with their simple geometries be seen as the successors of the great murals of Çatalhöyük? At one level there is a very different approach to the creation of designs, but in another sense both represent the efforts, whether conscious or not, of skilled individuals to reflect and maintain a sense of community in a changing world.

References

Arnold, P.J., 1999. *Tecomates*, residential mobility and early formative occupation in coastal lowland Mesoamerica. In J.M. Skibo & G.M. Feinman (eds.), *Pottery and People: a Dynamic Interaction*, 159 – 70. Salt Lake City: University of Utah Press.

Baird, D., 2002. Early Holocene settlement in Central Anatolia: problems and prospects as seen from the Konya Plain. In F. Gérard & L. Thissen (eds.), *The Neolithic of Central Anatolia. Internal Developments and External Relations During the 9th-6th Millennia cal BC*. 139 – 59. Istanbul: Eye Yayinlari.

Barrett, J.C., 1991. Bronze Age pottery and the problem of classification. In J. Barrett, R. Bradley & M. Hall (eds.), *Papers on the Prehistoric Archaeology of Cranborne Chase*. Oxford: Oxbow Monograph 11.

Bernstein, B. & Brody, J.J., 2002. *Voices in Clay: Pueblo Pottery from the Edna M. Kelly Collection*. Oxford, Ohio: Miami University Art Museum.

Boast, R., 2002. Pots as categories: British Beakers. In Woodward & Hill (eds.), 96 – 105.

Bourdieu, P., 1990. *The Logic of Practice.* Oxford: Polity Press.

Bunzel, R., 1929. *The Pueblo Potter: a Study of Creative Imagination in Primitive Art.* New York: Columbia University Press.

Cessford, C. forthcoming. Absolute dating at Çatalhöyük. In I. Hodder (ed.), *Excavating Çatalhöyük: South, North and KOPAL Area Reports from the 1995-99 Seasons.* Cambridge: McDonald Institute for Archaeological Research.

During, B.S., 2001. Social dimensions in the architecture of Neolithic Çatalhöyük. *Anatolian Studies* 51, 1 – 18.

Duru, R., 1994. *Kuruçay Höyük I: 1978-1988 Kazylarynyn Sonuçlary Neolitik ve Erken Kalkolitik Çag Yerlesmeleri.* Türk Tarih Kurumu.

Esin, U., 1993. Gelveri: ein Beispiel für die kulturelle Beziehiungen zwischen Zentralanatolien und Südosteuropa während des Chalkolithikums. *Anatolica* 19, 47 – 56.

Gibson, A. & Woods, A., 1997. *Prehistoric Pottery for the Archaeologist.* London: Leicester University Press.

Gibson, C., in prep. The Chalcolithic assemblages. In D. Baird (ed.), *The Konya Plain Survey Project, 1994-2001.* CBRL Monograph.

Hill, J.D., 2002. Pottery and the expression of society, economy and culture. In Woodward & Hill (eds.), 75 – 84.

Ingold, T., 2000. *The Perception of the Environment: Essays in Livelihood, Dwelling and Skill.* London: Routledge.

Last, J., forthcoming. Neolithic pottery from the East Mound. In I. Hodder (ed.), *Changing Materialities at Çatalhöyük: Reports from the 1995-99 Seasons.* Cambridge: McDonald Institute for Archaeological Research.

Lewis-Williams, D., 2004. Constructing a cosmos: architecture, power and domestication at Çatalhöyük. *Journal of Social Archaeology,* 4, 28 – 59.

Lucas, G., 2001. *Critical Approaches to Fieldwork: Contemporary and Historical Archaeological Practice.* London: Routledge.

Mellaart, J., 1965. Çatal Hüyük West. *Anatolian Studies,* 15, 135 – 56.

Mellaart, J., 1967. *Çatal Hüyük: A Neolithic Town in Anatolia.* London: Thames and Hudson.

Mellaart, J., 1970. *Excavations at Hacylar.* Edinburgh: Edinburgh University Press.

Mellaart, J., 1975. *The Neolithic of the Near East.* London: Thames and Hudson.

Morris, E., 2002. Staying alive: the function and use of prehistoric ceramics. In Woodward & Hill (eds.), 54 – 61.

Orrelle, E. & Gopher, A., 2000. The Pottery Neolithic period: questions about pottery decoration, symbolism, and meaning. In I. Kuijt (ed.), *Life in Neolithic Farming Communities: Social Organization, Identity, and Differentiation,* 295 – 308. New York: Kluwer Academic/Plenum.

Pickup, J., 2004. Reassessing Halaf symbolism in the Mosul region of Iraq. Paper presented at BANEA conference, Reading, March 2004.

Rye, O.S., 1981. *Pottery Technology: Principles and Reconstruction.* Taraxacum: Manuals on Archaeology 4.

Schiffer, M.B. & Skibo, J.M., 1987. Theory and experiment in the study of technological change. *Current Anthropology,* 28, 595 – 622.

Schoop, U-D., 2002. Frühneolithikum im südwestanatolischen Seengebiet? Eine kritische Betrachtung. In R. Aslan, S. Blum, G. Kastl, F. Schweizer and D. Thumm (eds.), *Mauerschau: Festschrift für Manfred Korfmann,* Vol 1, 421 – 36. Remshalden-Grunbach: Verlag Bernhard Albert Greiner.

Skibo, J.M. & Schiffer, M.B., 1995. The clay cooking pot: an exploration of women's technology. In J.M. Skibo, W.H. Walker & A.E. Nielsen (eds.) *Expanding Archaeology,* 80 – 91. Salt Lake City: University of Utah Press.

Woodward, A. & Hill, J.D. (eds.), 2002. *Prehistoric Britain: The Ceramic Basis.* Prehistoric Ceramics Research Group Occasional Publication 3. Oxford: Oxbow.

CHAPTER 4

Organic Pigments in Pottery Decoration of Early Agrarian Cultures in the Vistula Drainage: 4th-3rd Millennium BC

Aleksander Kośko, Jerzy Langer, Sławomir Pietrzak, Marzena Szmyt

Introduction

The question of organic pigments used by cultures in the Vistula drainage in the 4th-3rd millennium BC can be now narrowed down to the issue of wood-tar pigments.[1] Beginning in the mid-1980s, prehistoric wood tar has been subject to more careful physicochemical analyses including its remains on the surfaces of ceramic vessels (Kośko & Langer 1986). Evidence of its use in three roles was successively gathered, namely as a binder for ornaments cut out from birch bark (Vogt 1949; Langer & Kośko 1992, 67; 1999, 74), as a pigment used in making painted ornaments (Langer & Kośko 1992; 1999) and as a hypothetical "glazing"[2] (Józwiak, Langer & Pietrzak, 2001: Józwiak 2003, 233 – 4). Our paper addresses the state of research into the second of these roles. It summarizes the techno-archaeological and cultural-historical assessments of wood-tar pigments identified so far as having a decorative character.

The techno-archaeological description of Late Neolithic wood-tar pigments

Wood-tar pigments have been recorded in the decoration of ceramic vessels of three Late Neolithic cultures: the Funnel Beaker culture (FBC), Globular Amphora culture (GAC) and Corded Ware culture. However, the techno-archaeological analyses have covered only the ornaments of FBC and GAC pottery (Fig 1).

The physico-chemical examinations have been carried out by the archaeometry group of the Laboratory for Materials Physicochemistry and Nanotechnology, Faculty of Chemistry (Adam Mickiewicz University, Poznań). Use was made of standard methods of analysis which were treated as preliminary, although, for technical reasons, these were often the only methods employed. These comprise analyses such as measurements of melting point, solubility in organic solvents, water and aqueous solutions of acids (HCl) and bases (NaOH), thin layer chromatography (TLC), infrared (FTIR), visual and ultraviolet (UV-VIS) absorption spectra, electron paramagnetic resonance EPR, optical and scanning electron microscopy (SEM). In some cases mass spectrometry (MS and GCMS) have also been applied.

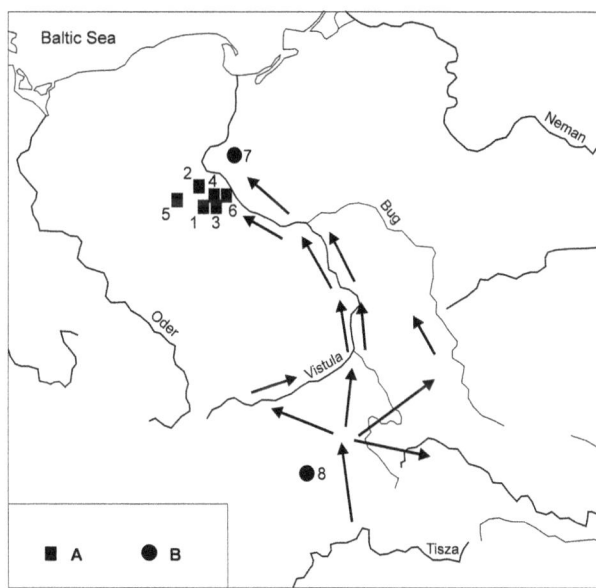

Fig 1. Location of the sampled sites. Key: A – Late Neolithic sites: the Funnel Beaker culture (1 – Opatowice site 33, 2 – Inowrocław-Mątwy site 4, 3 – Opatowice site 42, 4 – Kuczkowo site 5) and the Globular Amphora culture (5 – Bożejewice site 22, 6 – Kuczkowo site 1); B – Early Neolithic sites: the Linear and post-Linear Pottery circle (7 - Ryńsk site 42, 8 - Šariš Michaľany). Arrows show directions of influences of the East Linear Pottery circle (foll. Grygiel 2001).

The Funnel Beaker culture

"Wood-tar decoration" has been recorded on pottery from Kujawy dated to phases IIIB, IIIC, IVB, VA, (i.e. to 3600-2500 BC). The studies carried out so far do not allow us to make any detailed reconstructions of forms, elements or decoration patterns. What can only be said is that we deal here with belly decoration, most probably non-zonal ("filling in a noticeable space on a vessel surface with an ornament" – Kośko 1981, 40 – 41).

To describe the technology of making a pigment we shall use the four following samples as examples of a larger set of data:

Sr1[3] = Opatowice site 33 (Radziejów district, Poland), phase IIIB (radiocarbon dating of the wood tar: Poz-9835 4590±50 BP), Fig 2;

---

[1] Cf. Langer, Kośko 1992 and 1999 for the question of sporadic use of blood and a bituminous dye in the production of pigments.

[2] As "pots with glazing" we consider vessels covered with a rather thick and uneven layer of wood tar and showing no signs of prior preparation of the surface.

[3] Sr-... = lab. signature.

Fig 2. Sample Sr1. Opatowice site 33 (Radziejów district, Poland). A fragment of the Funnel Beaker culture vessel with traces of black pigment.

Fig 5. Sample Sr14. Kuczkowo site 5 (Aleksandrów Kuj. district, Poland). A fragment of the Funnel Beaker culture vessel with traces of black pigment.

Fig 3. Sample Sr3. Inowrocław-Mątwy site 5 (Inowrocław district, Poland). A fragment of the Funnel Beaker culture vessel with traces of black pigment.

Sr3 = Inowrocław-Mątwy site 5 (Inowrocław district, Poland), phase IIIC (radiocarbon dating of the site: Bln-2186 4470±60 BP), Fig 3;

Sr12 = Opatowice site 42 (Radziejów district, Poland), phase IVB (radiocarbon dating of the site: Gd-2764 4460±80 BP), Fig 4;

Sr14 = Kuczkowo site 5 (Aleksandrów Kuj. district, Poland), cultural layer, trench B1a, phase IVA/VA (radiocarbon dating of the site: Ki-6499 4620±35 BP; Ki-6501 4560±55 BP; Ki-6500 4630±35 BP), Fig 5.

Fig 4. Sample Sr12. Opatowice site 42 (Radziejów district, Poland). A fragment of the Funnel Beaker culture vessel with traces of black pigment.

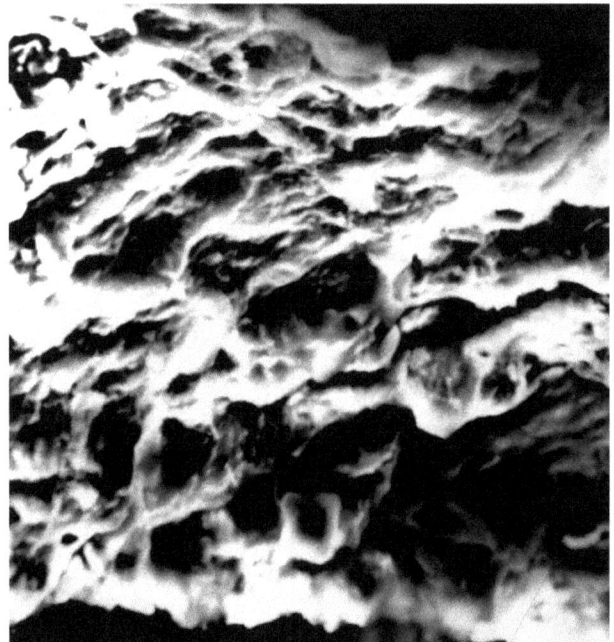

Fig 6. Sample Sr3 - SEM. Outer surface. Picture shows a wood tar layer applied with a "brush" (traces of "brush" strokes can be seen).

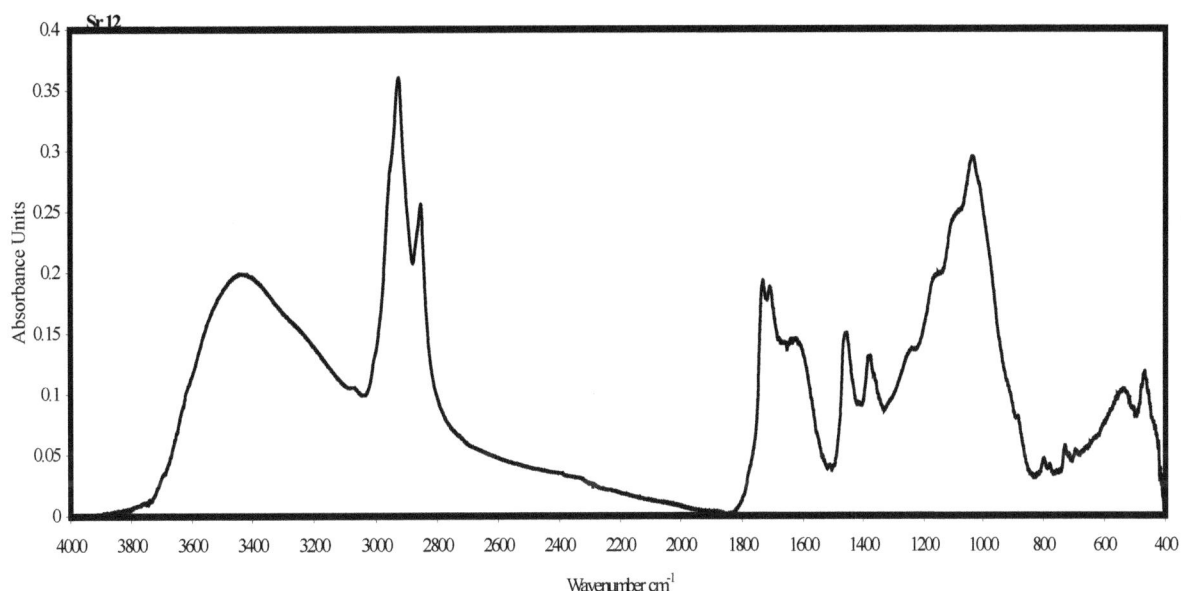

Fig 7. Sample Sr12 - FTIR spectrum. The high content of minerals in the wood tar results from deliberate additions.

Sample *Sr1* is an example of a pigment that has undergone extensive thermal degradation giving it a "mineral" character while the other samples are typical organic substances. The colour layer is up to 1mm thick. Under a microscope it shows signs of action of high temperatures (micro-bubbles) and deliberately added minute mineral crystals. In the outer surface of the sample *Sr3* a wood-tar layer was applied with a "brush" (traces of "brush" strokes can be seen in SEM examinations - Fig 6). Pigment *Sr14* was applied onto a smoothed mineral base. The nature of the black colouring substance is varied. Characteristic infrared absorption (FTIR) shows that, except sample *Sr1* (strongly carbonized, with a high mineral content) and sample *Sr14* (having characteristics of a bituminous (geogenic) substance of peculiar properties (Langer & Pietrzak 2001)), the basic material of pigment layers is a medium fraction of birch wood tar. This fraction melts at approx. 120° or 150°C (which means that it can be used only below this point), it can be dissolved in organic solvents, but does not dissolve in water. In the outer layer of samples *Sr3* and *Sr14*, there are aromatic organic acids (FTIR 1700 cm^{-1}, $\nu_{C=O}$), which is evidence of the action of high temperatures (*Sr3*) or of the different nature of the tar used (*Sr14*). Whereas the inner layers of sample *Sr3* and sample *Sr12* are characterized by the presence of unsaturated fatty acids (FTIR 1707-1710 cm^{-1}, $\nu_{C=O}$), the high content of which is a result of the way the tar was made (modification by adding fats, *Sr12*) or of the contact between the vessel and vegetable fats during its use (*Sr3*). The latter reason is validated by the difference in chemical composition of the tar layer between the outer and inner surfaces of the vessel.

Materials examined here differ from other uses of wood tars in that the present material contains a substantial addition of mineral substances including iron oxides and salts (Fig 7). The additions aid adhesion to the ceramic base and the mechanical properties of the pigment layer (increased resistance to wear). There could also be other reasons for the presence of iron compounds, as for instance, the addition of blood (Fig 8). It can be seen in sample *Sr1* in the form of micro-concentrations of iron the size of blood cells. The practice of adding blood seems to be of a more universal nature despite the fact that it was not required by the physico-chemical demands of the colouring-layer technology. This is indicated by the fact that a similar picture of iron decomposition is observed in sample *Sr3* (which is rich in mineral additions introducing iron), however, only on the surface of the free layer of pigment — the sedimentation of heavier mineral admixtures relieves the surface of the excess of iron. The high iron content of mineral origin observable inside the material allows us to trace blood cells that may occur there without being, in this case, the main carrier of iron. The action of high temperature and the hybrid, organic-mineral character of the pigments are confirmed by EPR examinations: the spectra show sharp, narrow lines typical of organic radicals generated in thermal processes and wide, bold lines attributed to paramagnetic mineral components (Fig 9).

It must be added that the observations made here have been supported recently by the analyses of 44 samples of FBC pottery carried out within the "Opatowice – Prokopiak's Mount" project (Kujawy region, Poland).[4]

---

[4] Project no. 2 H01H 028 25 financed by the Ministry of Science and Information Technology in 2003-2006.

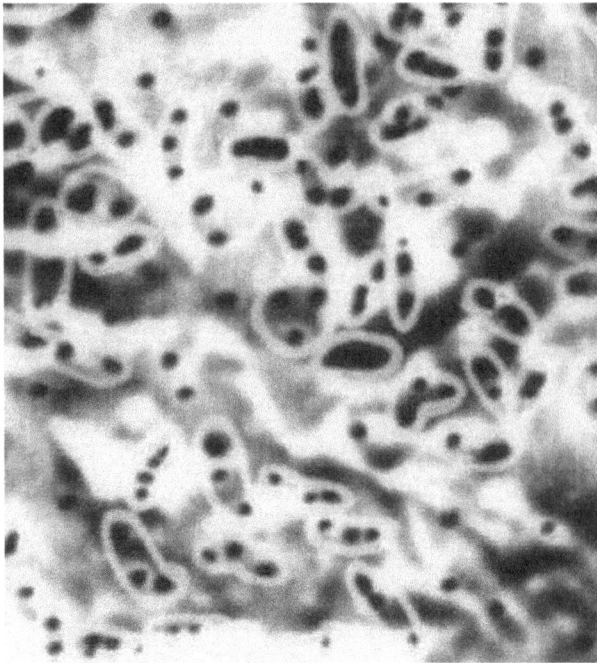

Fig 8. Sample Sr1 – SEM. Blood cell distribution.

Fourteen of the samples were found to be similar to *Sr1* (*i.e.* having a strongly marked mineral character), while the other 30 samples contained remains of wood tars (specifically, birch tar) with admixtures of mineral components.

Globular Amphora culture

"Wood-tar decoration" has been identified so far on pottery from two sites in Kujawy dated to phase IIb of the GAC (Kośko, Langer & Szmyt 2000):

Sr18 – Bożejewice site 22 (Strzelno district, Poland), feature A10, phase IIb (a set of radiocarbon date from the site: Ki-6912-Ki-6914 4335±45 – 4275±45 BP), Fig. 10;

Sr19 – Kuczkowo site 1 (Aleksandrów Kuj. district, Poland), site 1, feature A136, phase IIb (a set of radiocarbon dates from the feature: Ki-6917, Ki-6926-6929 4420±55 – 4370±50 BP), Fig. 11.

In both cases, a detailed study of the two fragments has revealed that a thin layer of pigment covered the external surface of the ceramic fragments. It is not possible, however, to reconstruct in any detail the exact scheme of decoration.

The black pigment (as above) is a hybrid material of an organic character containing mineral additions. It is a heavy fraction of wood tar with the softening point above 200°C (240°C and 210°C respectively), which allowed the safe use of the vessel to boil water (*i.e.* 100°C) or even to melt or heat fat (*i.e. c.* 150°C). The mineral ingredients contain silica and iron compounds thus improving the adhesion of the pigment layer to the ceramic base and resistance to wear.

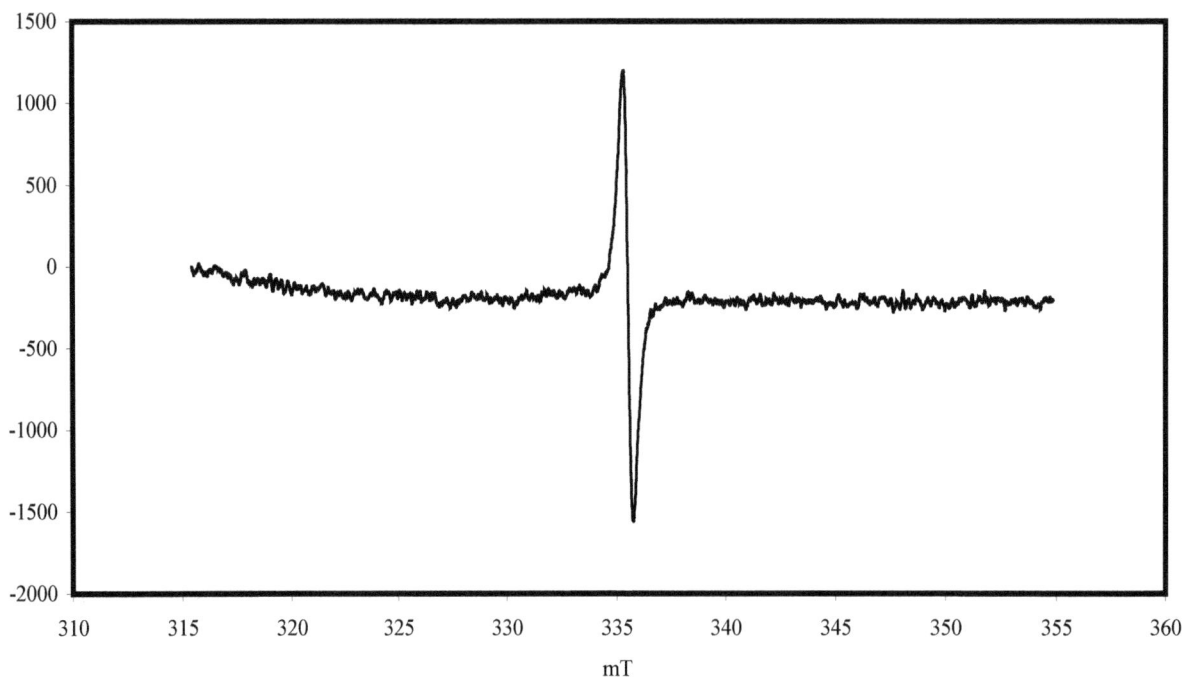

Fig 9. Sample Sr3 – EPR. Examinations show the action of high temperature and the hybrid, organic-mineral character of the pigments.

Fig 10. Sample Sr18. Bożejewice site 22 (Strzelno district, Poland). A fragment of the Globular Amphora culture vessel with traces of black pigment.

Fig 11. Sample Sr19. Kuczkowo site 1 (Aleksandrów Kuj. district, Poland). A fragment of the Globular Amphora culture vessel with traces of black pigment.

The position of wood-tar pigments in the circle of painted pottery cultures

The evidence of the use of "wood-tar decoration" coming from Kujawy is a stimulus for broader research into the cultural and historical contexts. The questions concern:

1   the establishment of the prologue of the phenomenon on the scale of the European Neolithic and Eneolithic cultures;
2   the sequence of stages of the phenomenon's development (topogenesis), and
3   reception mechanisms prevailing on the Central European Lowland.

Pottery painted with a wood-tar pigment in the circle of Linear cultures

The crucial findings of the studies carried out so far, albeit limited in terms of space and the scope of analysis,

include the establishment of the presence of wood-tar pigments in the decoration of pottery coming from the Linear and Post-Linear cultures of eastern Slovakia as well as from regions remaining under their influence and lying to the north of them (Fig 1) (Grygiel 2001). It has been also found that such techniques of pottery decoration are absent from the Eastern Carpathian frontier of the Black Sea Eneolithic cultures, for instance, Cucuteni-Tripolye (Stos-Fertner & Rook 1981: Langer & Kośko 1992; 1999, 64: Trąbska *et al.* 2003). This conclusion is substantiated by the analyses of painted ware from:

Sr10 -   Šariš Michalăny (Sabinov district, Slovakia), the Eastern Linear Pottery culture (younger phase = Tiszadob),[5] Fig 12;

Sr151 –   Šariš Michalăny (Sabinov district, Slovakia), the Bükk culture, Fig 13 and

Sr438 –   Ryńsk site 42 (Wąbrzeźno district, Poland), the Linear Band Pottery culture (LBPC), genetically related to the Eastern Linear Cultural Circle (Kirkowski 1994:64),[6] Fig. 14.

Fig 12. Sample Sr10. Šariš Michalăny (Sabinov district, Slovakia). A fragment of the Eastern Linear Pottery culture (younger phase = Tiszadob) vessel with traces of black pigment.

Sr10 is a case that has already been identified (EPR examinations) as an organic pigment on a birch-tar base with mineral additions (EPR spectrum shows a narrow intensive signal having spectral parameters corresponding to organic radicals (g = 2.0029, ΔH = 0.51 mT) and a broad signal of mineral components (g=2.0893, ΔH = 42.63 mT)), which is resistant to high temperatures.

---

[5] We are grateful to Dr. Juraj Pavùk for the samples from Šariš Michalăny.
[6] We are grateful to Mr. Ryszard Kirkowski, M.A., for the sample from Ryńsk (collection of the Museum in Grudziądz).

Fig 13. Sample Sr151. Šariš Michalǎny (Sabinov district, Slovakia). A fragment of the Bükk culture vessel with traces of black pigment.

Sample **Sr151** comes from a vessel bearing a motif of incised bands filled with a black pigment forming an even layer 0.5-1mm thick. The layer was applied when the pigment was liquid with a brush (or dauber), which is seen in the microtraces visible on the layer surface under a microscope. Also in this case, deliberately added mineral substances, different from the ceramic base, were identified. This is indicated by FTIR results (absorption in the range of 1000-1200 cm^{-1}) and specifically by EPR results (Fig 15-17). The EPR spectrum of Sr151 pigment consists of two lines: a narrow weak one (g=2.0035,

ΔH=0.47 mT), attributed to organic radicals resulting from a high temperature (pigment firing), and an intensive broad one corresponding to mineral ingredients contained in the pigment layer. The spectral parameters of this line (g=2.0931,ΔH=59.25 mT) are significantly different from the spectrum of the ceramic base g=2.1385, ΔH =102.5mT. These results, together with microscope observations, allow one to draw conclusions about purposeful introduction of mineral additions to the organic colour layer.

Pigments **Sr10** and **Sr151** show important similarities. In both cases, the organic material was birch tar, which is evidenced by characteristic IR absorption in the range of 880 cm^{-1} and 725 cm^{-1} as well as 3070 cm^{-1} (C-H in unsaturated compounds), 2924, 2852, 1453 and 1385 cm^{-1} (CH$_2$ and CH$_3$ groups), 1730 cm^{-1} (ester), 1710 cm^{-1} (unsaturated carboxylic acids) and 1603 cm^{-1} (carboxylic acid salts). The organic substance, when subjected to further heat treatment, turns out to contain purposefully added mineral ingredients (this is shown by EPR tests). Similar EPR spectra are observed consisting of a thin line having similar spectral parameters and attributed to organic radicals (g=2.0029, ΔH=0.51 mT and g=2.0035, ΔH=0.47 mT, respectively), and a broad line reflecting mineral ingredients, among which iron salts can be traced but not those of manganese.

Similar data were obtained for sample **Sr438**, which comes from a vessel with a painted pattern. Here also the pigment layer was deliberately applied; it is thin and has a hybrid, organic-inorganic character. This has been confirmed by FTIR spectra (Fig 18), where we have observed absorption attributed to inorganic components (e.g. 3697, 3620 cm^{-1}, 1026 cm^{-1}, 520 and 467 cm^{-1}), but also absorption bands typical of organic materials, including

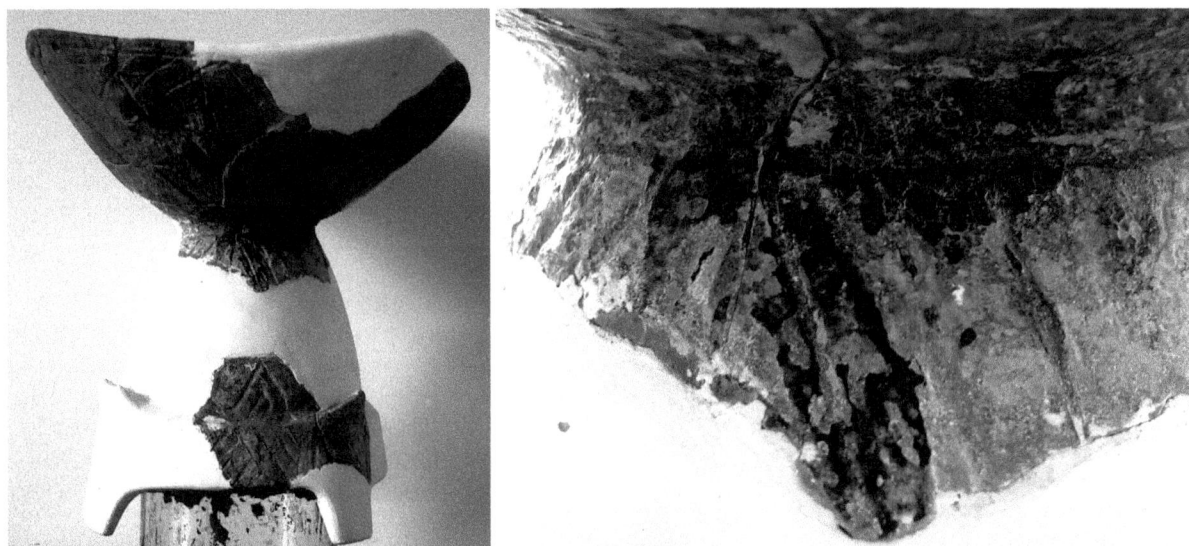

Fig 14. Sample Sr438. Ryńsk site 42 (Wąbrzeźno district, Poland). A vessel of the Linear Band Pottery culture with traces of black pigment.

Sr 151

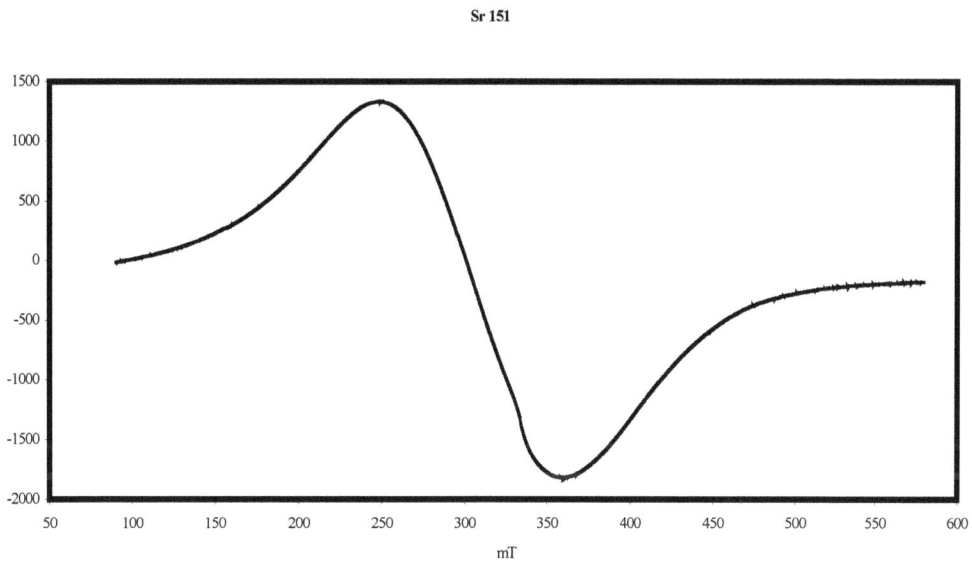

Fig 15. Sample Sr151 – EPR. Spectrum of ceramic substratum.

Sr 151

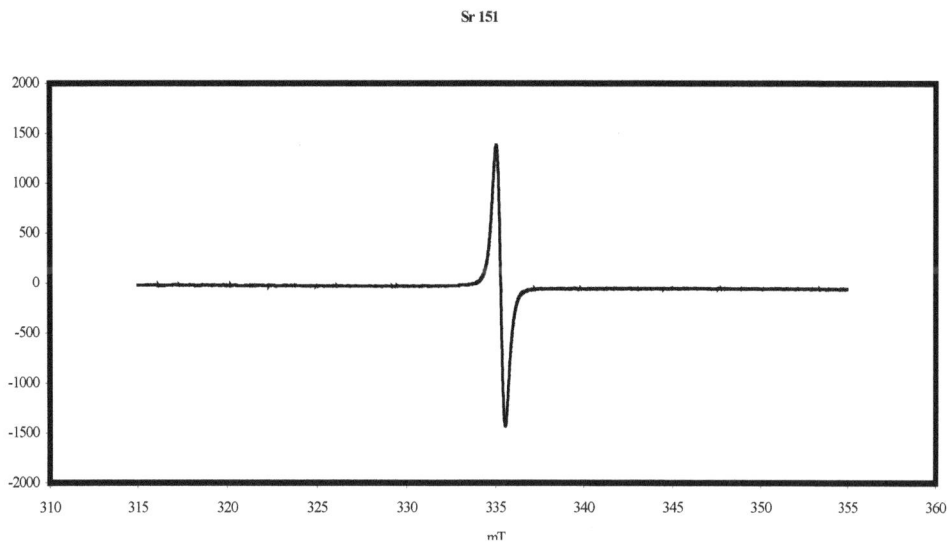

Fig 16. Sample Sr151 – EPR. Spectrum reveals the presence of organic radicals in a wood tar sample.

Sr 151

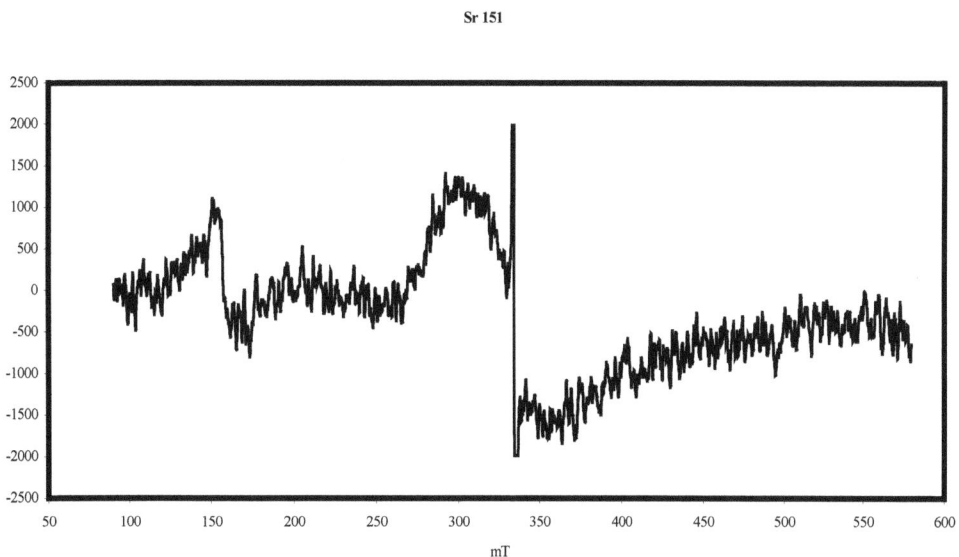

Fig 17. Sample Sr151 – EPR. Spectrum of mineral ingredients (purposeful admixture) present in the wood tar.

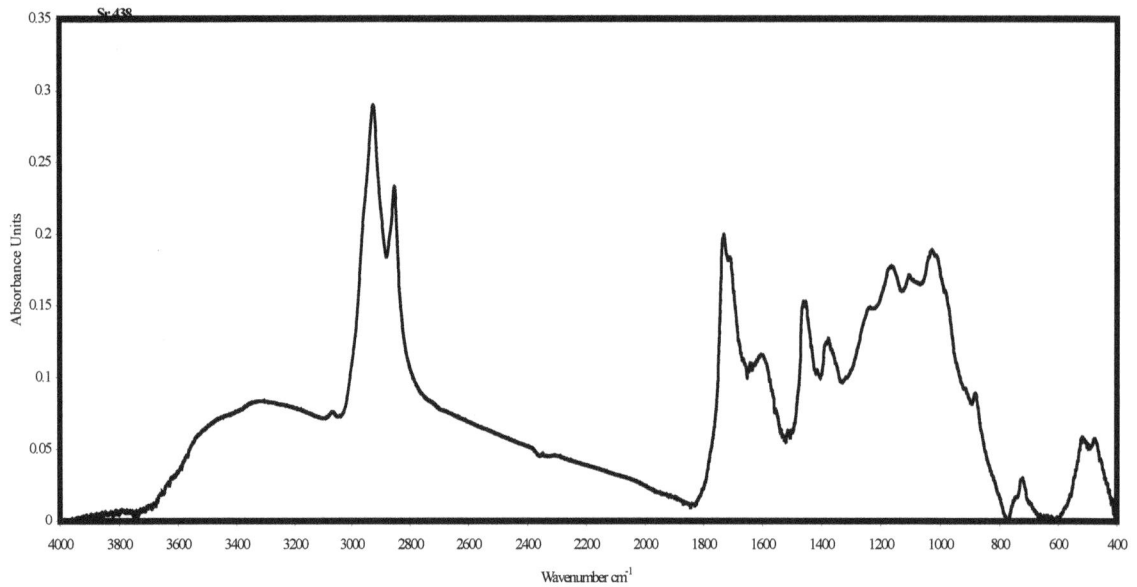

Fig 18. Sample Sr438 – FTIR spectrum. The high content of minerals in the wood tar results from deliberate additions.

wood tar (e.g. 2924 cm^{-1}, 2853 cm^{-1}, 1457 cm^{-1} and 1384 cm^{-1} (CH_2 and CH_3 groups), approx. 1730 cm^{-1} (group C=O, esters), 1653 cm^{-1} (C=O, salts of carboxylic acids). The small amount of the substance available has prevented us from identifying the raw material from which the tar was made. The hybrid nature of the pigment is reflected in the EPR spectrum: against a strong broad line (g=2.2357, ΔH=95.84 mT) attributed to inorganic ingredients, there is a weaker narrows signal (g=2.0020, ΔH=0.59 mT) originating with organic radicals typical of wood tars subjected to a high temperature. Microscopic examinations (SEM) reveal the complex structure of the pigment layer (Fig 19) and the fact that the base, of a different structure, was deliberately prepared. A clearly visible outer layer, about 0.1 mm thick, is microporous, non-homogenous and bears traces of directional application of the pigment, while it was semi-liquid, with a brush. This resulted in the horizontal direction of pigment microlayers and partial tightening of the pores. The base differs from the pigment layer in the size and shape of micropores (Fig 20).

It is hard to assess for the time being whether the technique of painting vessels with a black wood-tar pigment, which appeared in the upper Tisza (e.g. Šariš Michaľany) and lower Vistula drainages (Chełmno Land – Ryńsk site 42) in the second half of the 6th millennium BC, is an "invention" (technological-symbolic/stylistic) that could be limited to eastern Slovak settlement communities at least in its original form. An analysis of black pigments of the following cultures is urgently needed: Körös, Vinča and the groups of the western LBPC, in particular from the drainage of the Morava and upper Elbe rivers. Notice should also be taken of the broad range of wood-tar used as a glazing covering "kitchen" ware in the LBPC.

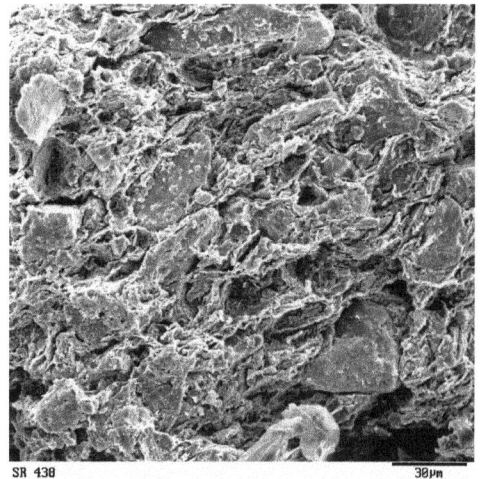

Fig 19. Sample Sr438 – SEM. A deliberate mineral admixture is present in the organic layer (wood tar) as a pigment modification.

Fig. 20. Sample Sr438 – SEM. A fracture of the layer of wood tar pigment (above) and a clear division line between the organic layer and the mineral substratum (below).

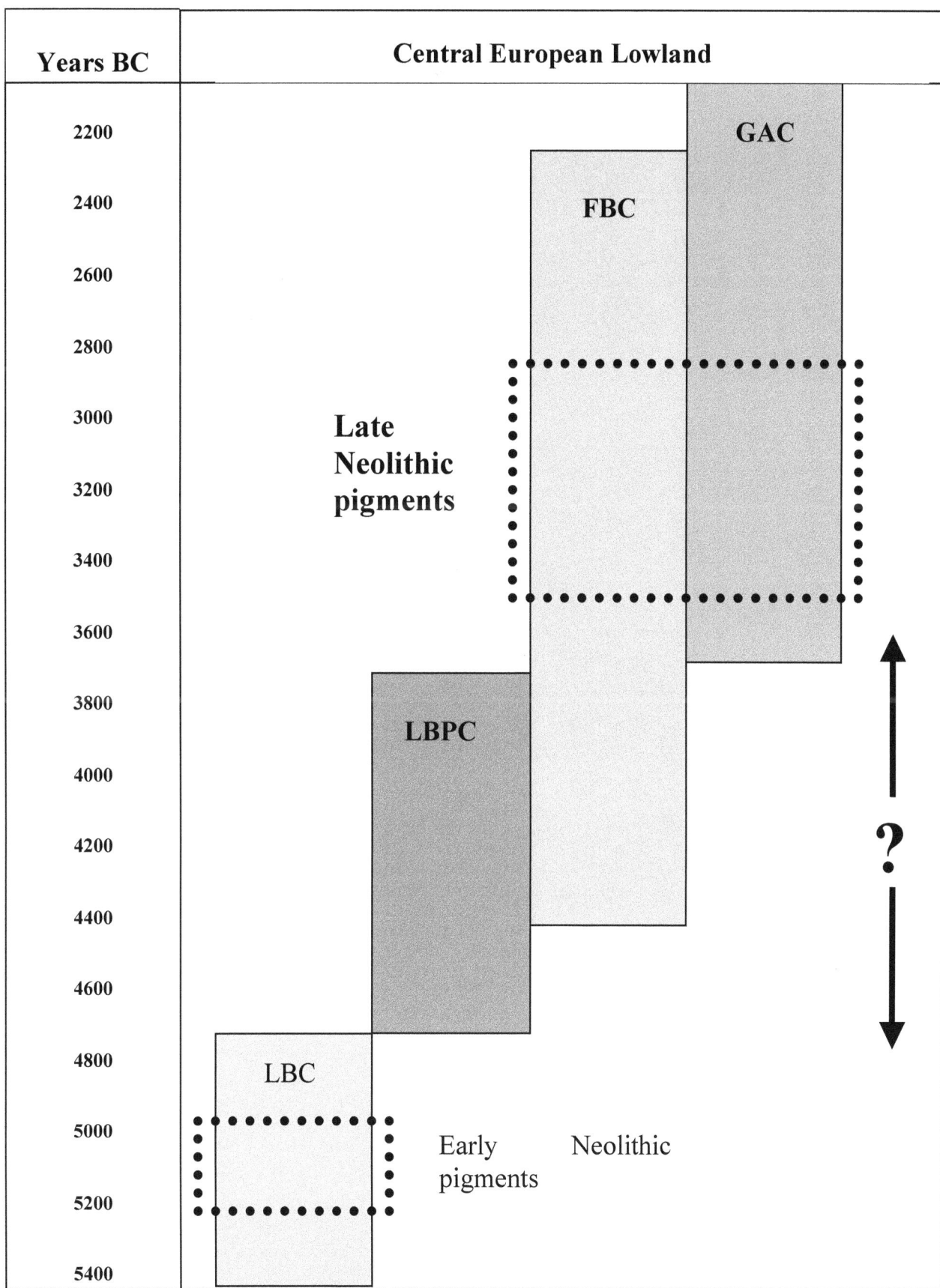

Fig. 21. Absolute chronology of the wood tar pigments used by the Lowlands societies (from the Vistula drainage: Kujawy region and Chełmno land) in the Neolithic.

The continuity/discontinuity of wood-tar decoration tradition? The Lowlands perspective

The Lowland pottery of post-Linear cultures does not show any signs of using wood tar in the forming of vessel surfaces, neither in making painted ornaments nor as a "glazing". Between the second half of the 6th millennium BC (Ryńsk site 42) and the middle of the 4th millennium BC (FBC in Kujawy), in the development of the techno-stylistic trait discussed here, there is a clear hiatus (Fig 21). However, it is hard to assess how far this phenomenon can be generalized in terms of space. This is caused above all by the absence of techno-archaeological data on pottery from the alleged cradle of the use of "wood-tar ornaments" in the upper Tisza drainage.

The problem is crucially important for the assessment of topogenetic ties between both, chronologically disjoint, processes of its Lowlands use; specifically the Early and Late Neolithic. For it must be noticed that in the development of both "Kujawy-Chełmno" LBPC societies and "Kujawy" FBC societies from phase IIIB — when "wood-tar ornaments" re-entered the Lower Vistula region — a special role was played by contacts with the cultural groups from southern Poland, including their Trans-Carpathian system of relationships with the Carpathian Basin (Grygiel 2001: Kośko 1988, 164ff). Can, therefore, the case in hand be treated as a renaissance of a set of already known — Trans-Carpathian — cultural patterns?

For the time being, the only chance for a preliminary testing of the hypothesis is offered by a comparative analysis of production techniques of wood-tar pigments and their uses as an Early (LBPC, Bükk culture - Slovakia, Chełmno Land) and Late Neolithic dye (FBC, GAC – Kujawy). The hypothesis is being tested now with the Late Neolithic resources having been considerably extended. Numerous data, to a large extent bearing out observations made in above, are supplied by the "Opatowice – Prokopiak's Mount" project now underway.

The role of "wood-tar ornaments". Reception mechanisms in the circle of painted ware cultures

In the set of known pottery dyes from the Balkans and Carpathian Basin, mineral pigments must be deemed developmentally earlier and by far dominant. This gives rise to the question: what cultural mechanism supplemented the set with wood-tar pigments?

The process of substitution — assumed in the above assessment — of black mineral dyes with similar coloured wood-tar ones could have had two reasons:

(a) raw material-technological or
(b) symbolic.

a. Black ceramic pigments can be obtained by using mineral raw materials such as iron and manganese oxides as well as (a less popular possibility) carbon and tar organic substances used directly or thermally fixed — turned into strongly carbonized layers. The latter technique enables one to obtain easily insoluble coatings and ornaments resistant to heat. When the traditional mineral substances, were locally in short supply, the use of wood-tar pigments was possible and gave similar effects. In addition, this technique did not require high temperatures (room temperature was enough or possibly 400-500°C in the case of fixation of the colouring layer) and the colouring process could be easily completed by the user on a finished, and fired vessel (to make it water-tight or for decorative purposes, as the need be).

b. The second reason concerned symbolic values — a prevailing system of decorative motifs conveyed new ideas and beliefs. Important clues for the assessment of symbolic values are supplied by the identification of ingredients. It has been found that black wood-tar pigments — in their Late Neolithic version — contained two ingredients heavily laden with symbolic meanings. These were birch, specifically birch bark, that was the main raw material in the destructive distillation of wood, and blood added to ready tar in the final stage of its production (Langer & Kośko 1992). It has already been pointed out that the addition of blood brings to mind many analogies to the symbolic behaviour of Middle East peoples and only to a lesser degree of European ethnic groups (such analogies are barely observable in the culture of Slavic peoples (Moszyński 1967, 256 – 7). On the contrary, the range where bark and wood-tar were treated "as means of complex magic functions" can be identified, in particular, with the Vistula drainage or more broadly with the North European zone, in particular the German-Baltic-Slavic Area (Szafrański 1949-1950, 481 – 2: Piotrowski 1997 ; Mańczak 1999). Recently, this question has been inspiringly developed in the archaeological and linguistic studies by A.P. Kowalski (2003).

To conclude, it can be suggested that "wood-tar ornaments" are one of many indications of changes in worldview and beliefs taking place in the early agrarian culture when it was adapting to Non-Balkan ("northern") environments.

Conclusions

In this paper, we wished to present research vistas in which we place the title issue: the production, use and significance of organic pigments in pottery decoration of early agrarian cultures in the Vistula drainage (4th-3rd millennium BC). At present, it has been possible to outline preliminary results of multi-faceted research providing guidelines for further work. They form a foundation for research projects that we are currently pursuing (Pietrzak 2005: Kośko, Langer, Pietrzak & Szmyt 2005).

References

Grygiel, R., 2001. Wpływy wschodniolinearnego kręgu kulturowego w kulturze ceramiki wstęgowej rytej na Kujawach. In *Księga Jubileuszowa dedykowana Januszowi K. Kozłowskiemu*, 297 – 310. Kraków: UJ.

Józwiak, B., 2003. *Społeczności subneolitu wschodnioeuropejskiego na Niżu Polskim w międzyrzeczu Odry i Wisły [Sum. The Societies of the East-European Subneolithic on the Polish Lowlands in the Area between the Oder and Vistula Rivers]*. Poznań: UAM.

Józwiak, B., Langer, J.J., & Pietrzak, S., 2001. Przyczynek do studiów nad wytwarzaniem i stosowaniem smół drzewnych wśród społeczności kultury niemeńskiej [Sum. A contribution to studies on production and use of wood tar in communities of the Neman culture]. *Sprawozdania Archeologiczne*, 53, 403 – 15.

Kirkowski, R., 1994. Kultura ceramiki wstęgowej rytej. Zarys systematyki chronologiczno-genetycznej [Sum. The development of the Linear Band Pottery communities in the Chełmno land. An outline of chronological-genetic systematization]. In Czerniak, L. (Ed) *Neolit i początki epoki brązu na ziemi chełmińskiej*, 57 – 99. Grudziądz: Muzeum w Grudziądzu.

Kośko, A., 1981. *Udział południowo-wschodnioeuropejskich wzorców kulturowych w rozwoju niżowych społeczności kultury pucharów lejkowatych [Sum. The share of the South-East European cultural models in the development of lowland communities of Funnel Beaker Culture]*. Poznań: UAM.

Kośko, A., 1988. *Osady kultury pucharów lejkowatych w Inowrocławiu-Mątwach, woj. Bydgoszcz, stanowisko 1 [Sum. Funnel Beaker Culture settlements in Inowrocław-Mątwy, Bydgoszcz voivodeship, site 1]*. Inowrocław: UAM.

Kośko, A., & Langer, J., 1986. Z badań nad wytwarzaniem i użytkowaniem dziegciu w neolicie [Sum. Des recherches sur la fabrication et l'emploi du goudron végétal à l'époque néolithique]. *Kwartalnik Historii Kultury Materialnej*, 4, 587 – 600.

Kośko, A., Langer, J.J., Pietrzak , S., & Szmyt, M., 2005. Substancje smoliste. In Kośko, A., Szmyt, M. (Eds), *Studia i materiały do badań nad późnym neolitem na Wysoczyźnie Kujawskiej. Opatowice – „Wzgórze Prokopiaka"*, part I. Poznań (in preparation).

Kośko, A., Langer, J.J., & Szmyt, M., 2000. Painted pottery as a symptom of Tripolye 'influence' in the circle of Neolithic Vistula cultures. In Kośko, A. (Ed.) *The Western Border Area of the Tripolye Culture*. Baltic-Pontic Studies 9, 282 – 8. Poznań: UAM.

Kowalski, A.P., 2003. Rola dziegciu i kory w zdobnictwie naczyń neolitycznych. Lingwistyczny przyczynek do prahistorii estetyki [Sum. Importance of birch tar and bark in the decoration of Neolithic vessels. A linquistic contribution to the prehistory of aesthetics]. *Folia Praehistorica Posnaniensia*, 10/11, 7 – 20.

Langer, J.J., & Kośko, A., 1992. Studies on the organic components in Neolithic pottery dyes. *Archaeologia Polona*, 30, 61 – 68.

Langer, J.J., & Kośko, A., 1999. Z badań nad zastosowaniem dziegciu w ornamentyce ceramiki neolitycznej. Perspektywa Niżu Polski [Sum. Studies on the application of birch-tar in the ornamentation of the Neolithic pottery from the view-point of the Polish Lowland]. *Folia Praehistorica Posnaniensia*, 9, 63 – 77.

Langer, J., & Pietrzak, S., 2001. Wytwarzanie i zastosowanie dziegciu w kulturach późnoneolitycznych [Sum. Production and use of tar in Late Neolithic cultures]. In Kośko, A. (Ed), *Archeologiczne badania ratownicze wzdłuż trasy gazociągu tranzytowego, vol. III, Kujawy, part 4, Osadnictwo kultur późnoneolitycznych oraz in terstadium epok neolitu i brązu*, 411 – 17. Poznań: Wydawnictwo Poznańskie.

Mańczak, W., 1999. *Wieża Babel*. Wrocław-Warszawa-Kraków.

Moszyński, K., 1967. *Kultura ludowa Słowian*, vol. II. Warszawa: Ossolineum.

Pietrzak, S., 2005. Zastosowanie i technologie wytwarzania dziegciu wśród społeczeństw międzyrzecza Dniepru i Łaby od VI do II tysiąclecia BC. Poznań (doctor's thesis, in preparation).

Piotrowski, W., 1997. Smoła drzewna i dziegieć w staropolskich przysłowiach i wyrażeniach przysłowiowych [Sum. Birch Bark Tar and Wood Pitch in Old Polish Proverbs and Sayings]. In Brzeziński, W., Piotrowski, W. (Eds), *Proceedings of the First International Symposium on Wood Tar and Pitch*, 279 – 96. Warszawa.

Stos-Fertner, Z., & Rook, E., 1981. Analiza pigmentów używanych do dekoracji neolitycznej ceramiki w miejscowości Bilcze Złote [Sum. Analysis of pigments used for decoration of Neolithic pottery from Bilcze Złote]. *Materiały Archeologiczne*, 21, 27 – 32.

Szafrański, W., 1949-1950. Wczesnohistoryczne smolarnie w Biskupinie w pow. żnińskim [Sum. Une goudronnerie protohistorique à Biskupin, distr. de Żnin]. *Slavia Antiqua*, 2, 453 – 82.

Trąbska, J., Trybalska, B., Gaweł, A., & Bytnar, K., 2003. I. Pigmenty i warstwy malarskie ceramiki neolitycznej kultury trypolskiej (Bilcze Złote). II. Zabytki kamienne z Bilcza Złotego [Sum. I. Pigmente und Malschichten an der Keramik der neolithischen Tripolje Kultur (Bilcze Złote). II. Steinartefakte von Bilcze Złote]. *Materiały Archeologiczne*, 34, 179 – 94.

Vogt, E., 1949. The birch as a source of raw material during the Stone Age. *Proceedings of the Prehistoric Society*, 15, 50 – 51.

CHAPTER 5

Bell Beaker Gendered Cups in Central Europe

Jan Turek

Symbols of gender

The people of Corded Ware and Bell Beaker cultures paid a great deal of attention to the symbolic differentiation of male and female phenomena within their funerary rituals. Their fundamentalistic rules of positioning the body in the grave strictly differentiated men with their heads orientated to the west (Corded Ware - CW) or north (Bell Beakers - BB) and women with their heads orientated to the east (CW) or south (BB). This habit has an obvious relation to sunrise/sunset symbolism. It is also clearly visible in the positioning of crouched bodies on the right (CW men and BB women) or left side (CW women and BB men). The male/female differentiation is also expressed in the selection of gendered artefacts that were parts of burial assemblages. Some male and female prestigious artefacts, such as weapons and jewellery appeared also in the graves of Corded Ware and Bell Beaker children, suggesting that the same system of the symbolic representation of different gender roles was already applied in the very early stages of life.

Humprey Case (1995) and Neil Brodie (1998) have demonstrated how the volumes of British and Irish Beakers differed according to male (largest volume), female (medium volume) and child burial (smaller volume) contexts. The gender specifics may, however, be found not only in the volumes of vessels, but also in their forms and decoration.

Some forms of Bell Beaker associated common pottery (in German *die Begleitkeramik*) are decorated by plastic ornaments of possible gender significance (Fig 1). These are mainly one handled cups that were the most popular funerary pots (Fig 2). The gendered cups were decorated with specific plastic ornaments that seems to be indicative of the gender of their owners. The male symbols are: moustache decorations protruding down the root of the handle, or phallic up side down inverted "Y" shapes distributed over the vessel body. Usually in even numbers, 2 or 4 times. The Y symbol is sometimes outlined from the top, which may resemble the schematic picture of sexual intercourse. Their female opposition seems to be nipple-like protrusions located in pairs on both sides of the handle's root and/or distributed over the vessel's body. The important observation is that the male and female symbols never appear on the same pot and they seem to be accordingly divided into male or female burial assemblages.

Examples may be given from Moravian cemeteries at Ostopovice (burial 14/73, see Ondruš - Dvořák 1992), Šlapanice (see Dvořák – Hájek 1990), Vyškov (burial 9/57) and Záhlinice (69/89 see Dvořák – Rakovský – Stuchlíková 1992), which represent individuals buried in the male position on the left side and all of them accompanied by cups with moustache decoration (Fig 3). The same observations were made in Bohemia, for example the cup from male grave 4 at Lochenice (distr. Hradec Králové, *Buchvaldek 1990*, 30, 38, Obr. 9:1). Unfortunately many more of these cups with male or female decoration are stored in museum collections without any details of their archaeological contexts and therefore it is impossible to reconstruct their possible gendered implications. It is certainly possible that these pots represent the role of gender not only in the funerary context but also in everyday gendered social activities. These 'labeled' pots may also have been distinguished in language as male and female pots and were possibly used in a much more personalised way than the remaining majority of pottery. The gender differentiation of some pottery types at the end of Eneolithic period and the habit

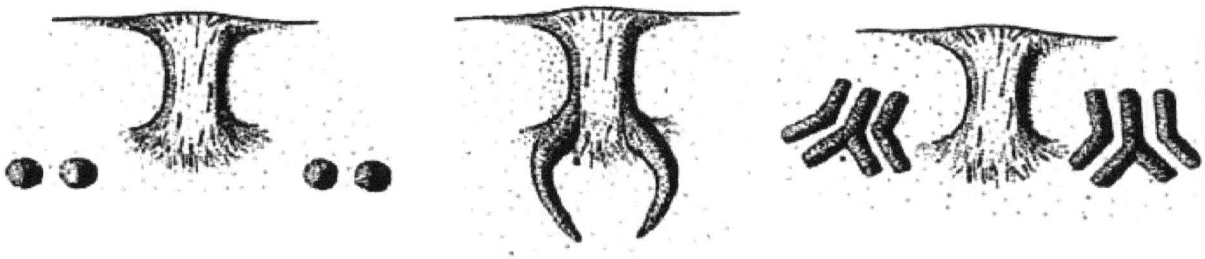

Fig 1. Plastic decoration of the area around the root of cup handles of so-called associated pottery of the Bell Beaker period. Left to right – 'nipple-like' - protrusions a female symbol?, the 'moustache pattern' and inverted Y – male symbols? (drawings after Heyd 2000, 199, Taf. 50).

Fig 2. Example of plastic decoration on a cup of so-called associated pottery from Bohemia (photographs by L. Hájek).

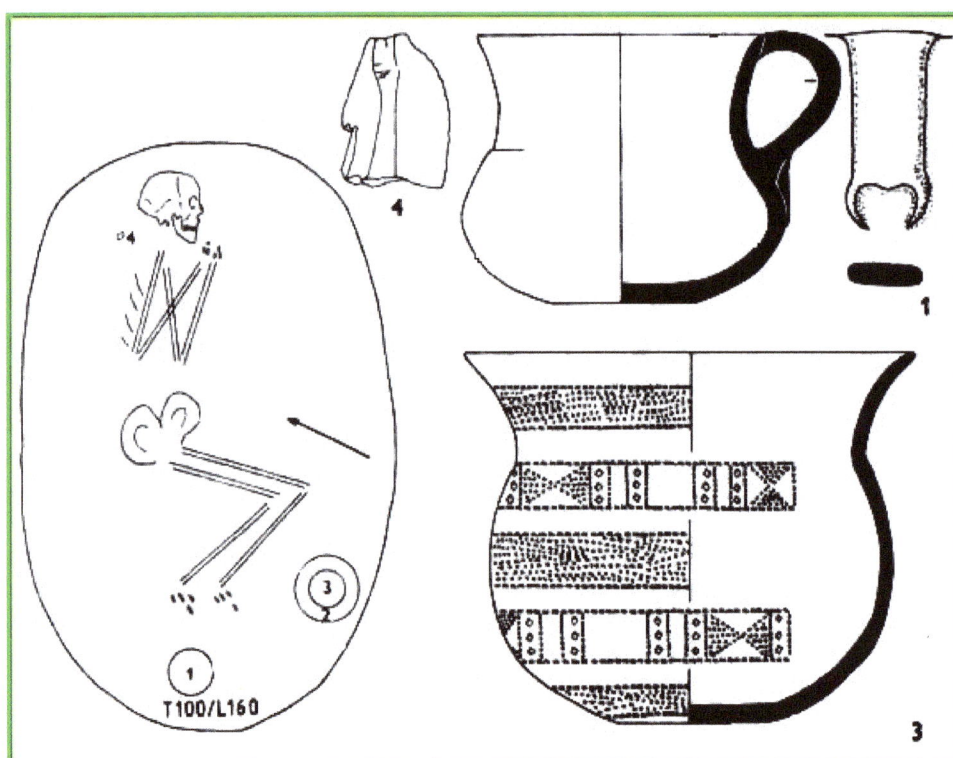

Fig 3. Male burial with *the 'moustache pattern' on a cup,* Šlapanice, Moravia (after Dvořák & Hájek 1990).

of labelling common cups with male or female specific symbols reflect the social need to distinguish gender roles and the positions of men and women in ceremonial as well as profane activities.

Pottery complex and drinking ceremonies

Bell Beaker pottery is part of a much greater symbolic artefactual system that was dominating pottery production in Central Europe from 4500 BC till at least 700 BC. Evžen Neustupný presented this concept as the Central European Eneolithic-Bronze Age pottery complex (cf. Neustupný 1995). This complex consists of:

large storage jars, amphorae, pots, handled pots, jugs, beakers, one handled cups and bowls (Fig 4). These types of pottery were created for specific purposes, but at the same time they became a distinctive cultural phenomenon. People in the earlier Neolithic period, as well as later in the Iron Age, Roman period and early Middle Ages did not use such an assemblage of pottery types; jugs, amphorae and beakers were unknown. Also looking through the Copper Age/Bronze Age pottery assemblages of Western or Eastern Europe we would hardly find a matching set of pottery types. This makes the pottery complex a specifically Central European phenomenon.

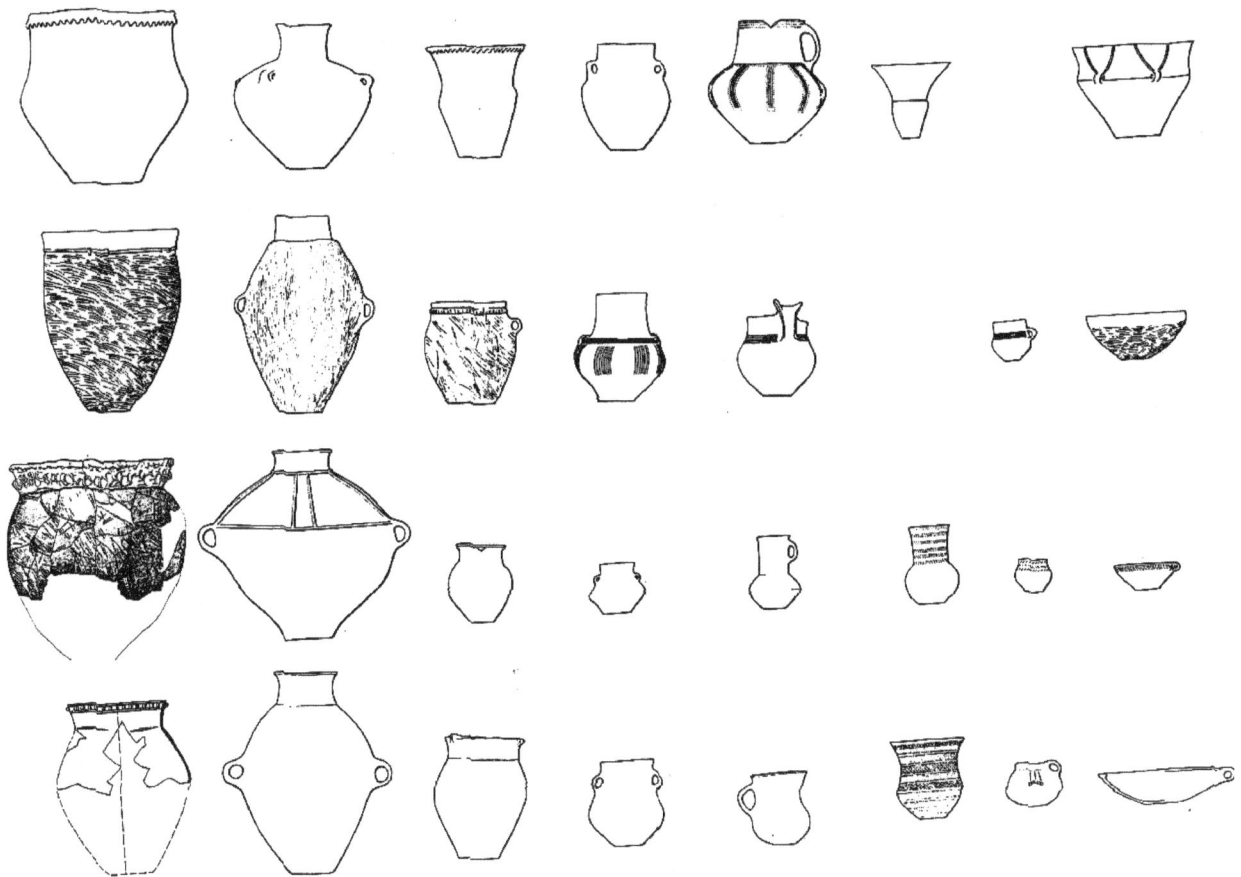

Fig 4. Central European Eneolithic-Bronze Age pottery complex (after Neustupný pers. comm. and Neustupný 1995). From the top, TRB, Rivnac, Corded Ware, Bell Beaker.

Some pottery types were specifically used for the storing and drinking of alcoholic beverages. The collective consumption of alcohol seems to have played an important role in social communications and the creation of hierarchies from as early as the early farming communities in Europe (cf. Sherratt 1987; Vencl 1994). Therefore it is possible to assume that some of the drinking pots were also used as attributes of particular social status and represented differences between social categories. Furthermore, the perfect finish and rich design of Bell Beakers differentiate this luxurious pottery from the rest of pottery production. In most cases the beakers are decorated all over their surface. It may be significant that the decoration is always arranged in a series of horizontal bands that might have marked the levels of drink inside during some collective drinking ceremonies. Andrew Sherratt (1987) has considered the possibility of the ritual consumption of alcoholic or narcotic beverages in a prehistoric environment. His interpretation is not exceptional in the context of the Central European Eneolithic period. The ceremonies involving the consumption of alcoholic beverages had already become an integral part of social communications in Europe at the beginning of the Eneolithic period and to a certain extent it has survived as a cultural phenomenon of Western society up to the present day.

The evidence of drinking rituals and feasts may already be seen in the pottery drinking sets of the Proto-Eneolithic (after 4500 cal. BC). These events played important roles in the creation and reinforcement of collective identity within communities as well as in communications with other neighbouring communities. The first jugs in Central Europe had already appeared in the Jordansmühl Culture and later there are the very specific tulip-beakers of the Michelsberg Culture. The higher production of wheat and barley, which was caused by more effective Eneolithic agricultural systems, established the more or less common opportunity for beer making. This was a very effective way to turn excess barley into a commodity of a higher value. People invited to such a beer feast might be invited as a reward for their work power and the host may have highlighted his social and economic superiority. The ceremonial drinking feasts had great potential for social communications within prehistoric communities, including the strengthening of social ties within the community as well as emphasising its collective identity.

Considering the pottery production of the Bell Beaker period, there are certain types of pots that are suitable for direct drinking, such as the one handled cups and small jugs, but the shape of Bell Beakers does not at first sight seem to be particularly suitable for the consumption of liquids. Bell beakers, as well as, for example earlier Michelsberg tulip-beakers, have sometimes extremely everted rims, that make direct drinking almost impossible. Such pots may have been used as containers or vessels for the manipulation of liquids prior to their consumption, or they may have been designed for drinking using a straw as has been identified on beer drinking scenes from ancient Mesopotamia or Egypt. Gibson, however, has also pointed out that kudos can be obtained by drinking from stylised impractical forms (2003, xi).

Only for women! Gendered pottery in the Late Eneolithic period

The gender differentiation of the late Eneolithic pottery in Central Europe is also represented in a less explicit way, without using specific gender symbols. In the Corded Ware (2900-2500 cal. BC) and Bell Beaker (2500-2300 cal. BC) funerary contexts it is possible to distinguish certain specific female types of pottery, such as egg-shaped storage pots and tall one handled jugs that exclusively appear in female graves (Fig 5). It seems likely that some pottery types were indicative of female burials and that perhaps even in day to day practice there were certain pots that were taboo to be touched by men and *vice versa*. Similar behaviour was observed, for instance, in the Mandara Valley amongst the Sub-

Saharan populations of present day Cameroon (Černý *et al.*) where women are not permitted to touch some of the male pots and they can only manipulate them using wooden "isolation" sticks. The gender differentiation of Bell Beaker pottery may also be a key to the problem of missing female burials in Bohemia and perhaps some other regions of Central Europe.

Missing women

I have recently discussed the question of the lack of evidence for female burials in certain regions of Central Europe during the Bell Beaker period (Turek 2002). The lack of female inhumations is characteristic of the Bohemian and central German group. However, the situation is different in Moravia and southern Germany where both sexes are equally represented in common burial rites. The lack of female burials in some regions must result from an alternative method of burial used for certain women. There are certainly many ways of disposing of the body without leaving any retrievable archaeological traces. In the case of Bell Beaker burial rites, it is important to note that secondary burials were often placed into the above ground parts of burial mounds as we know from regions where intact barrows survive (eastern Moravia, some sites in central Germany). The above ground elements of prehistoric burial mounds however have disappeared in most of the regions in Central Europe due to a long history of agricultural cultivation. These destroyed burial mounds and perhaps

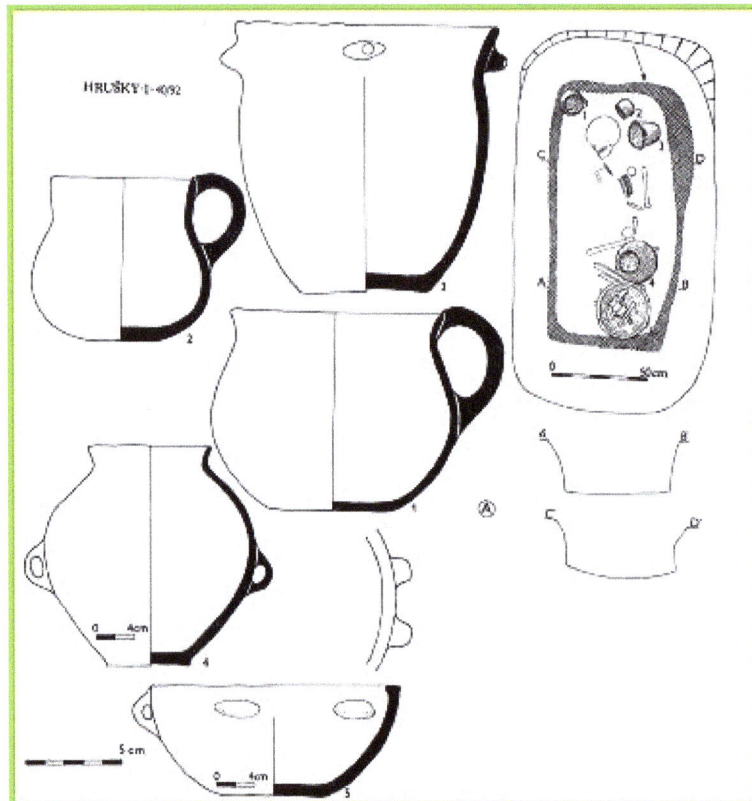

Fig 5. Amphora and a pot from a female inhumation burial in southern Moravia.

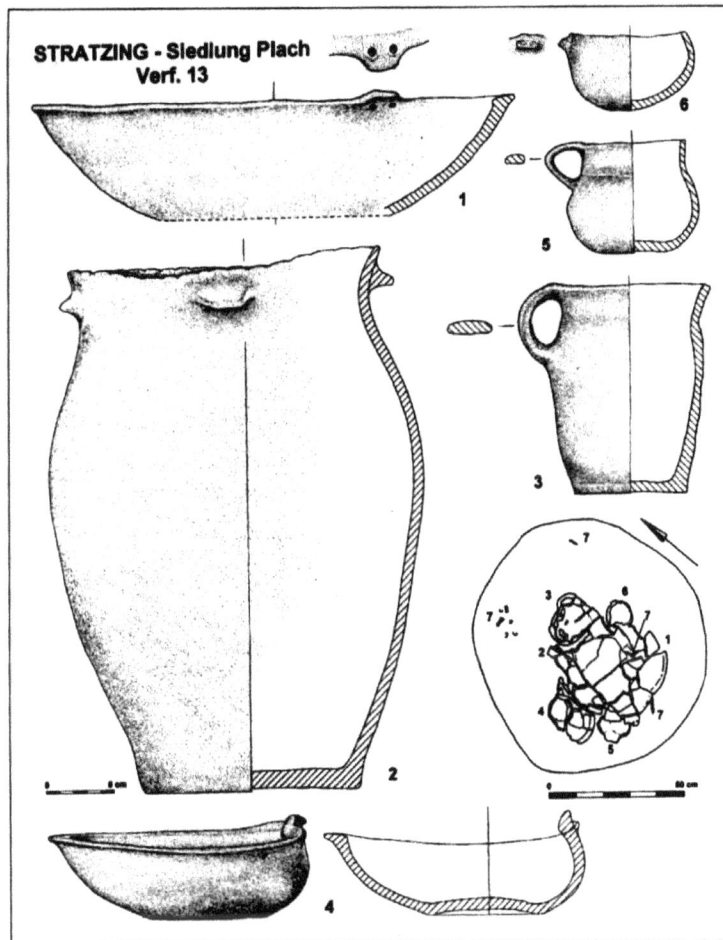

Fig 6. Settlement pottery from Stratzing.

the preference for cremation burial may be a key to the question of "missing" Bell Beaker women in Bohemia and central Germany.

In this context it should be emphasised, that the rare Bell Beaker cremation burials in Bohemia often contain large ovoid storage jars or amphorae used as urns containing the cremation. It is very possible that these are the cremations of women, and this method of disposing the body may have been specifically reserved for women. In several cases there is evidence for smaller pots, such as cups and bowls, being affected by burning, presumably from the cremation pyre, while the large urn has a smooth unburned surface. It seems that the smaller items of the pottery assemblage were placed near to the cremation pyre (probably not right inside it, as then the fire damage would likely have been much greater cf. Turek 2004). The amphorae or ovoid storage jars were selected as containers for the ashes after the cremation ceremony was completed (Fig 6).

References

Brodie, N. 1998: British Bell Beakers: Twenty five years of theory and practice. In M. Benz, & S. van Willigen (Eds), *Some New Approaches to The Bell Beaker 'Phenomenon' Lost Paradise...?*, 43 – 56. BAR International Series 690. Oxford: British Archaeological Reports.

Buchvaldek, M. 1990: Pohřebiště lidu se zvoncovitými poháry. Ein Gräberfeld der Glockenbecherkultur. Praehistorica 16 - Lochenice. Z Archeologických Výzkumů na Katastru Obce, Praehistorica 16, 29-50.

Case, H. 1995: Beakers: loosening a stereotype. In I. Kinnes & G. Varndell (Eds.) *'Unbaked Urns of Rudley Shape'. Essays on British and Irish Pottery for Ian Longworth*, 55 – 67. Oxbow Monograph 55. Oxford: Oxbow Books.

Černý, V., Gautier, J-G., Brůžek, J., Gronenborn, D., Velemínský, P. & Budil, I. T. 2001. *Mezi Saharou a tropickými pralesy* – Between the Sahara and the tropical rain forests, Praha.

Dvořák, P. 1992. *Die Gräberfelde der Glockenbecherkultur in Mähren I* (Bez. Blansko, Brno-město-Stadt, Brno-venkov-Umgebung). Katalog der Funde, MAQ, Brno.

Dvořák, P. & Hájek, L. 1990. *Die Gräberfelder der Glockenbecherkultur bei Šlapanice* (Bez. Brno-venkov), Katalog der Funde, MAQ, Brno.

Dvořák, P., Rakovský, I. & Stuchlíková, J. 1992. *Pohřebiště lidu s kulturou se zvoncovitými poháry u Záhlinic, okr. Kroměříž – Gräberfeld des Volkes mit Glockenbecherkultur bei Záhlinice*, Pravěk NŘ 2, 215 – 32.

Gibson, A.M. 2003. Prehistoric Pottery: Peope, pattern and purpose. Some observations, questions and speculations. In A. Gibson (ed) *Prehstoric Pottery: People, Pattern and Purpose*, v-xii. BAR International Series 1156. Oxford: BAR Publishing.

Heyd, V. 2000. *Die Spätkupferzeit in Süddeutschland. Dokumentations- und Tafelband.* Saarbruücker Beitrage zur Altertumskunde, Bd. 73, Habelt Gmbh. Bonn.

Neustupný, E. 1995: The significance of facts. *Journal of European Archaeology* 3 (1), 189 – 212.

Ondruš, V. & Dvořák, P. 1992. *Pohřebiště kultury zvoncovitých pohárů v Ostopovicích – Gräberfeld der Glockenbecherkultur bei Ostopovice*, ČMMB 77, 81 – 94.

Sherratt, A. G. 1987. 'Cups that cheered' In W.H. Waldren & R.C. Kennard (eds.), *Bell–Beakers of the West Mediterranean*, 81 – 114 BAR International Series 331. Oxford: British Archaeological Reports.

Turek, J. 2000 Being a beaker child. The position of children in late eneolithic society – Děti v období šňůrové keramiky a zvoncovitých pohárů. Postavení dětí ve společnosti pozdního eneolitu. *In memoriam Jan Rulf, Památky archeologické – Supplementum 13*, 424 – 38.

Turek, J. 2002. "Cherche la femme!" Archeologie ženského světa a chybějící doklady ženských pohřbů z období zvoncovitých pohárů v Čechách. "Cherche la femme!". The archaeology of woman's world and the missing evidence of female burials in the Bell Beaker Period in Bohemia, In E. Neustupný (Ed), *Archeologie Nenalézaného*, 217 – 40, Plzeň – Praha.

Turek, J. 2004. Žárové pohřby z období zvoncovitých pohárů na Nymbursku – Bell Beaker cremation burials from the district of Nymburk. *Archeologie ve středních Čechách*, 8, 229 – 33.

Vencl, S. 1994. Archeologie žízně – The Archaeology of thirst. *Archeologia rozhl*, 46, 283 – 305.

CHAPTER 6

Report on the University of Bradford Pilot Project into the Absorbed Residue Analysis of Bronze Age Pigmy Cups from Scotland, England and Wales

Alex Gibson & Ben Stern

Introduction

There is a range of small and miniature vessels within the ceramic record of the later Neolithic through to the middle Bronze Age (Fig 1). Occasionally, these take the form of smaller versions of the larger ceramic forms and, for example, there are small Beakers, Food Vessels and Collared Urns that stand no more than 10cm high. These vessels warrant the term 'miniature' because they are small versions of more usual, larger forms. Other diminutive vessels appear only in a small form. These comprise, for example, the splayed and geometrically decorated Aldbourne Cups, globular Grape Cups with multiple perforations and with their outer surfaces covered in close-set applied pellets, Fenestrated or Perforated Wall Cups with sections cut out of the walls of the vessels, and Biconical Cups often with one or two opposed pairs of perforations on the shoulder. In addition to these classic forms, there is also a range of less well-defined small pinch pots, thumb cups and tubs of varying form and quality. These cups are principally found in graves, usually with cremations, though small cups have been found in ostensibly domestic contexts at Kilellan Farm, Islay (Ritchie 2005) or Ardnave, Islay (Ritchie & Welfare, 1983, fig10:26). Stray finds have also been made and at Hungerford (Berks) an Aldbourne cup was found in association with a timber circle (Ford 1991). Cups may often be associated with Collared Urns and are common in 'Wessex' graves (Annable & Simpson 1964: Longworth 1983; 1984).

When the practice of miniaturisation first appeared in the ceramic record is currently under review. Certainly small vessels occur in the early Neolithic assemblages from Causewayed Enclosures such as Windmill Hill (Smith 1965) though these can often be explained in practical terms as, for example, cups or scoops in keeping with a 'domestic' assemblage. None seem to be deliberately small versions of larger forms. However, a small Mortlake style bowl from Co. Dublin, probably dating to around 3000 cal BC on stylistic grounds, may be the earliest recognised attempt at deliberate miniaturisation (Gibson 2004). This small vessel, less than 3cm high, is very much a copy in miniature of larger Impressed Ware vessels. Also in the later Neolithic the small highly decorated Grooved Ware tubs from Woodlands are, of course, well known. Beakers also occur in small variants as do Food Vessels and Collared Urns. These smaller versions of larger ceramic forms are difficult to explain

practically and despite the formal traits that they share with the larger variants, they are usually interpreted as Pigmy Cups.

The roles of miniature vessels or Pigmy Cups in the ceramic record of the earlier Bronze Age has been debated for almost 200 years since Colt Hoare. In describing the types of vessels usually encountered in the barrows of Wiltshire, Colt Hoare drew attention to these small cups in the following way:

> *The third species of vase differs very decidedly from either of the other two [i.e. Various Urn types and Beakers]; is smaller in its proportions, and more fantastic in its shape and ornaments. It is in general too diminutive to have contained the ashes, or even the* viaticum *of the deceased. We frequently find them perforated on the sides, and one of them in the bottom, like a cullender, which circumstances induces me to think that they were filled with balsams and precious ointments and suspended over the funeral pile. I shall therefore distinguish these vases by the title of INCENSE CUPS, as in the description of the numerous* tumuli *we have opened, it is absolutely necessary that these urns, so different in their nature, should be properly and distinctly discriminated. The name of* Thuribulum *might also be given to this small vase, as containing the* thus *or frankincense, which was burned at funerals.* (1810, 25)

From the above, it is chiefly the size of the vessels that Colt Hoare finds so distinctive and this is the trap into which many have fallen since.

Some 60 years later, Canon Greenwell may not have been a model excavator but was very much ahead of his time in his analysis of prehistoric ceramics and in his *British Barrows* he critically discussed the various theories associated with these pots (1877, 74-83). Greenwell first described the variety to be found in these small cups concluding that what we now know as the simple biconical cup (Longworth 1984) was the most common. He went on to write that 'various opinions have been expressed as to their use, none of which can be regarded as altogether satisfactory' (1877, 81). Of these theories, he listed:

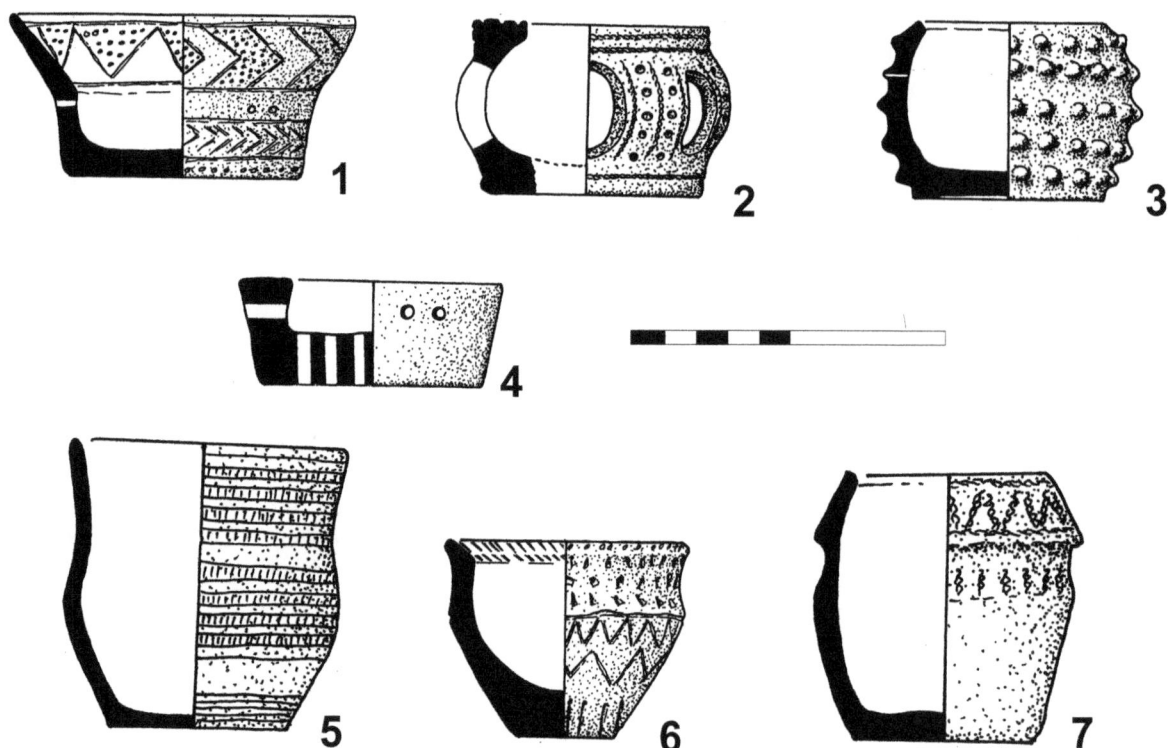

Fig 1. Various Cups and Miniature Vessels sensu stricto. 1 – Aldbourne Cup from Durrington, Wilts. 2 – Perforated Wall Cup from Great Shefford, Berks. 3 – Grape Cup from Preshute, Wilts. 4 – perforated Splayed Wall Cup from Wilsford, Wilts. 5 – miniature Beaker from Balblair Inverness, 6 – miniature vase Food Vessel from Craigdhu, Fife, 7 – miniature Collared Urn from near Bridlington, East Yorkshire. 1, 3 & 4 after Annable & Simpson 1964, 2 after Longworth 1983, 6 after Hanley & Sheridan 1994, 7 after Longworth 1984.

Cups removed from a domestic environment:
Burning of incense or aromatic oils:
Lamps:
Receptacles for special or particular body parts (e.g. the heart):
Cups for bringing embers/flame from its source to the pyre.

Greenwell was dismissive of each of these explanations but prefers the last-mentioned which he saw as most plausible given the cups' association with cremation and the importance of pyro-ritual activity in the earlier Bronze Age. Most of Greenwell's reasons for rejecting the other theories were somewhat subjective (incense burners 'imply a state of refinement to which we can scarcely consider the people who used them to have attained' (1877, 81)) but nevertheless he also based his rejections on his close observation of the pots themselves. He noted no charring on the cups to suggest their use as lamps and drew comparison with Roman terracotta lamps which, by contrast, were often sooted. He was also at pains to point out that the perforations in the walls of these small cups are often so low, or indeed in the base, that they could not have served as containers for liquids or oils. However with regard to flame transferers (or censers) 'neither the form nor the peculiarity of the holes and piercings is inconsistent with this explanation of their use. Their size is what we might

expect to find in vessels made for the purpose of carrying a piece of ignited touchwood or other suitable material, and the holes and piercings are not ill adapted for keeping it, by means of a draught, in a state of ignition' (1877, 83).

Greenwell's account was based on many years of collecting and observation. He seems not to have been aware of (or at least not to have acknowledged) J.A. Smith's (1872) discussion of these vessels, particularly those in the collection of the Museum of the Society of Antiquaries of Scotland. Smith makes the added suggestion that these vessels may also have been made for the graves of children having noted infant bones amongst some cremated remains. This idea has seen somewhat of a resurgence in popularity (e.g. McLaren 2004) but while it must be acknowledged that some cups undoubtedly are associated with the remains of children, others most certainly are not.

Abercromby (1912, 24-37) concurred with Greenwell that the term 'incense cup' had 'nothing to recommend it' and invented the term 'pygmy cup' to refer to their diminutive size. However, even this term is inaccurate for 'pygmy' comes from the Greek meaning 'dwarf' and therefore it suggests that these cups are 'dwarf' forms of larger vessels but this is by no means always the case (see Gibson 2004) (Fig 1).

Despite the reservations of Greenwell (and later Abercromby) Colt Hoare's original 'incense cup' hypothesis (or at least terminology) has been difficult to shake off. Certainly the multi-perforate varieties could have been used for this purpose. Ultimately stemming from this original hypothesis modern scholars have suggested that these vessels may have been used to burn a range of aromatic materials from pine bark to imported hallucinogens or materials with 'mind altering' properties (Sherratt 1991: Allen & Hopkins 2000).

Modern researchers, however, have shied away from explanations of function and the words 'incense' or 'pygmy' preferring the more descriptive terms of particular cup shapes – biconical cups, perforated wall cups and so on (Longworth 1983; 1984: Allen & Hopkins 2000: Gibson 2004) none of which have a functional implication. Abandonment of the term 'pygmy' also acknowledges that not all these cups are miniature versions of larger forms (Gibson 2004). However even if the ostensibly simple and inoffensive term 'cup' is used, then the study of these small vessels is hampered by the tendency to consider them as a class.

Despite the distinguished history of this method of study, it is fundamentally flawed. No student of the Neolithic and Bronze Age would consider studying Beakers, Food Vessels or Collared Urns together as a single class because they happened to be between 12cm and 20cm high. Distinctions are made largely on form and decoration rather than purely on size. Why, then, should cups be regarded as a single class just because they are all less than 10cm high? The future for these vessels lies in a comparative study based on a workable typology.

Residue Analysis of Bronze Age Cups

As a prelude to a larger study of prehistoric cups, a programme of analysis of absorbed residues was undertaken at Bradford University's Department of Archaeological Sciences to assess the value of this method of analysis to the study of these vessels (Table 1). Generously funded by the British Academy, this pilot programme was intended to include Britain, Ireland and Northern France however no vessels in the collection of the Ulster Museum or the National Museum of Ireland were deemed suitable and permission to sample was not forthcoming from French colleagues despite repeated requests.

Method

Samples were removed by scraping a portion of the inside of the cup with a scalpel and the resultant sherd powders were extracted with 3 aliquots of ~1 ml DCM:MeOH (dichloromethane:methanol 2:1, v/v), with ultrasonication for 5 min. followed by centrifugation to aid separation of the solvent and powder (5 min. at 2000 rpm). The extract was transferred to a clean glass vial. The solvent was then removed under a stream of nitrogen. Excess BSTFA (N, O- bis(trimethylsilyl)

trifluoroacetamide) with 1% TMCS (trimethyl-chlorosilane) (*Pierce*) was added to derivatise the sample which was warmed overnight. Excess derivatising agent was removed under a stream of nitrogen. To selected samples a known amount of internal standard (C_{34} *n*-alkane) was added and the sample diluted in DCM for analysis by GC and selected samples were also analysed by GC-MS. For comparative purposes, a method control was included in the sample extraction, derivatisation and analysis. All solvents were of AnalaR grade. All glassware was rinsed with DCM three times prior to use.

Instrumental (GC-MS)

Analysis was carried out by combined gas chromatography-mass spectrometry (GC-MS) using a Hewlett Packard 5890 series II GC connected to a 5972 series mass selective detector. The splitless injector and interface were maintained at 300°C and 340°C respectively. Helium was the carrier gas at constant inlet pressure. The temperature of the oven was programmed from 50°C (2 min.) to 340°C (10 min.) at 10°C/min. The GC was fitted with a 15m X 0.25mm, 0.1µm OV1 phase fused silica column (MEGA). The column was directly inserted into the ion source where electron impact (EI) spectra were obtained at 70 eV with full scan from m/z 50 to 700.

Results (Table 1)

No lipids were extracted from seven of the samples (Breach Farm, Salmonbry (X2), Northmanton, Westwood, Stainton quarry and Yarnton). From twelve samples (Gilchorn, Carfrae, Preshute, Upton Lovell, Wylye, Lesmordie, Burton Waters, Ponton (X2), Strathern, Lenton and Sutton) fatty acids were recovered, however the yields are similar to the method blanks and therefore cannot be regarded as indigenous to the sample but may originate from contamination. For Sutton this is despite the presence of a visible 'tide mark' on the inner surface of the pot. This was specifically targeted for sampling but now must be regarded to be inorganic. These fatty acids are ubiquitous at such low abundances and the contamination may include a number of phthalate plasticisers - these are modern synthetic compounds most likely absorbed by the sherds from plastic containers during storage.

Four samples (Drymmie Wood (e.g. Fig 2), Gairney Bank, Wilsford and Amesbury) have significant abundances of $C_{16:0}$ and $C_{18:0}$ fatty acids and/or an extended range of fatty acid carbon numbers (e.g. $C_{12:0}$ to $C_{20:0}$). Whilst this may be indicative of an oil or fat, it is however extremely difficult to identify any source origin for these lipids and again contamination cannot be excluded as without analysis of associated soil or the exterior surfaces, it is difficult to assess the level of potential contamination from the burial environment,

No	Cup Provenance	Museum	Description	Residue Analysis	References
1	Whitford	NMGW 12.130/2	Globular Cup. From a barrow. No details	C_{28}, C_{30} and C_{32} long chain alcohols. Wax esters	Grimes 1951: Savory 1980, No466
2	Sutton 268', Glamorgan	NMGW 40.179/10	Miniature Food Vessel. Cremation deposit of an adult male, Copper alloy knife, bone bead	Trace C_{16} and C_{18} fatty acids	Fox 1959: Savory, 1980 No.371
3	Breach Farm, Glamorgan	NMGW 38.37/2	Biconical Cup from a pit below a barrow. Cup and associations lay on top of a deposit of cremated bone representing three individuals. Associated with bronze axe, dagger, chisel and a fourth unidentified object, decayed wood, and two sandstone arrow-shaft smoothers. Flint associations, located below the bronzes, comprised 2 unworked pieces, convex scraper, leaf-shaped point, 3 triangular points, 3 discoidal implements and 13 barbed and tanged arrowheads. The cup has traces of red inlay in the decoration.	Nothing	Fox 1959: Grimes 1938
4	Upton Lovell G2e, Wiltshire	Devizes (228)	Grape cup. Cremation deposit, copper alloy awl, 11 gold beads, amber spacer necklace, copper alloy dagger, Collared urn (possibly), 2 gold cones, rectangular sheet of gold, shale button with gold cover.	Trace C_{16} and C_{18} fatty acids	Colt Hoare 1812: Annable & Simpson 1964
5	Preshute G1, Wiltshire	Devizes (248)	Grape cup. Adult contracted inhumation. Cow and pig teeth. Gold bound amber disc, gold bound shale bead, ribbed shale bead, chalk bead, Open cup, halberd pendant, ceramic stud, steatite bead, necklace of 150 shale disc beads, fossil encrinite, 3 copper alloy awls, amber pommel, copper alloy knife.	Trace C_{16} and C_{18} fatty acids	Cunnington 1908: Annable & Simpson 1964
6	Wilsford G36, Wiltshire	Devizes (170)	Open cup with perforated base. Cremation.	Trace C_{16} and C_{18} fatty acids. Trace n-alkanes	Colt Hoare, 1810: Annable & Simpson 1964
7	Amesbury 61a, Wiltshire	Salisbury	Biconical cup from a chalk-cut pit below a round barrow. Cremation of an adult male. Associated objects: beaver incisor, 3 amber beads copper-alloy awl, 2 segmented faience beads, steatite ring or bead, 2 cowrie shells, 2 flint flakes, small piece of copper alloy, fossil crinoid.	C_{12} to C_{20} fatty acid range: C_{16} and C_{18} dominant	Ashbee 1985
8	Wylye 2, Wiltshire	Salisbury	Perforated Wall Cup. From below a round barrow. On a layer of wood ash and charcoal containing burnt bone. Traces of white inlay in the decoration.	Trace C_{16} and C18 fatty acids	Passmore, 1942
9	Salmonby, Lincolnshire	Lincoln 54.67	Globular cup. Pit containing the cremation of a young adult female. Collared Urn lay to the S of the cremation, Cup to the N and a copper alloy dagger to the E. Charcoal.	Nothing	Allen & Hopkins 2000, No.11
10	Dowsby, Lincolnshire (pot)	Lincoln 132.94	Perforated Wall Cup. In a shallow scoop beside the remains of a cremation deposit within a damaged Collared Urn.	-	Allen & Hopkins 2000, No.1
11	Dowsby, Lincolnshire (earth outside pot)	Lincoln 132.94		Long chain alcohols C_{28} and C_{30}. n-alkanes. Wax esters	

No	Cup Provenance	Museum	Description	Residue Analysis	References
12	Dowsby, Lincolnshire (earth from inside pot near base)	Lincoln 132.94		Trace C_{16}, $C_{18:1}$ and C_{18} fatty acids. Wax esters	
13	Normanton, Lincolnshire	Lincoln EBP 22	Globular Cup. With a similar but larger bowl within an iron quarry. Contained dark earth and a few fragments of bone.	Nothing	Allen & Hopkins 2000, No.10
14	Lenton, Lincolnshire	Lincoln EBP 132	Thumb Cup. No contextual data.	Trace C_{16} and C_{18} fatty acids	Allen & Hopkins 2000, No.16
15	Salmonby, Lincolnshire	Lincoln 6.54	Biconical Cup. In a pit with *in situ* cremation since the surrounding area had been blackened.	Nothing	Allen & Hopkins 2000, No.15.
16	Ponton, Lincolnshire	Lincoln EBP 150	Open Cup. No contextual data.	Trace C_{16} and C_{18} fatty acids	Allen & Hopkins 2000, No.12
17	Ponton, Lincolnshire	Lincoln EBP 151	Open Cup. No contextual data.	Trace C_{16} and C_{18} fatty acids	Allen & Hopkins 2000, No.13
18	Strathern, Lincolnshire	Lincoln EBP 38	Globular cup. No contextual details	Trace C_{16} and C_{18} fatty acids. *n*-alkanes	Unpublished. Inf T. Cadbury
19	Burton Waters, Lincolnshire	Lincoln 222.98	Biconical Cup. Found during topsoil sieving in an area of flint scatter.	Trace C_{16} fatty acid	Allen & Hopkins 2000, No14.
20	Wilsford, Lincolnshire	Lincoln 25.73	Open Cup. No contextual data.	Trace C_{16} and C_{18} fatty acids	Allen & Hopkins 2000, No7.
21	Westwood, Fife	NMS EC12	Globular Cup. Within Collared Urn with cremated bone.	Nothing	Jervise 1867.
22	Gilchorn, Tayside	NMS EQ223	Biconical cup. Within a Collared Urn with a second cup and a cremation deposit.	Trace C_{16} and C_{18} fatty acids	Hutcheson 1890.
23	Carfrae, Lothian	NMS EC27	Open Cup. No contextual details.	Trace C_{12}, C_{16} and C_{18} fatty acids	Anon 1889.
24	Gairney Bank Farm, Tayside	NMS 1970.249	Open Cup. In cist with adult male inhumation and copper alloy dagger.	Trace C_{12}, C_{16}, C_{17} and C_{18} fatty acids	Cowie & Ritchie 1991.
25	Straiton Quarry, Fife (pot)	NMS unreg	Globular Cup. With an adult cremation deposit within a Collared Urn. Cup contained soil.	Nothing	Unpublished. Inf A Sheridan
26	Staiton Quarry, Fife (soil within pot)	NMS unreg		Nothing	
27	Lesmordie, Aberdeen	NMS unreg	Bipartite Cup. With cremation deposit within a Food Vessel Urn.	Trace C_{16} and C_{18} fatty acids	Unpublished. Inf A Sheridan
28	Drymmie Wood, Fife (residue retained from pot)	NMS EA33	Small bipartite vase food vessel.	C_{13} to C_{20} fatty acid range: C_{16} and C_{18} dominant	Anderson 1849, 109.
29	Yarnton	OAU P55	Perforated Wall Cup.	Nothing	Unpublished. Inf A. Barclay

Table 1: List of cups sampled and synopsis of results.

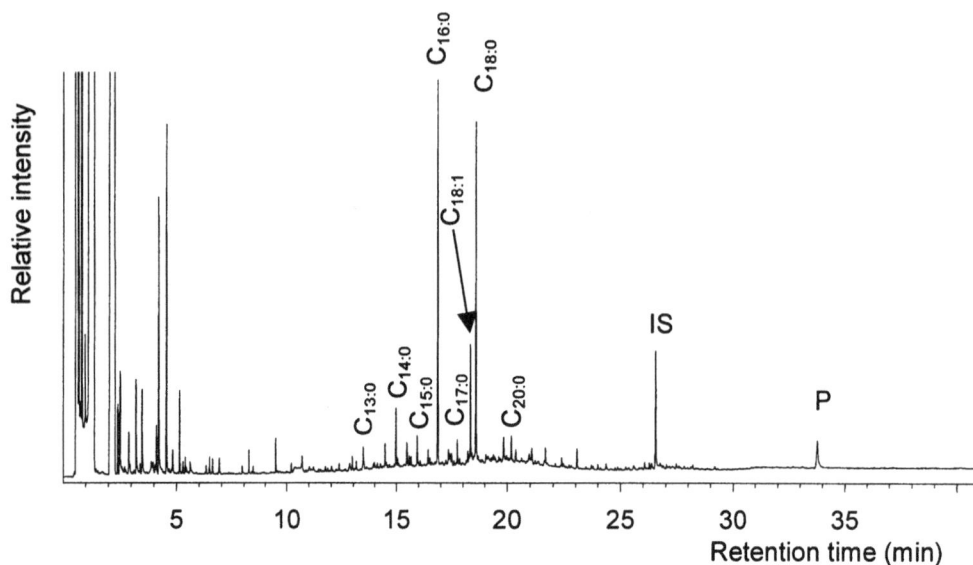

Fig 2. Mass chromatogram of the solvent extract of the visible residue from Drymmie Wood, BSTFA derivatized. IS = C_{34} n-alkane internal standard, C = fatty acid with carbon number, P = phthalate plasticiser.

handling and/or storage. Some of these samples also have a homologous series of *n*-alkanes. This distribution looks similar to fossil fuel contamination, possibly resulting from conservation and/or storage.

The Whitford and Dowsby (X2) samples have a more complex lipid distribution (Figs 3-4). These samples all contain a series of even carbon numbered wax esters and in some samples there are traces of *n*-alkanes, fatty acids and long chain alcohols. Although these samples can be defined as containing a wax it would be difficult to assign it as beeswax in particular as the composition of beeswax is quite distinctive (dominant C_{30} alcohol, with C40 to C48 wax esters, (Regert *et al.* 2001). There are other potential sources such as plant waxes (Bonfield 1997).

Conclusions
The results of this project, therefore, are disappointing. It would appear that biomolecular studies, as they currently stand, are unlikely to throw further light on the uses of these vessels and given the destructive nature of the technique, no further analyses can justifiably be recommended.

Of course we may be wrong to look for a function (practical use) rather than considering the symbolism of these vessels. McLaren (2004) has discussed the symbolism of some miniature artefacts, particularly of battle-axes, and has even noted that the Doune miniature battle-axe was of a stone too soft to have had a practical use. She suggests that these miniature 'useless' artefacts may have instead carried much of the symbolism of their larger 'usable' versions. As such it might be tempting to see their associations with children as symbolic of the child's intended role in the society however as McLaren

herself points out, the association of small artefacts with children is not always consistent (2004, 299) and cups with purely adult burial associations are common.

It has been mentioned elsewhere that across Europe there seem to be various pots and zoomorphic figurines from the Neolithic which, by their crudeness and unevenness, may possibly be regarded as the work of children or 'apprentices' learning the potters' art (Gibson 2002, 39-41; 2003). These ostensibly non-utilitarian (even naïve) artefacts are missing from the British archaeological record, particularly the anthropomorphic and zoomorphic figurines. New potters would have needed training. Potters' skills need to be learned (though some students might learn faster than others) and passed down to future generations albeit at an early age. It would appear that figurines were taboo in the British Neolithic and early Bronze Age however some pots themselves are of dubious quality whether in their form, decoration or fabric mix and it may be that these represent the work of inexperienced trainee potters. Might cups also represent the work of children learning potting skills? Certainly, like the larger vessels, there is variation in quality amongst these small pots: some asymmetrical in shape, some with haphazard decoration, others poorly fired, yet others in over-coarse fabrics. Perhaps these cups are made *by* children rather than for burial with children.

Another observation made during a study of Scottish Bronze Age cups but also noted elsewhere in Britain, is that some of these pots are primary firing wasters (Gibson 2004, figs 97 & 98). Some would have still been serviceable as the damage is limited to slight spalling on the outer surfaces. Other pots, however, have catastrophic spalling where the spalls have broken both surfaces. In some cases the pots have shattered and have

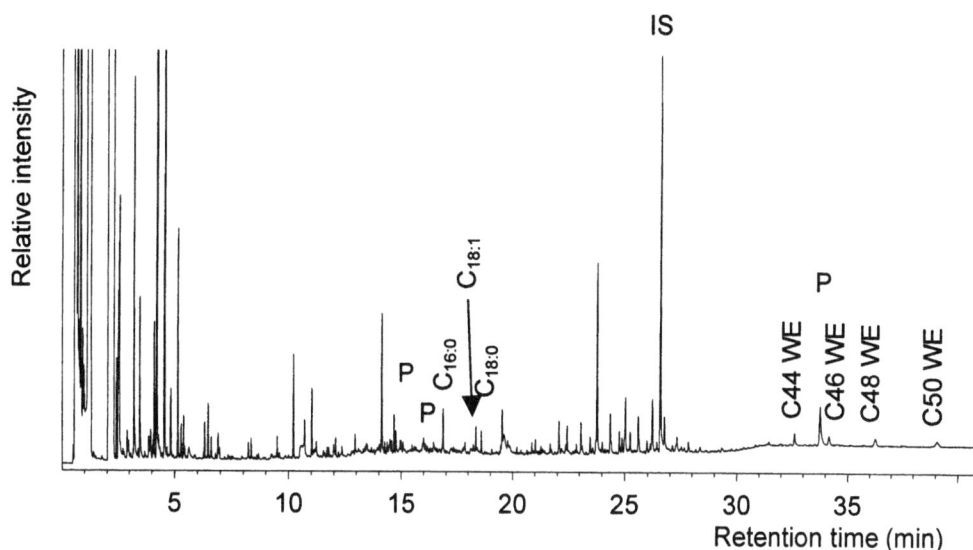

Fig 3. Mass chromatogram of the solvent extract of soil from outside pot Dowsby, BSTFA derivatized. IS = C_{34} n-alkane internal standard, C = fatty acid with carbon number, P = phthalate plasticiser, WE = wax ester with carbon number.

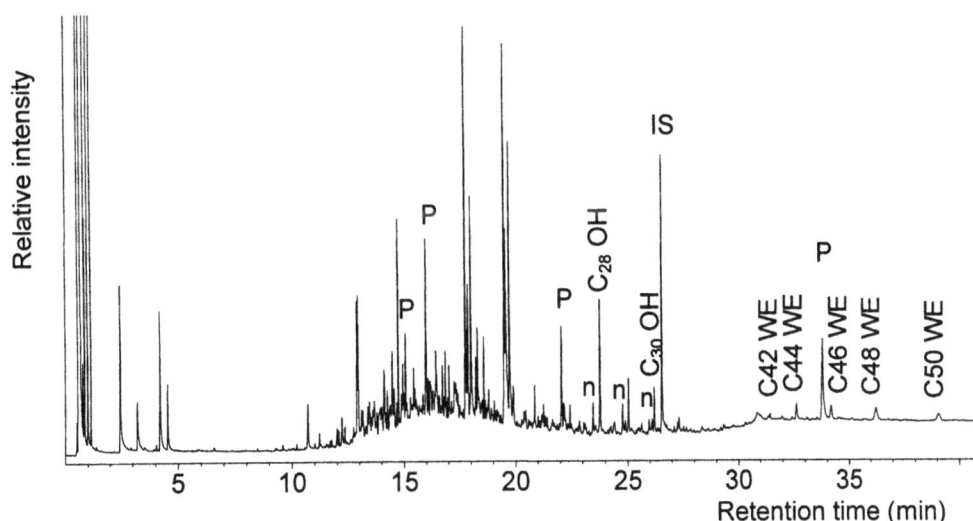

Fig 4. Mass chromatogram of the solvent extract of soil from inside pot Dowsby, BSTFA derivatized. IS = C_{34} n-alkane internal standard, P = phthalate plasticiser, WE = wax ester with carbon number, C OH= long chain alcohol with carbon number, n = n-alkane.

been pieced together from fragments. This damage could not have occurred post-firing: the spalls are indicative of primary firing wasters. Given that many are associated with cremation burial, were they made for firing on the funeral pyre? In other words they may have been pots specifically made for incorporation with the dead and may never have had a 'function' beyond the burial ritual.

Fire is a transformative medium. It transforms food from a raw to a cooked, palatable state. It changes cold to warmth, dark to light and wood to embers. It changes clay to ceramic and a human body from a corporeal state to ashes. It's chemistry would not have been known, but its mythology would undoubtedly have been rich. Changing clay cups to ceramic in the same fire in which a

cremation was taking place and in which other, organic funeral objects were being destroyed (food gifts, clothing, wooden items) may have had a deep significance and, if made by a child, may have linked past, present and future generations.

In order to carry this research forward, we must first of all recognise that pigmy cups, incense cups, miniature cups, grape cups or Aldbourne cups do not represent a class of prehistoric ceramics. There are several different grammars at play amongst these small vessels and only rarely do these grammars coincide just as with 'conventional' Bronze Age ceramics – Beakers, Food Vessels and Collared Urns. We must also stop asking the question as to their 'use'. The possible answers to this question were in place in pre-Greenwell times but are, of course, unprovable even, it would appear, with chemical analyses. Perhaps the questions to be posed, specific to each type, should be 'what do they mean?' and 'what is the origin of the original grammar?' Detailed contextual analysis within a theoretical framework might be able to answer the former question while the latter appears more difficult and would require a wider archaeological and ethnographic study even into the realms of skeuomorphism.

Acknowledgements

I am most grateful to the British Academy for funding the travel, subsistence and laboratory costs involved in this pilot study and to The Society of Antiquaries of Scotland for a travel grant to study the Scottish examples. The samples were taken by A Gibson and processed and analysed by B Stern and thanks are due to Carl Heron for allowing the analysis in the facilities of the Department of Archaeological Science at the University of Bradford and for offering advice on the interpretation of the chromatograms. Ian Kinnes advised on the French connections. Although the collections were not sampled, Mary Cahill and Andy Halpin allowed access to the cups in the National Museum of Ireland and Sinead McCartan provided assistance in the Ulster Museum. Martin Wright, Paul Robinson and Thomas Cadbury respectively of Salisbury and South Wiltshire Museum, Museum of the Wiltshire Natural History and Archaeological Society and Lincoln Museum kindly facilitated access to the collections. Alistair Barclay of Oxford Archaeology allowed the Yarnton vessel to be sampled. Alison Sheridan not only helped with the sampling of the collections in the National Museum of Scotland but also shared her extensive knowledge of the Scottish material. Special thanks are due to Ian Longworth for allowing me access to his corpus of cups and to both Ian Longworth and Andrew Lawson for their support for this project.

Postscript

Since preparing this article in 2004, the writers were involved in the manufacture and analysis of ceramics from an experimental pig cremation carried out by Alison Sheridan and others of the National Museum of Scotland. Two small replica biconical cups were made (by AMG) of a mixture of potters' modelling clay and river silts. These were made deliberately porous to try and ensure firing success. The cups were sent to NMS and one was coated internally with beeswax while the other was untreated. Both cups were then successfully fired in the cremation pyre and subsequently analysed at the University of Bradford (by BS).

Wax was clearly identified in one of the vessels and this was confirmed as being the coated vessel by Dr Sheridan. Interestingly, neither of the vessels had absorbed pig fats from the burning carcass, or if they had, these had been swiftly burned out. One vessel also provided a signature of pine wood, presumably from the pyre fuel.

While the blind testing does indeed confirm the accuracy of the process, more interesting is the lack of fats absorbed from the cremation itself. This means that if AMG's hypothesis is correct, in that these vessels were made with the intention of being pyre furniture, they would not necessarily display a lipid signature derived from the corpse.

References

Abercromby, J. 1912. *A Study of the ronze Age Pottery of Great Britain and Ireland and its Associated Grave Goods*. Oxford: Clarendon Press.

Allen, C. & Hopkins, D., 2000, Bronze Age Accessory Cups from Lincolnshire: Early Bronze Age Pot? *Proceedings of the Prehistoric Society*, 66, 297 – 318.

Anderson, J. 1849. Notice of a small cemetery, containing deposits of cinerary urns and burnt bones on the estate of Balbirnie in Fife; and of a similar cemetery, also containing deposits of urns and burnt bones, at Sheriff-Flats, Lanarkshire; with notes on the classification of the different varieties of urns found in Scotland. *Proceedings of the Society of Antiquaries of Scotland*, 13 (1848 – 9), 107 – 24 .

Annable, K. & Simpson, D.D.A. 1964. *Guide Catalogue of the Neolithic and Bronze Age Collections in Devizes Museum*. Devizes: Wiltshire Archaeological & Natural History Society.

Anon1889. Donations to the Museum. *Proceedings of the Society of Antiquaries of Scotland*, 23 (1888 – 9), 270.

Ashbee, P. 1985. The excavation od Amesbury Barrows 58, 61a, 61, 72. *Wiltshire Artchaeological and Natural History Magazine*, 79, 39 – 91.

Bonfield K.M. (1997) *The analysis and interpretation of lipid residues associated with prehistoric pottery: pitfalls and potential*. Unpublished PhD thesis, University of Bradford

Colt Hoare, R. 1810. *The Ancient History of Wiltshire: Part 1 – South Wiltshire* London: William Miller

Cowie, T. & Ritchie, G. 1991. Bronze Age Burials at Gairneybank, Kinross-shire. *Proceedings of the Society of Antiquaries of Scotland*, 121, 95 – 110.

Cunnington, M.E. 1908. Notes on the opening of a Bronze Age barrow at Manton, near Marlborough. *Wiltshire Archaeological and Natural History Magazine*, 35 (1907-8), 1 – 20.

Ford, S. 1991. An Early Bronze Age Pit Circle from Charnham Lane, Hungerford, Berkshire. *Proceedings of the Prehistoric Society*, 57 (2), 179 – 81.

Fox, C. 1959. *Life and Death in the Bronze Age*. London: Routledge, Keegan Paul.

Fox, C. 1943. A Bronze Age Barrow (Sutton 268') in Llandow Parish, Glamorgan. *Archaeologia*, 89, 89 – 125.

Gibson, A.M. 2002. *Prehistoric Pottery in Great Britain and Ireland*. Sroud: Tempus.

Gibson, A.M. 2003. Prehistoric Pottery: People, Pattern and Purpose. Some Observations, Questions and Speculations. In A. Gibson (ed) *Prehistoric pottery: People, Pattern and Purpose*, v – xii. BAR S1156, PCRG Occasional Publication 4. Oxford: BAR Publishing.

Gibson, A.M. 2004. Small, but Perfectly Formed? Some Observations on the Bronze Age Cups of Scotland. In A. Gibson & A. Sheridan (eds) *From Sickles to Circles: Britain and Ireland at the Time of Stonehenge*, 270 – 288. Stroud: Tempus.

Grimes, W. 1951. *The Prehistory of Wales*. Cardiff: National Museum of Wales.

Grimes, W.F. 1938. A Barrow on Breach Farm, Llanbledian, Glamorgan. *Proceedings of the Prehistoric Society,* 4, 107 – 121.

Hanley, R. & Sheridan, A. 1994. A Beaker cist from Balblair, near Beuly, Inverness District. *Proceedings of the Society of Antiquaries of Scotland*, 124, 129 – 39.

Hutcheson, A. 1891. Notice of the discovery and examination of a burial cairn of the Bronze Age at the farm of Gilchorn, near Arbroath. *Proceedings of the Society of Antiquaries of Scotland*, 25 (1890 – 1), 447 – 63.

Jervise, A. 1867. Account of the discovery of a circular group of Cinerary Urns and human bones at Westwood, near Newport, on the Tay. *Proceedings of the Society of Antiquaries of Scotland,* 6 (1866 – 7), 388 – 94.

Longworth, I.H. 1983. The Whinny Liggate Perforated Wall Cup and its Affinities. In A.C. O'Connor & D. V. Clarke (eds), *From the Stone Age to the Forty-Five*, 65 – 86. Edinburgh: John Donald.

Longworth, I.H. 1984. *The Collared Urns of Great Britain and Ireland.* Cambridge: Cambridge University Press.

McLaren, D. 2004. An Important Child's Burial from Doune, Perth and Kinross, Scotland. In A. Gibson & A. Sheridan (eds) *From Sickles to Circles: Britain and Ireland at the Time of Stonehenge*, 289 – 303. Stroud: Tempus.

Passmore, A.D. 1942. Barrow N.2, Wylye, Wilts. *Wiltshire Archaeological & Natural History Society Magazine*, 49, 117 – 8.

Regert M., Colinart S., Degrand L. & Decavallas O., 2001. Chemical Alteration and Use of Beeswax through Time: Accelerated Ageing Tests and Analysis of Archaeological Samples from Various Environmental Contexts. *Archaeometry*, 43, 549-569.

Ritchie, A. (ed) 2005. *Kilellan Farm, Ardnave, Islay. Excaations of a Prehistoric to Early Medieval Site, 1954 – 76, by Colin Burgess and Others*. Edinburgh: Society of Antiquaries of Scotland.

Ritchie, G. & Welfare, H. 1983. Excavations at Ardnave, Islay. *Proceedings of the Society of Antiquaries of Scotland*, 113, 302 – 66.

Savory, H. 1980. *Guide Catalogue of the Bronze Age Collections.* Cardiff: National Museum of Wales.

Sherratt, A. 1991.Sacred an Profane Substances: The Ritual Use of Narcotics in Later Neolithic Europe. In P. Garwood, D. Jennings, R. Skeats & J. Toms (eds) *Sacred and Profane. Procdings of a Conference on Archaeology, Ritual and Religion, Oxford, 1989.* 50 – 64. Monograph 22. Oxford: Oxford Committee for Archaeology.

Smith, I.F. 1965. *Windmill Hill and Avebury*. Oxford: Clarendon Press.

Smith, J A. 1872. Notice of a Cinerary Urn, containing a small-sized urn (in which there were the bones of a child), Discovered in Fifeshire; with notes of similar small and cup-like vessels, in the Museum of the Society of Antiquaries of Scotland. *Proceedings of the Society of Antiquaries of Scotland*, 9 (1870 – 72), 189 – 207.

Stern, B., Heron, C., Serpico, M. & Bourriau, J., 2000. A comparison of methods for establishing fatty acid concentration gradients across potsherds: a case study using Late Bronze Age Canaanite amphorae. *Archaeometry*, 42(2), 399 – 414.

CHAPTER 7

Holes: A Review of the Interpretation of Vessels with One or More Extra Holes From the Late Bronze Age and Iron Age in South Scandinavia

Ole Stilborg

A hole is a necessity for a ceramic vessel to be a practical container, but how are we to understand the meaning of more than one hole? To some extent there is an arithmetical logic involved here – 2 holes are a problem, while 3, 5 and 7 might be fairly easily explained, at least in certain special cases and many holes again make interpretation difficult. I will start clarifying this oversimplification. In the cases, where fully reconstructed prehistoric vessels display one orifice and two, four or six smaller, paired drilled holes, we are most often dealing with repairs of cracks in the vessel wall. Repaired vessels occur from time to time in the whole of Scandinavian prehistory. The highest frequency of repairs, I have come across, is on the earliest pottery in western Latvia called Sarnate pottery (Bērziņs 2000, 60). Clearly, curation of these vessels seems to have been important. It must be said, though, that in some cases, these holes must have another explanation because of their number and spread all over the vessel (Fig 1, Vankina 1970, plate LVII, 2).

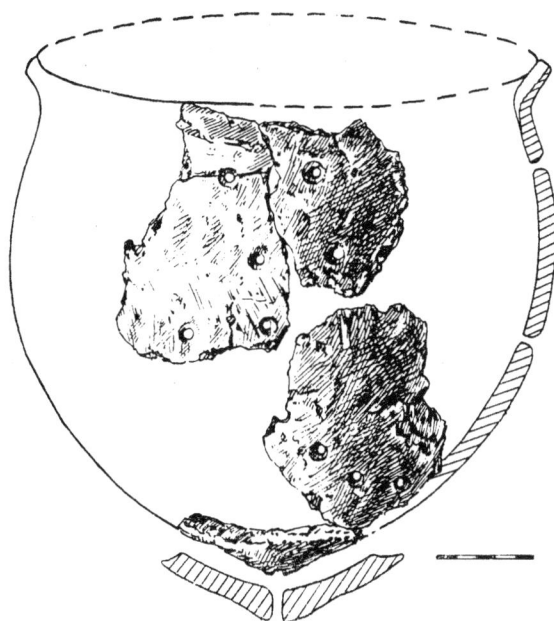

Fig 1. Vessel with multiple holes from the Sarnate site, Latvia. Notice the hole in the apex of the pointed base. After Vankina 1970.

Another case is the four suspension holes that occur on cooking vessels in parts of Southern Scandinavia during the Early Preroman Iron Age (Becker 1961, 204f) and the two similar holes with the same function on some later Viking Age pots (Fig 2). Repair holes and suspension holes are fairly easy to understand, but how are we to explain just one additional hole – primary or secondary – in the vessel wall or the base of a vessel? The second problem or group of problems concerns vessels with perforated walls and/or bases. In this paper, I will present and try to delineate these problems as well as describe the approach by which I am trying to solve them. My main aim, however, is to get responses and suggestions to further the work with the interpretations of a potentially important source of knowledge on household activities or craft processes.

Research in Sweden

Pots with more than one hole have of course been known to Swedish archaeology for a long time. Perforated sherds are especially conspicuous in ceramic assemblages. Vessels with multiple holes first appear during the Late Bronze Age – from around 1000 BC – in the whole of southern Scandinavia. They are subsequently found during the whole of the Early Iron Age (c.500 BC – AD400) and in parts of Sweden even in the beginning of the Late Iron Age. Recently, a find of a perforated wall sherd appeared in a context dating to AD1000. The majority of the finds, however, belong to the Late Bronze Age. From an early date, the vessels were interpreted as strainers for cheese making and the term strainer has been used commonly since then. I suppose that the interpretation was based on the combination of an analogy to historical cheese making and the assumption that this was a natural part of the household activities. No real discussion of the practical use of these strainers or possible traces of the use was initiated. Subsequently, the interpretation became standardised by the term "silkärl" (strainer in English).

In the 1990's Birgitta Hulthén challenged this established view on the basis of ethnographic parallels and observation of traces of use (Hulthén 1995, 3 and Hulthén pers. comm.). She divided the perforated containers into two groups – perforated vessels and perforated cylinders (Fig 3). The first group has parallels in many parts of the world, where pots with perforated bases and/or sides are often used for steam-cooking vegetables or couscous for example (Hulthén 2000, 20). The perforated container holding the foodstuff is placed on top of a cooking pot with boiling water (Fig 4). Hulthén also argues convincingly that the introduction of

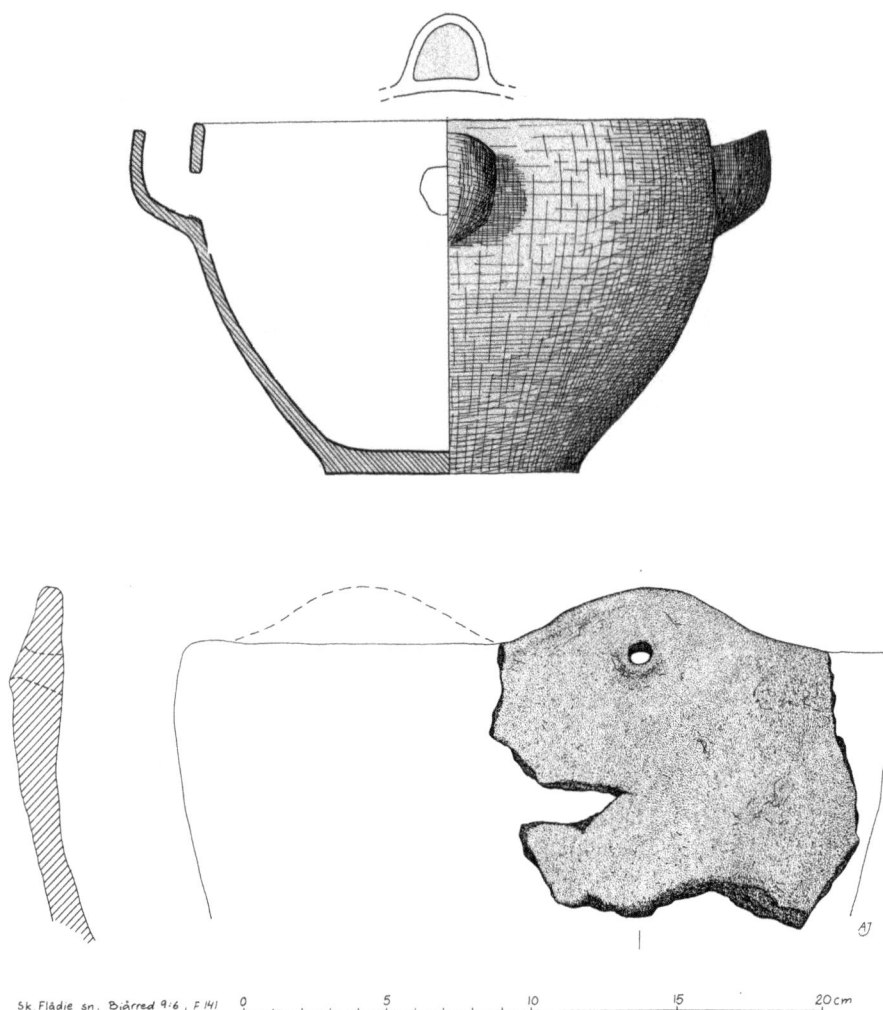

Sk.Flädie sn, Bjärred 9:6, F 141

Fig 2. Vessels with suspension holes from the Pre Roman Iron Age and the Viking Age respektively. 1:3. After Becker 1961 (H. Ørsnæss del.) and Lindahl et al 2002/the National Heritage Board, UV-South.

hulled barley (*Hordeum vulgare var. vulgare*) to South Scandinavia during the Late Bronze Age evidenced by archaeobotanical research could be the reason behind this ceramic innovation in the area. Since hulled barley is best used for cooking and demands a long cooking time in order to become digestible, steam cooking offers an easily managed way of preparation. It did not need to be stirred all the time (Hulthén *op. cit.*). I will return to this theory later.

The other group – the perforated cylinders – are most often represented by sherds with characteristic traces of use – a high fired to sintered inside and a totally oxidised core (Hulthén pers. comm., Stilborg 2002, 140f). The perforated vessels, on the other hand, are normal to low fired – *i.e.* around 500°C and for a fairly short time - leaving a distinctly dark core in the vessel wall. The fact that the cylinders seem to have been exposed to the highest temperatures on the inside indicates that the high firing is a secondary, use-related effect. Hulthén has

suggested that they could have been used as heat-containers being filled with glowing charcoal whenever heating a place away from the central hearth was needed (ibid). This explanation is also well-founded both in the natural need for heating different parts of the living space and in later parallels such as the Japanese Hibachis (ibid).

The third group of vessels with holes appear in significantly lower numbers from around 500 BC to AD100 in southern Scandinavia (Fig 5). It comprises containers with one primary or more commonly secondarily made hole in the base. The diameters of these holes are measured in centimetres as opposed to the millimetre sizes of the holes in the perforated vessels. These vessels have received far less attention except for studies of some larger assemblages. Most often, the holes described in literature seem to be a secondary change of the vessel design, but have been given no clear functional explanation so far (Becker 1961, 222; Arbman 1945, 105). In one of the largest concentrations of vessels with

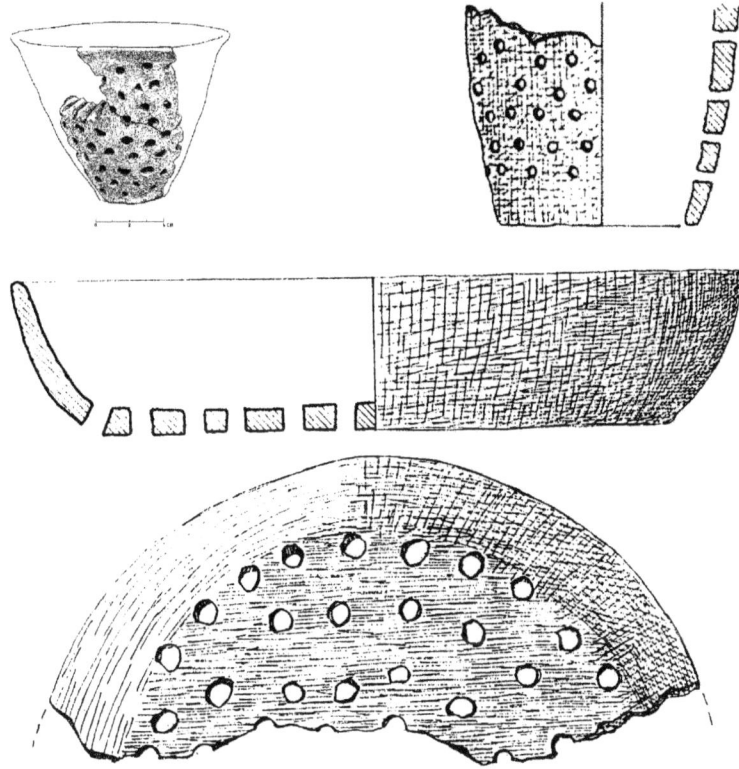

Fig 3. Vessels from the Early Iron Age with perforated walls and base respectively. 1:3. After Lindahl et al 2002/the National Heritage Board, UV-South and Becker 1961 (H. Ørsnæss del.). Perforated cylinder dated to the late Bronze Age. After Jensen 1997.

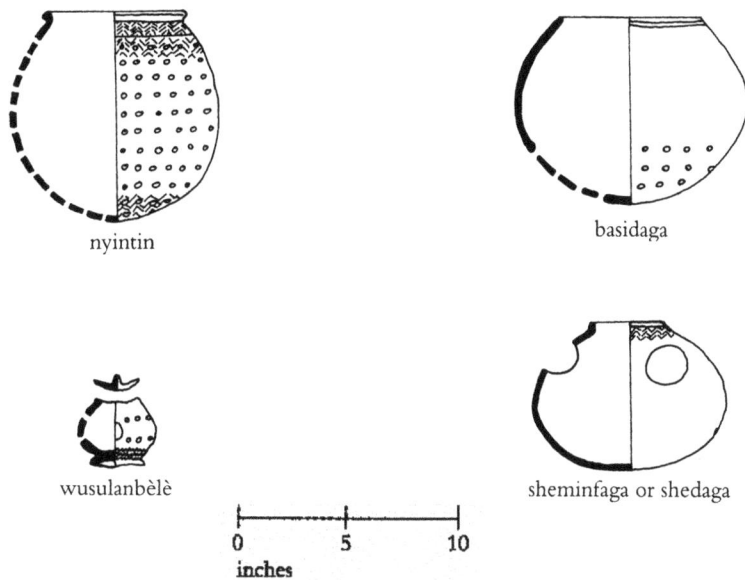

nyintin

basidaga

wusulanbèlè

sheminfaga or shedaga

0   5   10
inches

Fig 4. Perforated vessels used in present day Mali for steam cooking (nyintin), straining (basidaga), incense burning (wusulanbele) and watering the chickens (sheminfaga). After Frank 1998.

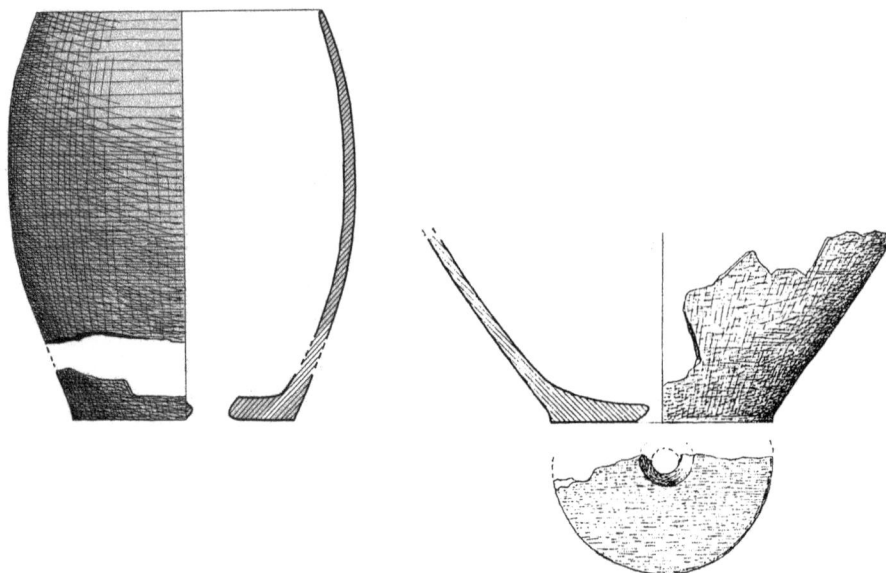

Fig 5. Vessels with one hole in the base from Early Iron Age contexts in southern Scandinavia, 1:4. After Becker 1961 (H. Ørsnæss del.).

a hole in the base occurring among deposited vessels on the shore of the small lake Käringsjön in Halland, Sweden, the holes were sealed with a stone in some of the vessels. A phenomenon which might indicate a tertiary function.

A closer look at one hole

The interpretations suggested by Birgitta Hulthén represent a huge step forward in relation to the cheese myth and inspires an even deeper scrutiny of the phenomenon of perforated vessels as well as the containers with just one extra hole.

I will start with the latter group. We can start by dismissing the simple explanation that these holes are only accidental damages from the use of the vessels. Both the limited occurrence in time, the centered position of the holes and the fact that there are also examples of primary holes are strong arguments that the holes were made for a reason. The vessels with a hole in the base occur both on settlements, in graves and in votive contexts as exemplified by the finds at Käringsjön in Halland. In this assemblage, the holes in some of the vessels were covered with a stone, while at the settlement of Övre Glumslöv in western Scania, a secondary hole in a large, storage-type vessel had been closed with a lump of clay (Fig 6). This is a hint that the holes had a very special function, which was not always in demand and that this function is not related to the secondary sacral use of the vessel. The idea that sacrificed vessels should be made un-useable cannot, however, be dismissed as an explanation altogether. In the case of the vessel from the

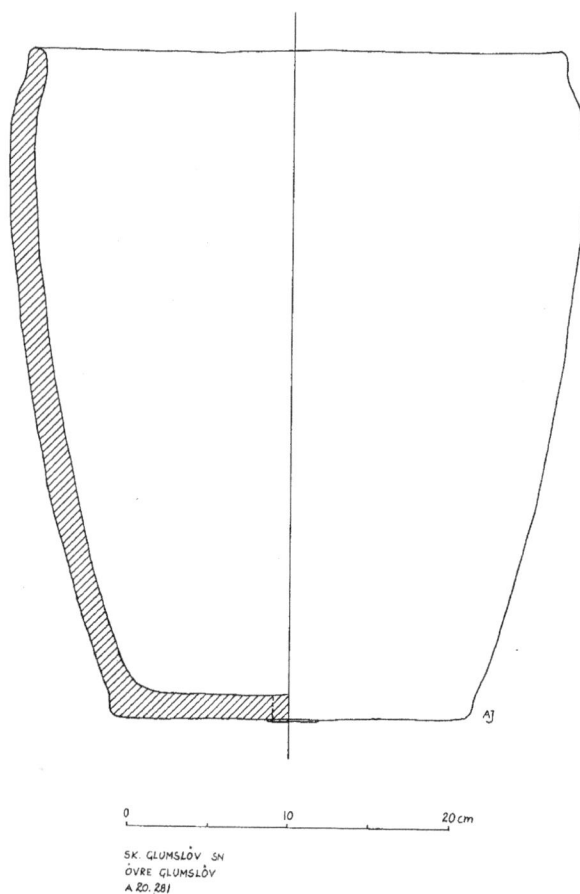

Fig 6. Large vessel with hole in the base from a pit house at the Pre Roman Iron Age settlement at Övre Glumslöv, Scania. The hole had later been plugged with a lump of clay. After Schmidt Sabo 1999 (A. Jeppson del.).

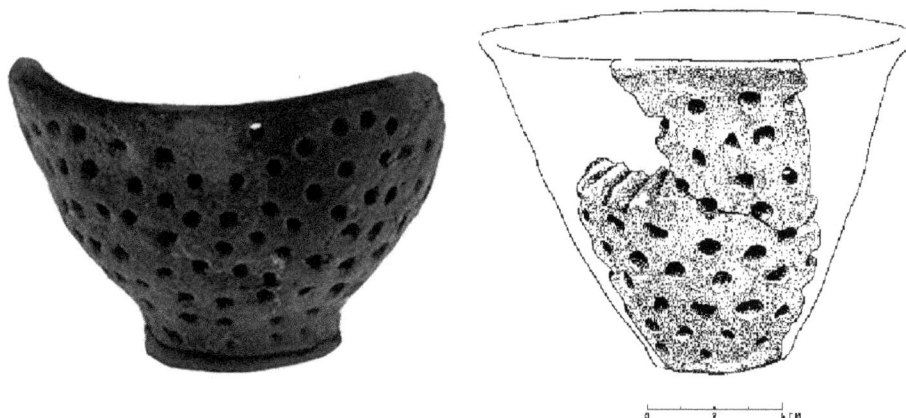

Fig 7. Vessels with perforated walls from Late Bronze Age and Early Iron Age contexts in southern Scandinavia, 1:3. After Lindahl et al 2002 /the National Heritage Board, UV-South and Lindahl et al 2002/ Malmö Culture Environment.

west Scanian settlement, instead of discarding an otherwise whole vessel, the hole was plugged and the vessel reused (Schmidt Sabo 1999, 25). The inside of the jar was covered with a thick layer of charred organic material, which may have been caused by fermentation/souring or other processing of organic substances. No lipid analyses have been performed on these use traces. They are in any case difficult to associate with either the primary (without a hole in the base), the secondary (with a hole in the base) or the tertiary function (plugged hole in the base) of the vessel. No apparent use traces were observed in the hole itself. The shapes and sizes of the vessels with holes in general do not give any good clues to the function. The medium sized to large vessels (c.5-15 litres in volume) are of simple shapes and even if some of them are sooted on the inside, it is difficult to relate these use traces to the function of the hole as mentioned above.

Thus, we have little data to indicate the possible uses for large vessels with holes in the bottom. However, one function, I happened to come across in the literature, involves the production of dye. In Nigeria sets of two pots standing on top of each other – the top one with a hole in the bottom – are used in one phase of the production of an alkaline solution needed to extract indigo (Folorunso 2002). A mixture of different ashes and water is placed in the upper pot on top of a sieve of sticks and plant fibres covering the hole in the base of the pot. Water containing potash will trickle trough the sieve and is collected in the lower pot (Ibid, 136).

Other plausable uses, which take the size of the vessels into account, are cheese making and music. A good portion of cheese in a cloth could fit in the vessels and the hole would allow the whey to seep out. The hole would also allow sound to better "escape" from the vessel, if it was used as a drum with a hide strapped across its mouth. In both cases, however, we are again left with the question: if the function is that simple and

logical, why then is the phenomenon limited in time?

A closer look at multiple perforations

While the interpretation of perforated vessels as steam cooking utensils has a sound base in ethnography and seems to fit in well with a new need for slow cooking of hulled barley in the Late Bronze Age, it does not explain the whole variation in the assemblages. There are also some problems with the frequency and distribution of perforated vessels on settlement sites. With one notable exception to which I will return later, most excavated settlements from the Late Bronze and Early Iron Age with perforated vessels have produced only a couple of sherds of one to two pots. The characteristic perforation is rarely missed by the archaeologist and this indicates, that the perforated vessels were not common utensils in the households. Furthermore, a specific study of the Early Iron Age site of Kvärlöv in Scania (Ericsson 1999) showed that the few perforated sherds were not found in connection with the hearths like the majority of the pottery. This is contrary to what one would expect had the utensil been used for steam cooking.

Even more problematic for the steam-cooking theory is that several of the few perforated vessels for which we know the shape and size, seem to be rather small "beakers" with walls perforated almost all the way up to the rim, but with no perforations in the base (Fig 7). It is of course not impossible to insert these vessels into larger pots containing boiling water but both the small size and the lack of holes in the base are curious in a steam cooking context. Another group of vessels of larger size and with perforations only in the base seems much more like what one would expect and is more similar to the ethnographic parallels (Fig 8 & 4). Most of the finds of vessels with perforated bases are dated to the Early Iron Age (Becker 1961).

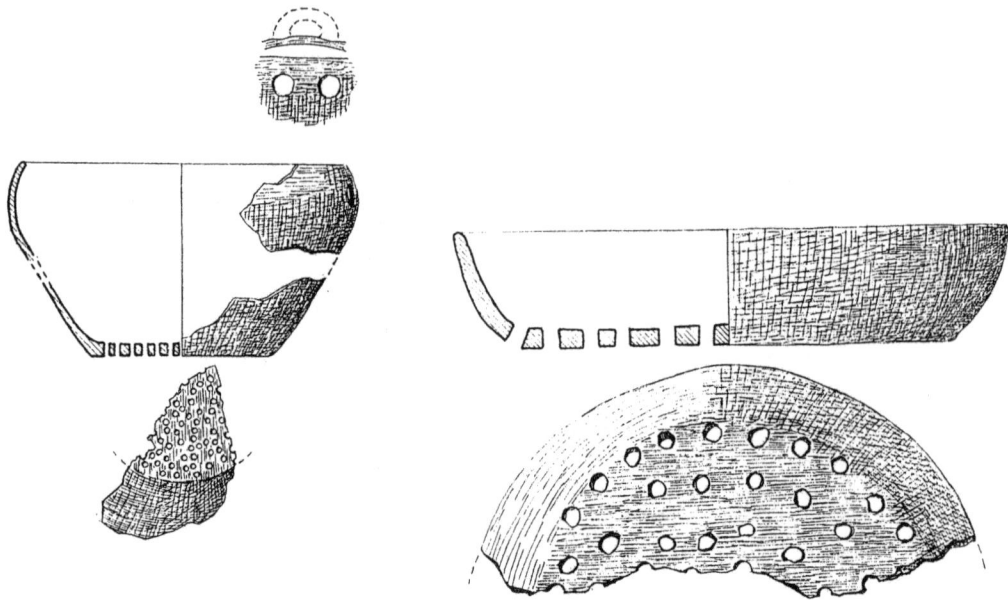

Fig 8. Vessels with perforated bases from Early Iron Age contexts. 1:4. After Becker 1961 (H. Ørsnæss del.).

The notable exception to the rule of only a few perforated sherds being found on each site is the Late Bronze Age settlement of Kristineberg near Malmo in the southwestern corner of Scania. The large assemblage from this site is presently under study and not yet published but I may reveal that it contained sherds of more than 10 perforated vessels. None of these seem to have had perforated bases and they were probably fairly small. The problems envisaged above in connection with this rich material prompted a new attempt to understand the perforated vessels better. Consequently, it was decided to record all possible relevant information about the Kristineberg perforated vessels and other available finds from southern Sweden in order to get an overview of the variation.

The database involves recording ware, vessel wall thickness, sherd type and shape, vessel shape and size, average diameter of the holes, average distance between holes, arrangement of the holes, surface treatment, firing, use traces and the context of the finds. This is a purely empirical exercise, but a necessary one in order to get a better knowledge of what we are actually trying to interpret. The work is still in progress, so I can only draw some preliminary conclusions. First of all, the variation is considerable – especially in ware, surface treatment and the arrangement of the holes. A more limited variation is found in the average hole size. Together with the very variable quality of the execution of the holes, the variation leaves the general impression of an *ad hoc* production – not controlled by too many conventions on ware quality and vessel design. This leads further on to the thought that these vessels may have served a number of different functions. One of the better preserved vessels seemed at first to have a new and fairly obvious function (Fig 9). Compared to other vessels, it had a very small

rim diameter of 35mm on top of a conical neck emanating from a convex body where the first rows of perforations occur. The inside of the perforated part was sooted. No other parts of the vessel were identified, so we have no information on the lower parts of the body or the base. However, the size and shape of the upper parts indicates a close resemblance to the perforated vessels named cheese moulds in British prehistory (Fig 9c, Gibson 2002, 14f). The first suggestion for the function of this vessel was, however, as an incense burner like the small vessels in Mali (Fig 9b, Frank 1998, 37f). The experiment performed by Jacqui Wood in England (J. Wood in Gibson 2002, 15) on the so-called cheese mould points to a very different function possibly as a Bunsen burner. The vessel was stuffed with dry reed which, on ignition, produced a high, narrow, hot flame useable for processes within fine metal work. The use as an ancient Bunsen burner is a different function indeed fom that initially envisaged but exploits the perforations, small size and narrow mouth of the vessel in much the same way as incense burning. The use traces are probably also very much the same, although the higher temperatures of the more fierce Bunsen fire ought to burn away most of the soot. The matter would remain undecided had it not been for the context of the Kristineberg vessel. In the pit dominated by ceramic household refuse also appeared remnants of a few crucibles and a mould for bronze casting. Even if the incense burner theory cannot be fully rejected, the Bunsen burner function seems the more plausible.

The interpretation of this one perforated vessel brings us a small step further in the attempt to interpret this phenomenon. Even if the shape of this vessel is so far unique, the suggested function strengthens the general impression of a group of utensils with very diverse

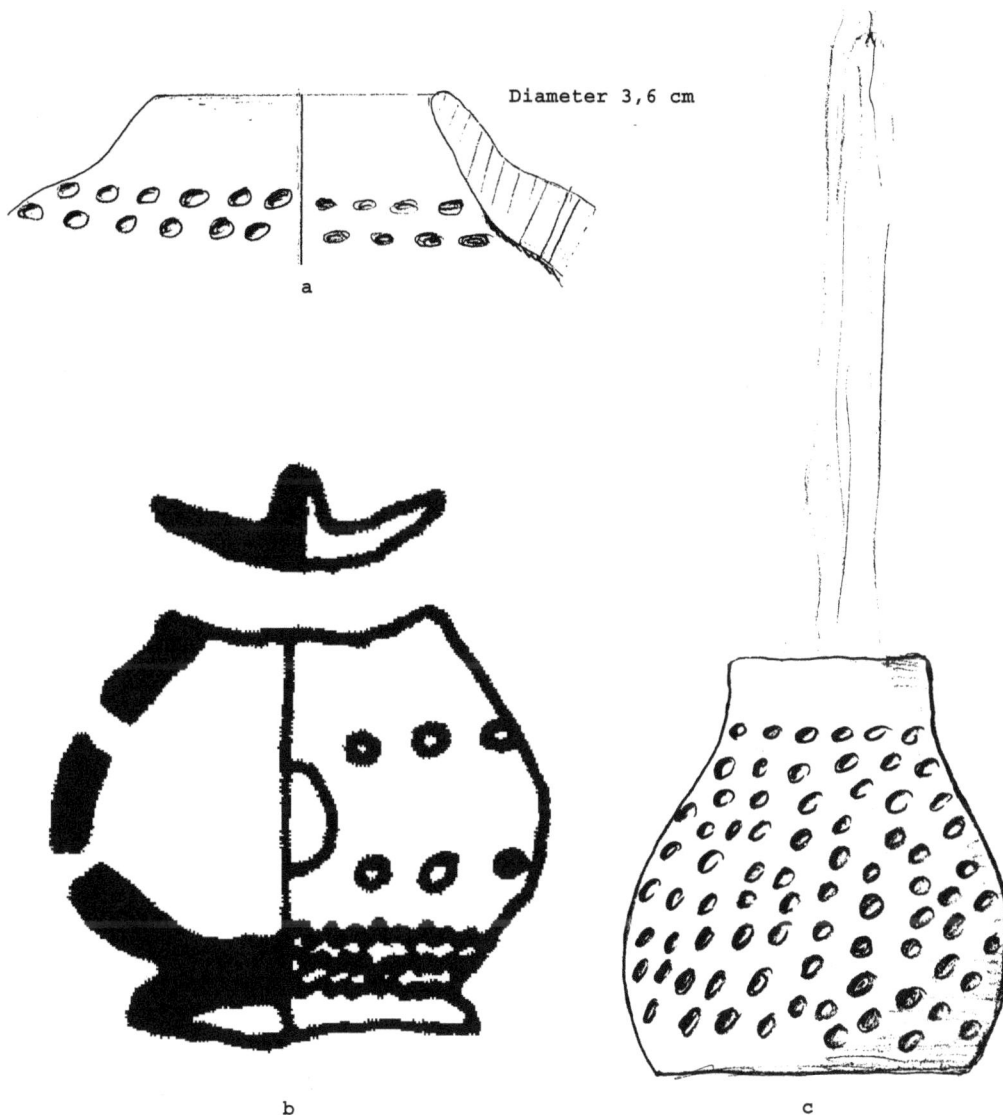

Diameter 3,6 cm

a

b

c

Fig 9. a. Reconstruction of the upper parts of a perforated vessel from the Late Bronze Age site of Kristineberg. 1:1.
b. Drawing of an incense burner (wusulanbele) from Mali 1:1. After Frank 1998.
c. Drawing inspired by an experiment performed by Jacqui Wood (Gibson 2002, 15) using a similar, perforated vessel as a Bunsen burner for metal work. 1:1,5.

functions and points to a connection with handicrafts, which has not been considered previously. In line with this connection is a suggestion given to me by a student working with experimental bronze casting. His idea was that the perforated vessels could have been used for cleaning wax later used for making the model objects for the lost wax method. The whitish and bluish discolorations that I have observed on the rims of some perforated vessels could be use-traces from this activity and would be interesting to analyse. All kinds of straining should of course also be considered – even the purifying of beverages as suggested by another Swedish archaeologist (Borna-Ahlkvist *et al* 1998, 139).

The other group of perforated utensils – the perforated cylinders – at first seemed a fairly straightforward group.

The almost sintered inside of these containers is a clear indication of a use in connection with high temperatures and the need for the spread of heat in the home might be a logical explanation. Remnants of a perforated cylinder found at the Iron Age site of Domprostehagen in eastern Sweden carrying the same use traces has, however, been interpreted in a different way on the basis of the find context (Hörfors 2001, fig 42 and 43). The perforated sherds were found at the edge of a hearth together with finds of metal slag. Fragments of at least one crucible were found in the vicinity. The excavating archaeologist has suggested that the cylinder had been placed in the centre of the hearth connected to radiating flues with bellows at the end. The cylinder should have served as a distributor of even heat in the charcoal heap around it. The details of this proposition should be tested by

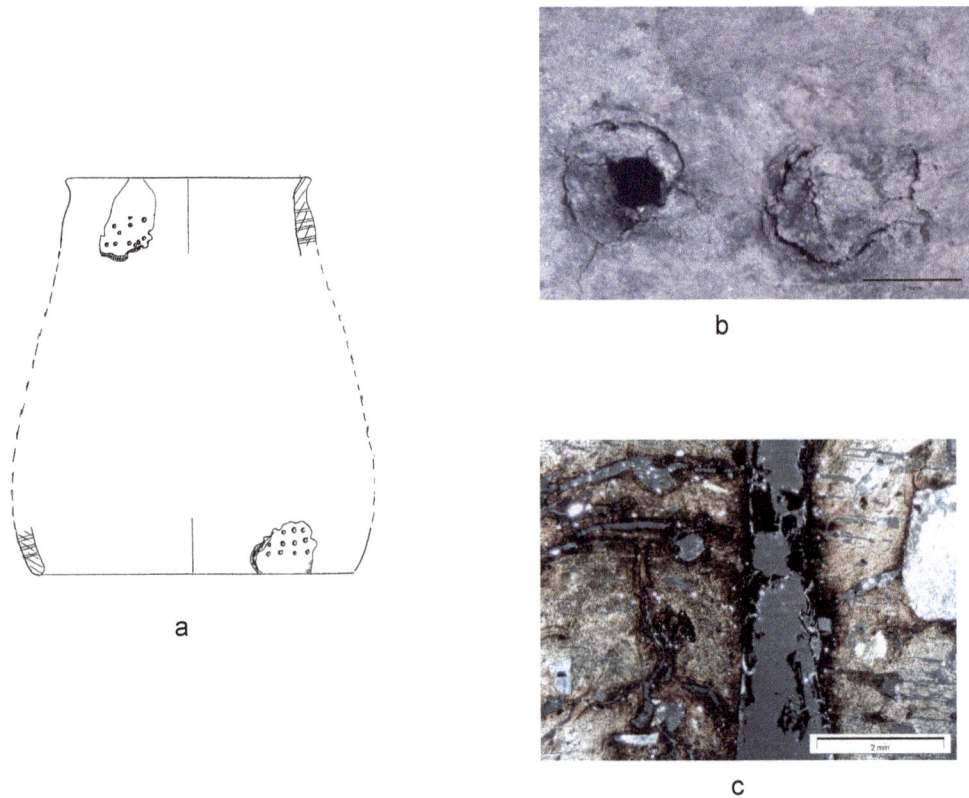

Fig 10. a. Reconstruction of a perforated cylinder from an Iron Age site in eastern Sweden. 1:4.
b. A close up photo of perforations clogged with charred organic material. c. A microscope photo of a cross section of a perforation (Thin section, crossed nicols).

practical experiments, but the association between the cylinder and metal work is without question. It is corroborated by at least three other finds of perforated sherds in metal working contexts in eastern Sweden (Gruber *et al* 2004, 56; Nordén 1929, 60f). In one case, the perforated sherds were the only pottery found in the smithy (Nordén 1929, 60f). However, in these other cases, the sherds were not fired to as high temperatures as in the case of Domprostehagen.

No parallels for this use of perforated cylinders in connection with metal working have been noted in the southernmost part of Sweden perhaps also indicating regional differences in the use of the perforated vessels. This is further underlined by another, recently studied, group of perforated cylinders in Iron Age contexts in eastern Sweden. Sherds of two perforated cylinders appeared in a stone setting on an Early Iron Age burial ground. Each of the two cylinders had been placed here together with one or two minor vessels and sherds of other pots. A tentative reconstruction of the cylinder from which most sherds had been preserved shows a high cylinder, *c.*200mm tall, with an S-like curving body and inward turned and outward turned rims respectively at the two orifices (Fig 10a). The ware was sparsely tempered and low fired. At between 1 and 2 mm in diameter, the perforations were smaller than is common on cylinders

found in southernmost Sweden. Even more remarkable is the thick layers of charred organic material lining the perforations and in several cases clogging them up (Fig 10b & c) on some of the sherds. The sherds from the narrower end of the cylinder with an outward turning rim profile had perforations with these heavy layers of charred material while the rim sherds from the other end did not. This observation raised of course doubts as to whether this was actually the same vessel, but the doubts were cleared away by the comparison of thin sections made on both rim types. Thus the uneven distribution of the sooting is an important part of the use-traces on this cylinder. A reasonable explanation would be that the soot was produced by a smouldering material placed in the lower, wider part of the cylinder. The soot would be deposited by smoke passing up and out through the perforations in the upper part of the cylinder while air was drawn into the lower part of the cylinder by the combustion via the perforations there. The inflow of air hindered the deposition of soot in the perforations.

Both the cylinder shape and the very narrow perforations through an 8-10mm thick vessel wall makes it unlikely that the material passing through the holes would have been fluent. Analyses of the organic layers are in progress at the Archaeological Research Laboratory, Stockholm University. According to a report of preliminary results (FTIR-analysis) the spectrum fits best with reference samples of oats and rye indicating a cereal origin. Pending the confirmation of this result by lipid analyses, it further complicates the interpretation of the use of this perforated vessel. Why were cereals burned in a perforated cylinder? Judging from the use traces, the temperatures have been fairly low and/or the heating brief, which makes it unlikely that the grains were burnt to produce heat. This brings us back to the incense burning function discussed and dismissed for the small Bronze Age perforated vessel from Kristineberg. The idea of incense, however, does not seem likely either – partly because of the cereal, partly because of the size of the cylinder.

We do not know whether this function of the perforated cylinder was enacted at the cemetery or whether the use-traces are remnants of an earlier practical function in a profane context. However, so far, I have only come across this type of use-trace on perforated sherds in a few similar ritual contexts in eastern Sweden. Consequently, the idea of cereal sacrifice, however difficult to test, should be included as a possible explanation. Only future finds and analyses can tell.

We may conclude that perforated vessels, found in sacrificial and sepulchral settings in this part of Sweden around the birth of Christ, seem to have been used for burning organic material possibly cereals, while at the same time other perforated vessels fulfilled as yet unknown functions within a metal working context.

A holistic conclusion

The title of the chapter is not just a pun. As so often in archaeological research, I cannot present the ultimate overview; not even clearly explain the functions of the vessels with holes in the base and the perforated vessels I have studied. But, hopefully, the study has brought us closer to a general understanding of these two different phenomena. The most essential conclusion of the study is that we are dealing with objects which in most cases were made on demand for a certain function.

The single holes in the base of the jars were secondary features perhaps related to the sizes of the vessels but not to specific type, and in some cases repaired afterwards when the secondary function was no longer in demand.

The perforated vessels and cylinders were made of very varying ware; shapes were almost as diverse, the perforations were placed irregularly over the surface and not always punched through and, finally, the firing was very short. The find contexts of the perforated vessels place them in household as well as craft and ritual settings with some regional differences. The use-traces indicate high as well as low temperatures.

Given this diversity, it would in reality be wrong to rule out any function for the perforated vessels or indeed for the jars with hole in the bottom. Incense burners, Bunsen burners, hibachi, "sacrificial burners", steam cookers, strainers and maybe even vessels for cheese-making are probably all included in these groups of objects. Only a close scrutiny of find circumstances, associations, use traces as well as of the technical parameters of the object itself may lead to a functional determination of each find. On the other hand, through this holistic approach we may extract new and very interesting information on the different processes for which the vessels with holes were used.

Acknowledgments

It is only fair to start by extending thanks to all the people making holes in their vessels during prehistory. I would also like to thank the Prehistoric Ceramics Research Group for arranging a most inspiring conference in Bradford. For the permission to write about unpublished results I thank v. A. Rostovanyi (antiquarian at Malmö Heritage) and H. Menander (antiquarian at the National Board of Antiquities, UV-Linköping). A warm thanks to FD S. Isaksson at the Archaeological Research Lab., Stockholm University, for performing the lipid analysis and for sharing my fascination in perforated vessels. My colleagues A. Lindahl and T. Brorsson at the Laboratory for Ceramic Research are thanked for discussions and comments on perforations and for inspirations for this article.

References

Arbman, H. 1945. *Käringsjön. Studier i halländsk järnålder.* KVHAA Handlingar 59:I. Stockholm. Kungliga Vitterhets, Historie och Antikvitets Akademin.

Aspeborg, H. 2003. *Arkeologisk undersökning Rydebäck station. Gårdar från förromersk järnålder. Skåne, Kvistofta socken, Rya 1:30.* Riksantikvarieämbetet, UV syd, Doff 2003:14.

Becker, C. J. 1961. *Førromersk Jernalder i Syd- og Midtjylland.* Nationalmuseets Skrifter VI. København. Nationalmuseet.

Bērziņs, V. 2000. Keramikas Darināšana un Lietošana Sārnatē. *Arheoloģija Etnogrāfija* 20. laid. Rigā, 44-59

Borna-Ahlkvist, H., Lindgren-Hertz, L. & Stålbom, U. 1998. *Pryssgården från stenålder till medeltid. Arkeologisk slutundersökning RAÄ 166 och 167, Östra Eneby sn., Norrköpings kommun, Östergötland..* Rapport UV Linköping 1998:13. Avdelningen för arkeologiska undersökningar. Linköping. Riksantikvarieämbetet.

Ericsson, T. 1999. Järnåldersbebyggelse vid Kvärlöv. *Riksantikvarieämbetet UV Syd. Rapport 1999:99.*

Lund. Riksantikvarieämbetet.

Frank, B. 1998. *Mande Potters & Leather-workers. Art and Heritage in West Africa.* Washington. Smithsonian Institution Press.

Folorunso, C. A. 2002.The Archaeology and Ethnoarchaeology of Soap and Dye Making at Ijaye, Yorubaland. *African Archaeological Review* Vol. 19, no. 3 September 2002. 127-46.

Gibson, A. M. 2002. *Prehistoric Pottery in Britain and Ireland.* Stroud. Tempus Publishing.

Gruber, G., Petersson, M., Österström, K. 2004. Resultat, område 10. In M. Petersson (Ed.) *Abbetorp – ett landskapsutsnitt under 6000 år. Arkeologisk undersökning av an boplats, ett gravfält, en offerplats, stenstränger och fossil åkermark.* Rinna och Väderstads socknar, Boxholm och Mjölby kommun, Östergötland. UV Öst Rapport 2002:43. Arkeologisk undersökning – Väderstadsprojektet, 73-93. Linköping. Riksantivarieämbetet.

Hörfors, O. 2001. *Domprostehagen 1993-1999. Arkäologisk undersökning. Raä 84:3.* Kulturmiljöavdelningen. Linköping. Östergötlands Länsmuseum.

Hulthén, B. 1977. *On Ceramic Technology during the Scandinavian Neolithic and Bronze Age.* Theses and Papers in North-European Archaeology 6. Stockholm. Akademilitteratur.

Hulthén, B. 1995. Ceramic Artifacts – A key to ancient society. In P. Vincenzini (Ed.) *The Ceramics Cultural Heritage. Proceedings of the International Symposium The Ceramics Heritage of the 8th CIMTEC-World Ceramics Congress and Forum on New Materials Florence, Italy June 28-July 2, 1994.* Monographs in Materials and Society, 2. Faenza.

Hulthén, B. 2000. *Keramikhantverket under sen bronsålder – tidig järnålder i Grevie socken, Skåne.* Arkeologisk undersökning. UV Syd rapport 2000:31 del 2. Lund. Riksantikvarieämbetet

Isaksson, S. 2005. *Analys av organisk lämning på ett perforerat kärl, F123 från RAÄ 17-18, Tannefors 1:107.* Unpublished report.

Jensen, J. 1997. *Fra Bronze- til Jernalder – en kronologisk undersøgelse.* Nordiske Fortidsminder Serie B, Bind 15. København. Det Kongelige Nordiske Oldtidsselskab.

Lindahl, A., Carlie, A. & Olausson, D. (Eds.) 2002. *Keramik i Sydsverige, en handbok för arkeologer. Monographs on Ceramics.* Lund. Keramiska Forskningslaboratoriet.

Nordén, A. 1929. *Östergötlands Järnålder I. Enskilda fyndgrupper och problem.* Norrköping.

Schmidt Sabo K. (Ed.). 1999. *Gårdar i Övre Glumslöv - från stenålder till nyare tid.* Riksantikvarieämbetet UV Syd. Rapport 1999:102. Lund. Riksantikvarieämbetet.

Stilborg, O. 2002. Lerskivor, glödkärl och lerblock – att flytta värme. In Lindahl, A., Carlie, A. & Olausson, D. (Eds.) *Keramik i Sydsverige, en handbok för arkeologer. Monographs on Ceramics,*140-141.

Lund. Keramiska Forskningslaboratoriet.

Vankina, L. 1970. *Sārnates purva apmetne.* Rigā. Latvijas PSR Vēstures Muzejs.

CHAPTER 8

The San Giovenale Pottery: Production and Raw Material

Anders Lindahl, Embaie Ferrow, Daniel Fuglesang and Pia Sköld

Introduction

The Swedish excavations at San Giovenale (Viterbo) have had great impact on Etruscological research (Fig 1). With the active participation and support of the late Swedish King, Gustav VI Adolf, the Swedish team worked between 1956 and 1965 in excavating large parts of the Etruscan settlement as well as several of the tombs in the surrounding necropolis.[1] The implications of this work would be far ranging. Previously, Etruscan research was based primarily on finds from the tombs. Now an Etruscan town came to light. Houses of varying size and importance were excavated as well as cult rooms, a large workshop area called *il Borgo* with preserved walls up to two metres in height, a large bridge complex, cisterns, wells, underground storage rooms, roads and many other architectural remains (Fig 2). The bulk of the archaeological record is from the Etruscan Archaic period but there is also much material and settlement remains from the Late Etruscan (Hellenistic) period as well as the earlier Protovillanova period, the Bronze Age and the Neolithic.

In common with international research, interest has been focussed primarily on the Archaic period, a time when Etruscan society and indeed San Giovenale experienced a climax in their civilisation. The Late Etruscan period (4[th]C BC onwards) has traditionally received less attention. With words like "decline" and "Romanisation" this period has been somewhat neglected.

San Giovenale holds an interesting position in this period of Roman expansion. Despite a general turbulence in southern Etruria at this time and the location of this site, only *c.*60km northwest of Rome, we see at San Giovenale an unbroken Etruscan presence until the end of the 3[rd]C BC, possibly later, when the settlement was apparently abandoned. There is no evidence of battles or strife at San Giovenale, which would suggest conflicts with the conquering Romans. Equally interesting is the total lack of contemporaneous Roman material, which could suggest peaceful trading relations. This is especially interesting when one considers the genesis of a permanent Roman presence in the area, with villas being

built from the 4th century onwards, showing a clear Roman knowledge of the area.

The Late Etruscan period at San Giovenale was first discussed by Ingrid Pohl (1985). The archaeological remains of this period are represented by a two-room house, a well, a cistern and an underground room. Late Etruscan material has also been found in a cistern and a well, on the acropolis (Pohl, forthcoming) as well as sporadic finds throughout the entire settlement. It was also during this period that a part of *il Borgo* was transformed for new industrial purposes with the construction of, among other things, wine presses. From the necropolis two Late Etruscan tombs have been excavated and published by Gierow (1969) and Fuglesang (1998), though a couple of hundred tombs were excavated already in the late 19th century, of which many were apparently Late Etruscan (Bazzichelli, 1877).

One can generally say that in common with the Archaic period, the Late Etruscan material remains suggest that San Giovenale was less wealthy than other contemporaneous communities. By far the greatest bulk of the material is undecorated Coarseware pottery used for food preparation and storage as well as a wide range of other domestic and industrial activities. Clays are gritty and shapes are generally simple, representing functional Italic tastes over several centuries. Apart from imported Black-glaze (also in more limited numbers and simpler forms than other settlements) other imports are surprisingly lacking in the pottery repertoire, despite the fact that they are present at nearby Blera, only *c.*6km from San Giovenale. Red-figured vases, for example, are represented by only three examples in the two Late Etruscan chamber tombs (Gierow 1969; Fuglesang, 1998) and there are only a few body sherds in the entire settlement. Lacking finer tablewares and with a limited amount of Black-glaze, a ware used even in less wealthy households, Late Creamware was probably used as primary tableware for the people of San Giovenale (Fig 3).

Late Creamware was first addressed while publishing material from a Late Etruscan tomb at San Giovenale (Fuglesang, 1998). The term Late Creamware was chosen as it appears that this ware was a development from the earlier Fine and Coarse Creamware, well-published above all at Veii (Threipland & Torelli, 1970). The earlier Fine Creamware was of a fine, well-depurated buff cream or pink fabric and usually coated with a thin slip of the same colour. Vases could also be decorated

[1] The excavations at San Giovenale are published in the Swedish Institute in Rome's series under volume number 26. Smaller articles are published in the Swedish Institute's journal, *Opuscula Romana*. See also *Etruscan culture: land and people*; *San Giovenale. Materiali e problemi*; *Architettura etrusca nel Viterbese*.

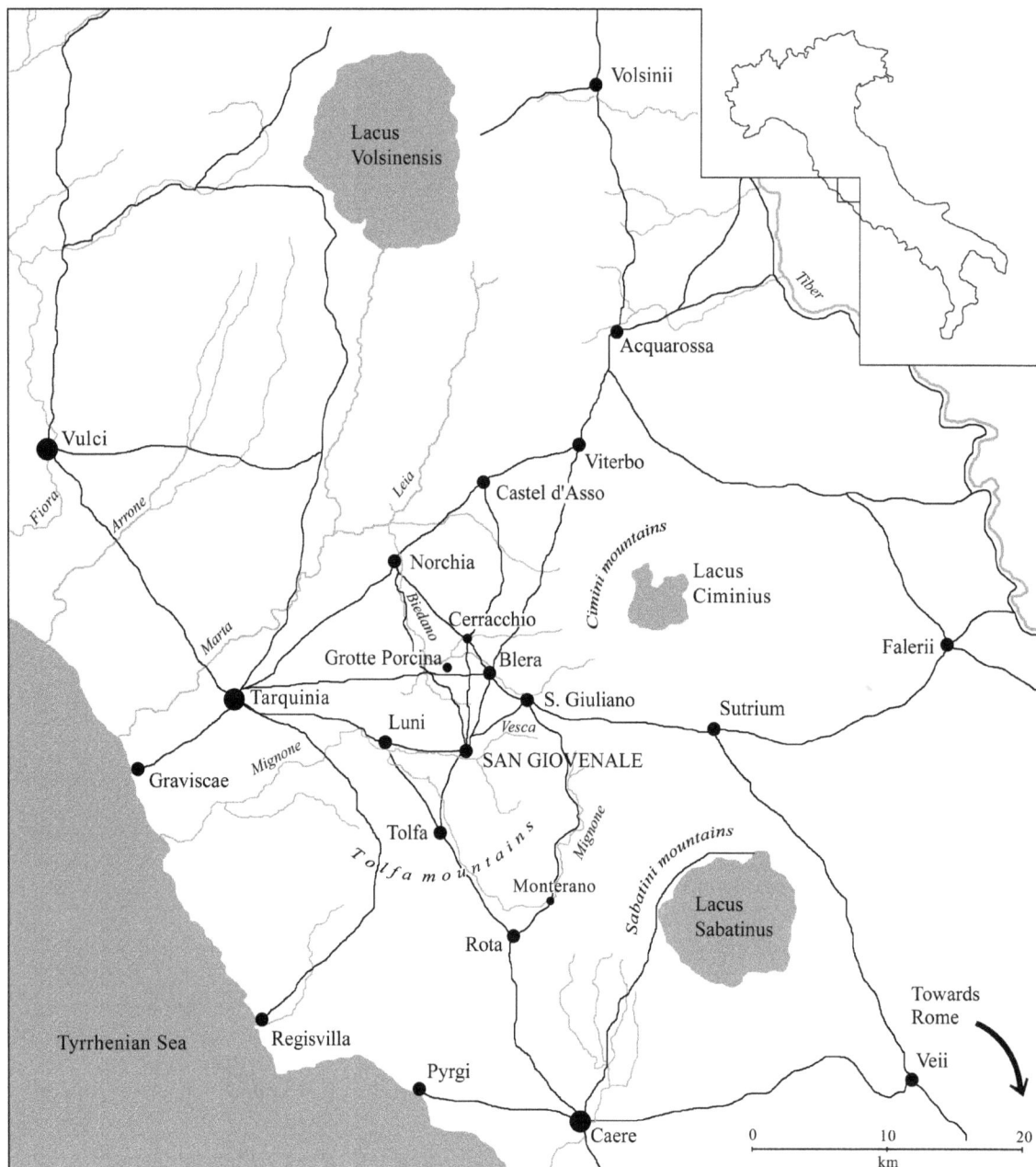

Fig 1. Plan of cities and main roads in southern Etruria (after Architettura etrusca 1986, 28).

with painted orange-brown bands and wavy patterns. These vases were used as primary tableware for the less wealthy. Coarse Creamware had a somewhat grittier fabric and was used for a wide range of domestic purposes, such as food preparation, serving vessels and storage. In the mid 4thC Black-glaze took over the role as primary tableware. Late Creamware, however, continues though in somewhat different forms. Though some clays are still well-depurated, similar to the earlier Fine Creamware and contemporaneous Black-glaze, many fabrics are quite gritty, bearing similarities to the earlier Coarse Creamware. Slips become even thinner, more of a wash than a slip, and were sometimes not applied at all. However, one interesting aspect of Late Creamware can be observed. Now that this ware was no longer the

primary tableware, one can observe a greater experimentation in the form repertoire with many new shapes appearing.

Very little is known of the organisation of Etruscan pottery production. It has been assumed that the earlier Creamware would have been produced in nucleated workshops, by specialist artisans, similar to the later production of Black-glaze. It has also been assumed that smaller communities would have lacked the resources for this production and that they would have instead depended on import from the larger centres. However, the Late Creamware repertoire suggests new possible modes of production. This ware with its often grittier clays and rather poor surface finish suggests a less

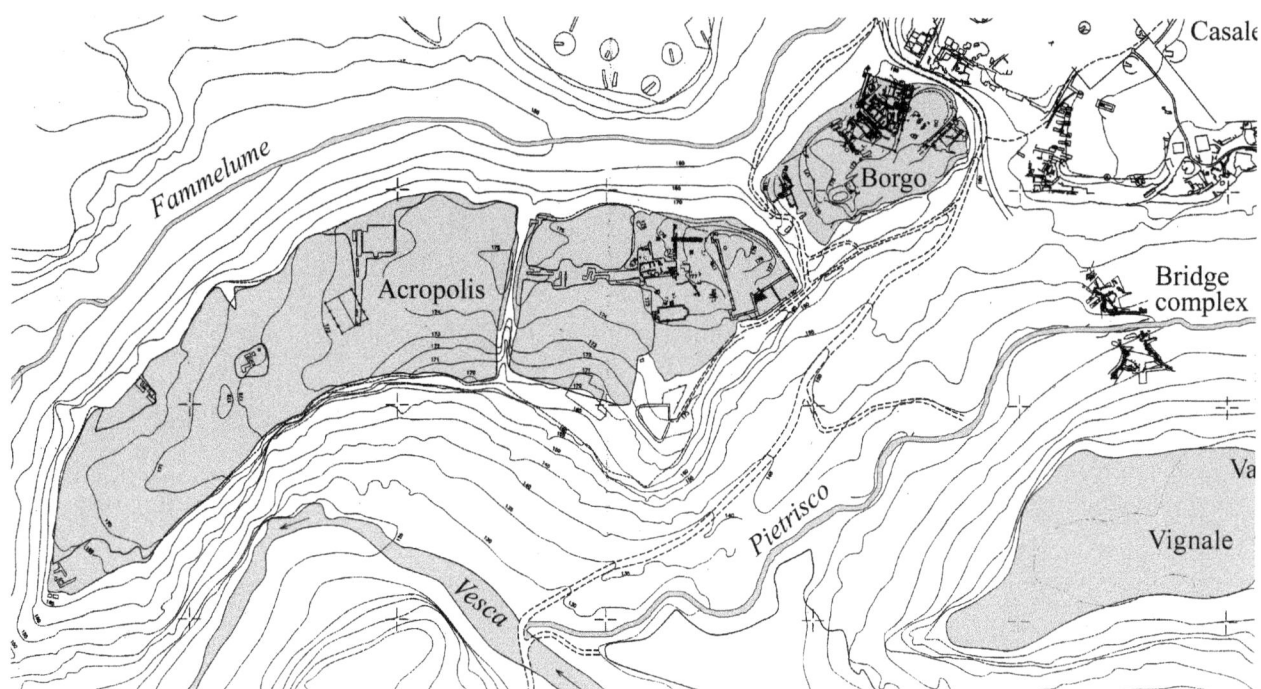

Fig 2. Plan of San Giovenale and its surroundings.

Fig 3. An example of a Late Creamware plate. Height 6.5 cm, Foot height 2.6 cm, Rim diameter 15 cm, Foot diameter 5.5 cm. The vessel was found in Tomb II San Giovenale.

specialised level of production. The vast range of shapes present at San Giovenale, many apparently unique to that site, would seem to support theories of a local production of Late Creamware, even at the smaller communities.

The short-stemmed plate is considered to be characteristic of the earlier Fine Creamware. This particular vase is also present in Late Creamware in a variety of different forms. One of the aims of this project was to take samples from selected short-stemmed plates in Late Creamware and compare them with the clays present in the San Giovenale area in order to gain clarity as to the possibility of a local production of this ware. In the spring of 2004 several clay samples in the terrain around San Giovenale were taken. Apart from a more random search of the terrain in order to find suitable clays the search was facilitated through discussions with the director of the experimental Etruscan workshop at

Civitella Cesi, who offered information as to their pottery clay sources. Samples were also taken from several short-stemmed plates, now preserved at the Swedish Institute in Rome. These plates, all from the late 4th to late 3[rd]C BC, came from a variety of different contexts at San Giovenale (Fuglesang 1998). Ingrid Pohl has long argued for a local production of most wares at San Giovenale, above all with regards to the Archaic material. This she has based on visual analyses of the fabrics and slips as well as the shapes present (Olinder & Pohl 1981, 55-78). The present project, however, is the first time laboratory analyses of the clays and pottery have been performed at San Giovenale. The results of this study will have important implications, not only for future research at San Giovenale but also for studies of the smaller inland communities as a whole, during the Late Etruscan period.

Material

The material comprises 9 sherds of Late Creamware (SG-1 – SG-9) and 2 sherds of Coarseware (SG-10 and 11). Samples SG-1, 3, 5, 8 and 9 came from a Late Etruscan tomb (Fuglesang1998). Samples SG-2, 6, 10 and 11 came from the underground room and samples SG-4 and 7 from the late Etruscan house and its cistern (Fuglesang, forthcoming) (Fig 4).

Altogether 16 clay samples were collected in the area around San Giovenale (Fig 5). (CSG-1 – 16) plus the finer fractions extracted after sedimentation of samples CSG-2, 7, 8, 15 and 16 (named FCSG-2, 7, 8, 15 and 16). Two clays were taken c.2km from the site, along the road

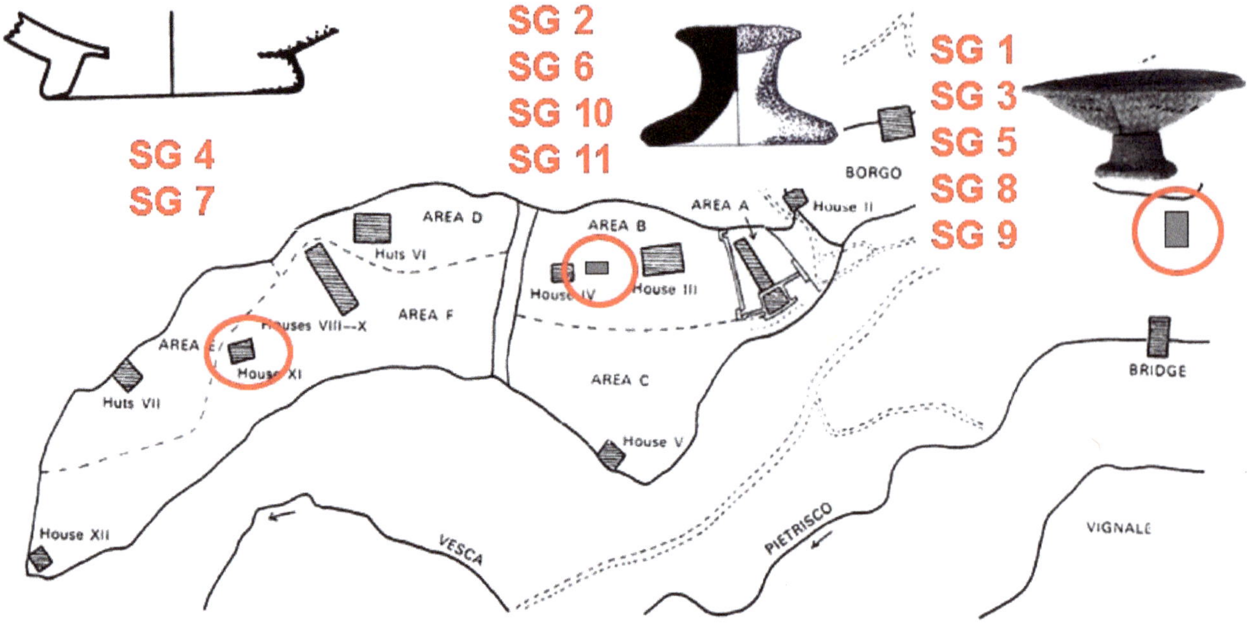

Fig 4. Plan of San Giovenale with the location of the sampled sherds.

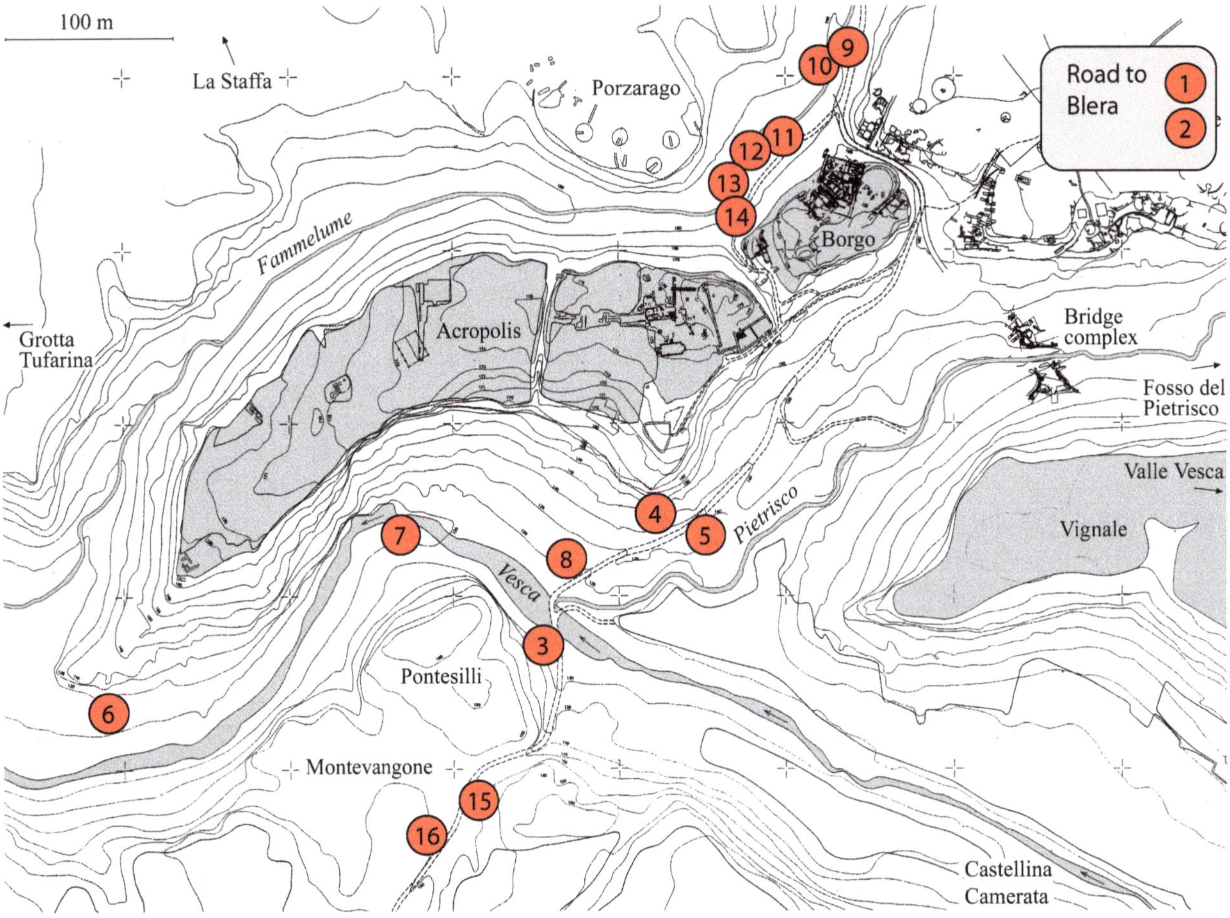

Fig 5. Plan of San Giovenale with the location of the sampled clays.

leading from the "Via Tarquiniese" to Civitella Cesi (CSG-1 and 2). The other 14 samples were taken in the immediate vicinity of the acropolis. Two of these samples were taken along the Via Dogana, heading down towards the Vesca river, at a spot where a smaller road branches off to the Pietrisco brook (samples CSG-4 and 5). Two samples were taken on the other side of the Vesca river, following the same road about 150m up the hill (CSG-15 and 16). Sample CSG-3 was taken at the ford over the Vesca river below San Giovenale and sample CSG-7 approximately 50 m downstream from this point. The sample CSG-6 was taken further downstream of the Vesca along the full length of the San Giovenale plateau at a point directly below the western tip of the acropolis. Samples were also taken in the immediate vicinity of the Fammilume brook, directly north of *il Borgo* (CSG-9 – 14).

Experimental technique

Microscopy

A polished surface of the cross-section of the sherds is studied under a stereomicroscope. It is a fast and inexpensive method of studying the type of temper (sand, crushed rock etc.) in order to gain an idea of the amount of coarse fractions (material ≥silt) in the clay. Furthermore, the study will also give an indication of the forming technique of the vessel. Microscopy of the polished surface in combination with photographs taken in the microscope is most useful for comparative studies of a large sherd assemlage in order to select sherds for thin-sections and Mössbauer spectroscopy.

The microscopy of thin-sections under a polarising microscope is a well-known method for petrographic studies of geological samples. The method is also widely used in archaeological science for the study of ceramic thin-sections. The thin-section is analysed at magnifications ranging from 20X to 630X in both parallel and polarised light. This analysis makes it possible to identify different minerals in the silt and sand fractions. Furthermore remnants of organic matter, diatoms and other impurities in the clay are studied. Particular observations of minerals and other features of the temper and clay are noted. An image analysis is performed in order to determine the amount and grain size variation of the coarse fractions using KONTRON KS 300 (Lindahl 2002, 2004). Two different grain fractions are measured – grains >0.1mm and grains <0.1≥0.01 mm – at two different magnifications – 20X and 100X respectively.

The variation in grain size in a ceramic ware varies, depending on the natural inclusions in the raw clay and any addition of temper by the potter. In raw clay, the grain size may vary, depending on the location of the clay deposit. It may also vary within one and the same clay deposit, depending on the depth from which the clay

was quarried. Both these factors are subject to the environment in which it was formed. Thus, the calculation of the grain-size variation of samples is a means of distinguishing different productions. In order to estimate the carbonate content of the clays and the sherds they were all tested with 3% hydrochloric acid (HCl).

Mössbauer spectroscopy

The physical and chemical changes associated during firing of iron rich (Fe-bearing) clays in the production of ceramics are governed by the prevailing firing parameters, such as temperature, time, and the mineralogy of the raw material used. Mössbauer spectroscopy is an established technique in studying the state of iron (Fe) in ceramics (Cousins & Dharmawardena 1969). It has been fully demonstrated that the technique could be used to retrieve the ancient firing conditions by comparing with clays fired under controlled experimental conditions. Moreover, the Mössbauer spectra of sherds could also be used to locate the provenance of the pottery from specific production sites.

In this study five of the sampled sherds (SG-1, 3, 5, 7 and 11) from San Giovenale were studied using room temperature Mössbauer spectroscopy. Three sherds, SG-1, SG-7 and SG-11, were fired in an oxidising environment for a total of 24 hours at temperatures ranging between 600°C and 1000°C. The resulting Mössbauer parameters of the temperature series will be compared to the Mössbauer parameters of the unprocessed sherds to estimate the possible firing temperature of the relevant samples. The samples were crushed to powder and homogenised in a crucible. Two grams of each sample were fired in an oxidising atmosphere in a Carbolite RHF1500 oven in three eight hours long heating, annealing, and cooling periods. The rate of heating and cooling depends on the annealing temperature. For example, for annealing at 800°C the rate of heating or cooling was 1.7°C/min while for annealing at 1000, the rate is 2°C/min. The fired samples were then crushed and homogenised in a crucible and portioned for Mössbauer spectroscopy.

All Mössbauer data were collected at room temperature. Samples of 200mg were mixed with petroleum jelly using the technique introduced by Rancourt (1994). This gives symmetric high- and low-energy components of the absorption lines, effectively eliminating the need for texture correction of the spectrum. The spectra were not corrected for thickness effects since the amounts of samples mixed with the petroleum jelly corresponded to <5mg/cm^2 of natural iron. The spectrum was collected in a 512 multi-channel analyser in conjunction with an electro-mechanical drive system running at constant acceleration. Spectrometer velocity was calibrated against natural iron foil with a source of [57]Co in Rh with a starting nominal activity of 55 mCi.

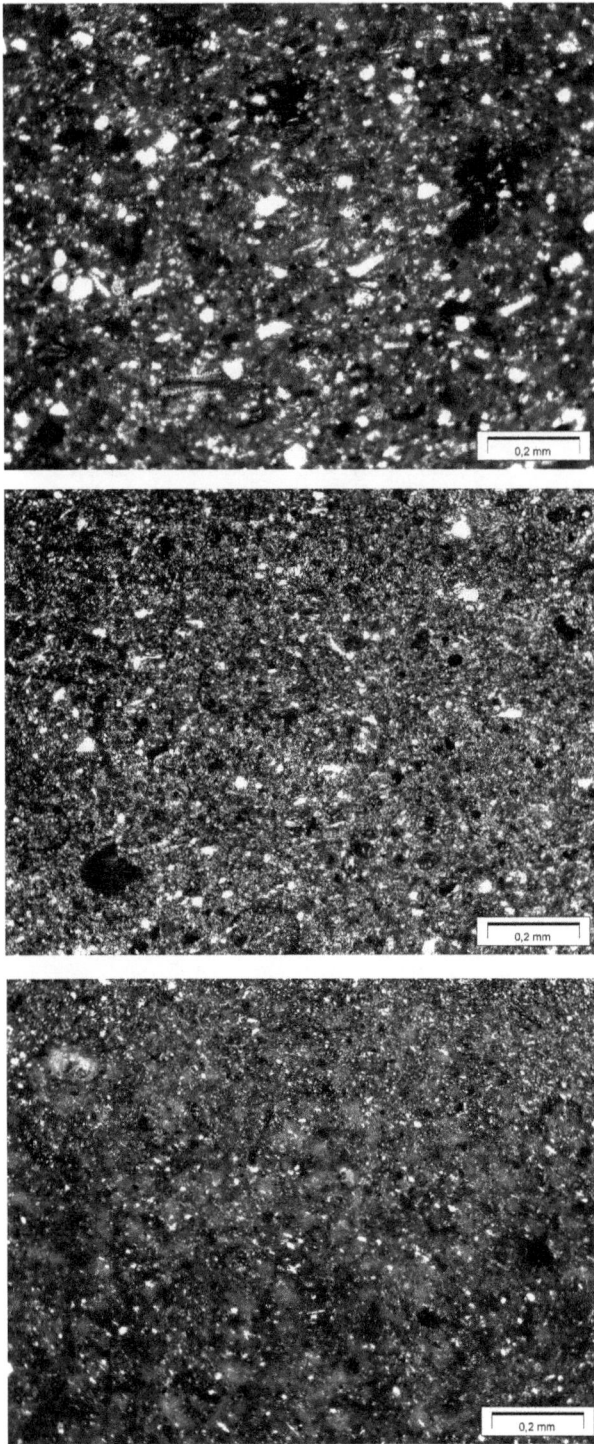

Fig 6. An example of the varied composition of the clays used for the manufacture of Late Creameware plates. Micrograph in polarised light. Top. SG-3, medium amount of coarse silt. Middle. SG-1, rich amount of silt. Bottom. SG-9, low amount of fine silt.

Carbon analyses

To investigate how the carbonates react during combustion a carbon analysis was performed using a multi phase carbon analyser (LECO RC-412). The majority of carbonates decompose within a range of temperatures ($500 - 1000°C$). Most forms of carbon (C),

both organic and inorganic, combust in an oxidizing atmosphere and is converted into carbon dioxide (CO_2). The evolution of CO_2 is associated with endothermic peaks at various temperatures, CO_3 (inorganic C) approximately between $500-1000°C$ and organic C mostly under $550°C$.

The clays (FCSG-7 and 15) were ground to powder and fired in an oxidised atmosphere in a laboratory furnace (Carbolite RHF 1500) at 700, 825 and $900°C$ for 45 minutes. To get an impression of how much of the carbon that combusts in the firing range up to $700°C$ a sample of the raw clay FCSG-7 was included in the analysis.

Experimental Results and Discussion

The fabric of all the analysed Late Creamware vessels is very fine. There are very few grains in sizes that exceed 0.5mm. The vast majority of inclusions are smaller than 0.1mm. The fabric of all the Late Creamware vessels (SG-1 – SG-9) may be classified as very fine even when seen under a stereomicroscope. However, analyses of the thin sections in a polarising microscope display a more varied composition both in grain size distribution and amount of inclusions (Fig 6).

The two sherds of Coarseware (SG-10 and 11), sampled as being of local production, have a gritty fabric with clearly visible inclusions of mineral grains even by the naked eye. In both these samples the maximum grain size is larger than 1.5mm. The analysis of the thin sections of samples SG-10 and 11 show that these vessels were made of different clays. The mineralogical composition differs in that SG-11 comprises a large quantity of diopside grains, a mineral that SG-10 lack almost completely. Furthermore, the amount of grains larger than 0.1mm varies in the two samples. In SG-10 it is 7% (vol.) and in SG-11 it is almost twice as much, 13% (vol.). The number of grains in this grain fraction also varies; SG-10 has a mean value of 65 grains and SG-11 a mean value of 85. The ratio between the number of grains and amount in these two samples should be interpreted as larger grains in SG-11 as compared to smaller grains in SG-10.

The plot (Fig 7) shows the relation between grain area in mm^2 (mean value) and number of grains (mean value) for grains in the size interval $<0.1\geq0.01$ mm. As illustrated here, there is a wide range of fabrics from the extremely fine with few inclusions to a ware with an abundance of comparatively large grains.

The vessel SG-6 found in the underground room on the acropolis and SG-9 found in a Late Etruscan tomb (Fig 4) have a ware that is almost identical, which suggests that they were made of the same clay (Fig 8). One other group may be distinguished in the material, vessel SG-2 found in the underground room, SG-4 from the house and SG-8 found in a Late Etruscan tomb display such similar

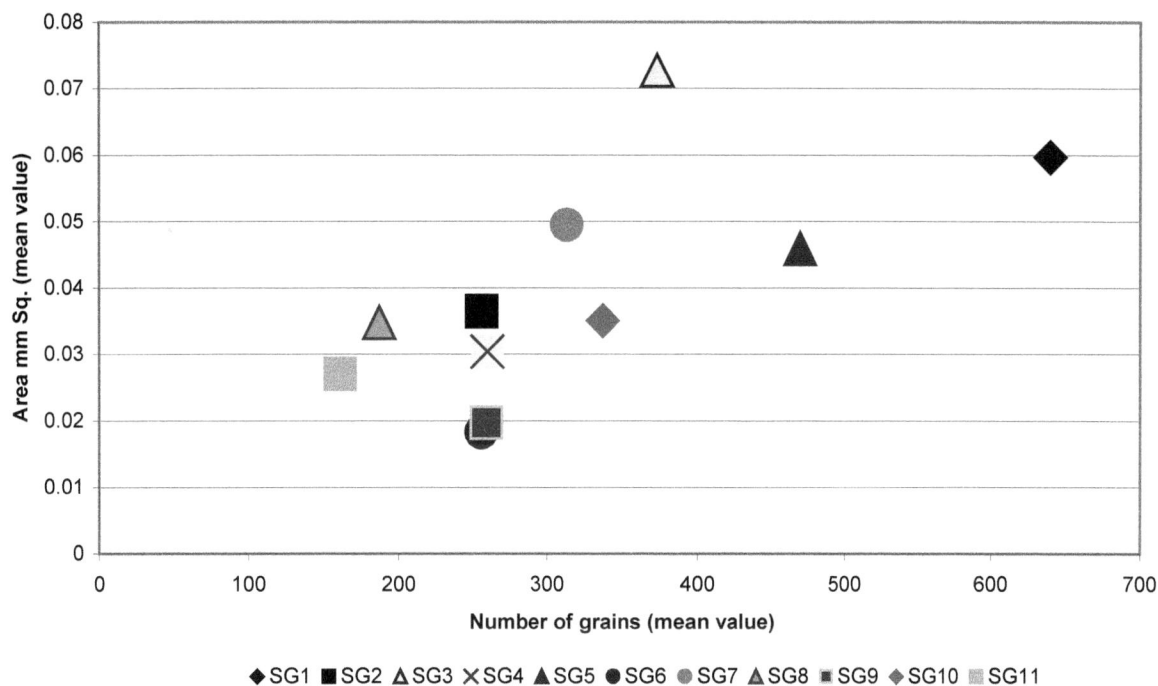

Fig 7. Scatter-plot showing the relation between area in mm^2 (mean value) and number of grains (mean value) for grains in the size interval <0.1≥0.01 mm for the sampled sherds. There is a wide range of fabrics from the extremely fine with few inclusions to ware with an abundance of comparatively large grains.

characteristics of the ware that they may be considered to be made of the same clay (Fig 9).

None of the vessel samples reacted to the treatment with HCl. This could be due to the fact that either they were all made of non-calciferous clays or that the carbonate content had escaped in the firing process[2]. Half of the clay samples (CSG-1, 3, 5, 6, 7, 9, 10 and 13) show a reaction when treated with HCl. Calciferous clays must normally be treated in some way (*e.g.* an addition of organic matter, mixture of salt water or fired in a reduced

atmosphere) to minimize breakage during and after firing. Thus the result of the HCl-test may implicate that these clays would have been a less likely choice for the manufacture of the pots.

Test-briquettes of all the sampled clays were made and fired in a laboratory furnace in an oxidising atmosphere at a temperature of 600°C for 30 minutes. All of them, even the calciferous ones, produced a solid ceramic ware. The majority of the clays have a rich red-brown colour after firing, indicating a very rich iron content. CSG-1, 3, 5, 7, 12 and 13 show a more buff colouration, though they too must be considered as iron rich.

The test-briquettes were also used to make ceramic thin-sections. The analyses of the thin-sections of the clays confirm and further give details on the result of the HCl-test. Samples CSG-1, 3 and 7 are, compared to the others, much more fine-grained. Max. grain size for SGL7 is only 1mm, CSG-3 has slightly larger grains (max grain 1.9mm). CSG-1 has a very fine grain matrix and a few large grains. the max. grain size is 3mm. These three clays have calciferous material in all grain fractions. In samples CSG-5, 6, 9, 10 and 13 the calciferous material is mainly concentrated to the sand fraction and can, in most cases, be described as grains of limestone. In addition to the limestone the major mineralogical components are grains of basaltic rock, tuff, volcanic glass, quartz and feldspar. The non-calciferous clays (CSG-2, 4, 8, 11, 12, 14, 15 and 16) display, with the

---

[2] In calciferous clay the calcium carbonates cause stress to the ceramic ware due to different chemical reactions during and after firing. When the calciferous clay is fired there is a de-carbonation of the calcium carbonate in that carbon dioxide (CO_2) leaves as a gas and calcium oxide (CaO) – burned lime – remains in a solid state – $CaCO_{3(s)}$ + heat → $CaO_{(s)}$ + $CO_{2(g)}$. The gas ($CO_{2(g)}$)has a larger volume than the carbon and oxygen in the carbonate, this gas-expansion is most damaging to the ceramic ware. Immediately after firing when the ceramic ware cools down the CaO reacts with the humidity in the air and there is a hydration of the CaO. This reaction forms calcium hydroxide, commonly called slaked lime – $CaO_{(s)}$ + $H_2O_{(l)}$ → $Ca(OH)_{2(s)}$ + heat. Since the clay has shrunk in the firing there is a great chance that the ware may break due to expansion of the forming of calcium hydroxide. Both the calcium oxide and the calcium hydroxide are soft and may be easily removed mechanically from the ceramic ware if for instance the vessel is rinsed in water. That the ceramics once contained grains of CaO and/or $Ca(OH)_2$ are often seen as voids in the ware.

The calcium hydroxide is not stable, it reacts with the carbon dioxide in the air (carbonation) and form calcium carbonate – $Ca(OH)_{2(s)}$ + $CO_{2(g)}$ → $CaCO_{3(s)}$+ H_2O. Unless there is an active supply of CO_2 this latter reaction is normally much slower than the other two.

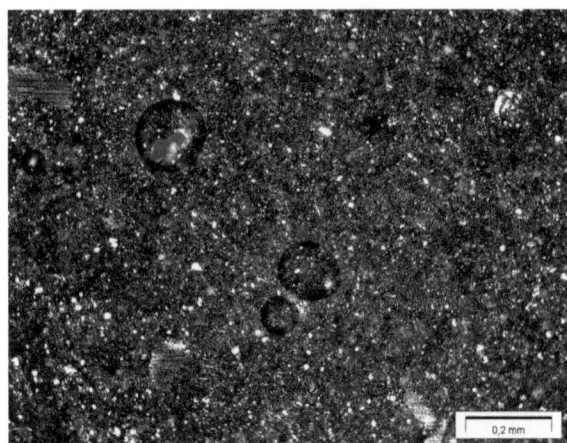

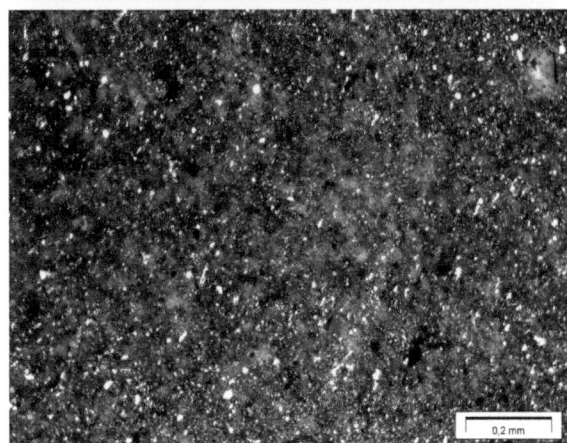

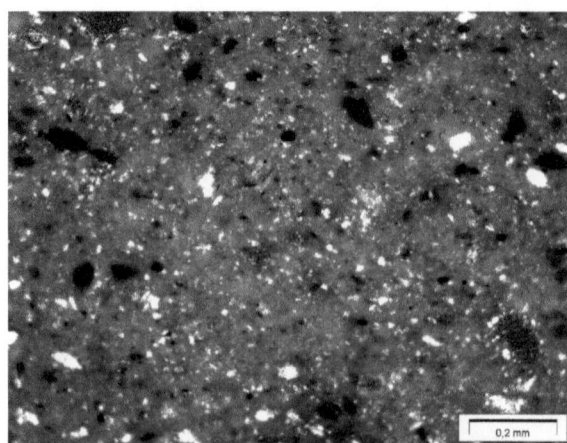

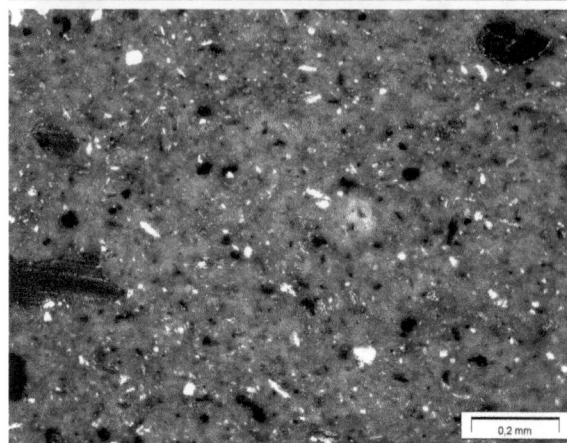

Fig 8. A comparison between SG-6 (a) and SG-9 (b). Both vessels are made of a very fine clay with a low amount of fine-grained silt. Micrograph in polarised light.

absence of limestone, a similar mineralogical composition of the coarse fractions as the carbonate bearing clays.

The most striking result of the analyses of the clays is the heterogeneous map of clays that is being displayed, for instance the various types of calciferous clays that are described above. To this can be added that practically every possible grain size distribution is represented in the material (Fig 10). The clays that, according to grain size distribution and absence of calciferous material, are considered to be the most suited for making pottery are CSG-2, 8, 12, 15 and 16. For instance, the grain size distribution and mineralogy of clay CSG-8 is very similar to the ware of the Coarseware sherd SG-10 (Fig 11).

The Late Creamware vessels were all made of extremely fine clay. Natural clays of such fineness are normally found in lacustrine environments, such as deep-water lake or sea sediments. However, they can also be made by grain-size fractionation. If the clay is dispersed in water, for example in a pit or barrel, the heavy particles (sand and coarse-silt fractions) settle first while the finer particles (fine-silt and clay fractions) stay in suspension for a longer time and then sediment on top. After the water has evaporated the fine-grained clayey top layer

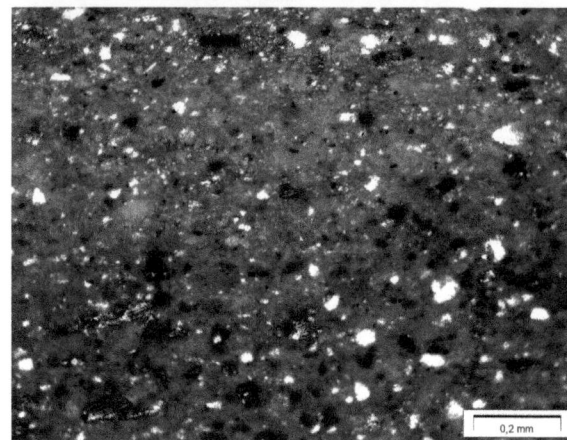

Fig 9. A comparison between SG-2 (a), SG-4 (b) and SG-8 (c). They are all made of a fine clay with a low amount of medium sized silt grains. Micrograph in polarised light.

can easily be collected. To disperse the clay in water is also a good method to rinse it from organic matter since this material will float on the water and thus can be skimmed off during this process of grain-size fractionation. The clay used to manufacture the vessels of Late Creamware was in all likelihood processed by this method of levigation.

In order to test if clays from San Giovenale could have been used for the Late Creamware plates five of the raw clays were selected for grain-size fractionation in the laboratory. In addition to the non-calciferous clays CSG-

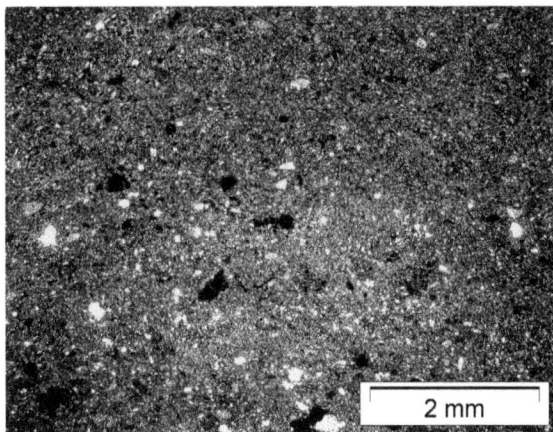

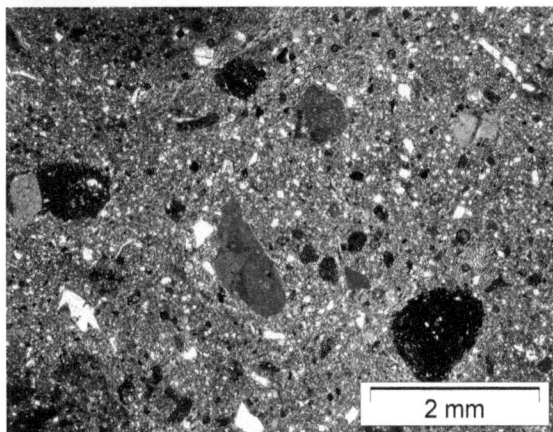

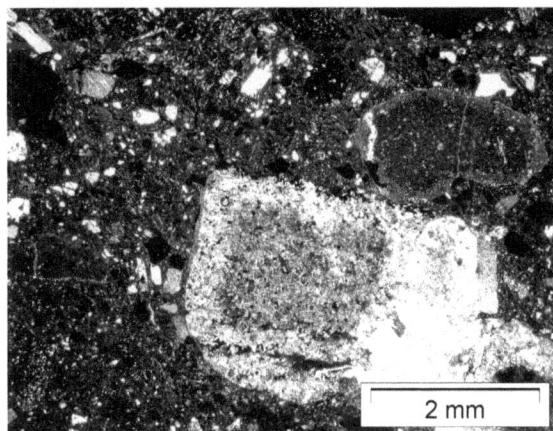

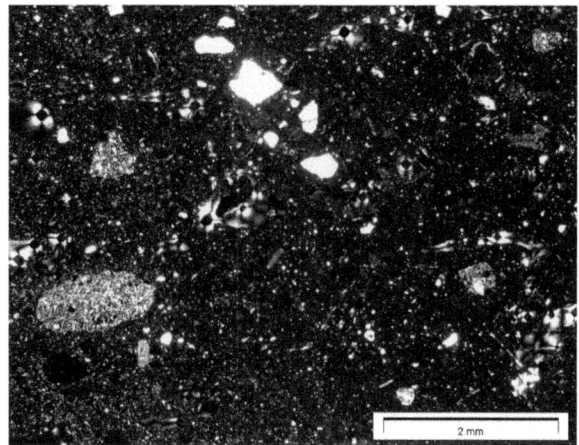

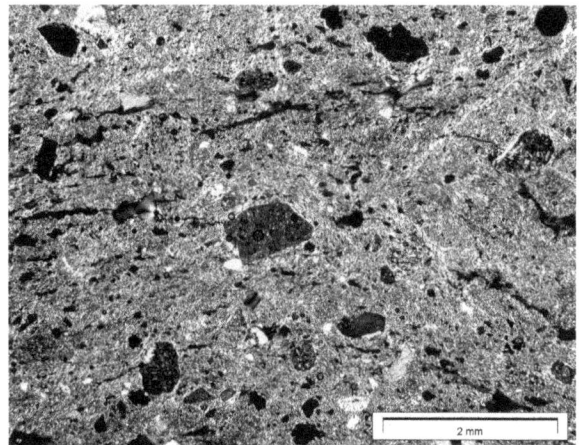

Fig 11. A comparison between the vessel SG-10 and the raw clay CSG-8. Both are examples of sandy silty clays and they have a very similar mineral composition.

Fig 10. An illustration of the heterogeneous assemblage of clays in the near surroundings of San Giovenale. a) CSG-7, a calciferous fine grained clay, b) CSG-15, a non calciferous silty sandy clay and c) CSG-6, a calciferous clay with several grains in the fraction larger than 2 mm.

2, 8, 15 and 16, the very calciferous clay CSG-7 was also chosen. The reason for this was three-fold:

1. It was a clay suggested by the director of the experimental Etruscan workshop at Civitella Cesi,
2. It was the most fine-grained clay of all the clay samples and
3. The fired test briquette of the clay showed good thermal qualities.

After sedimentation four test-briquettes were made of the fine-grained top-layer of each one of the clays. These were fired at 650, 700, 750 and 800°C for 30 minutes and successively thin-sections were made. The thin-section analyses show that the five clay samples prepared by grain-size fractionation are all very similar to the ware of the Late Creamware vessels. Samples FCSG-2, 7, 8 and 16 are more fine-grained than the vessels while FCSG-15 is found right in the middle of the sampled vessels (Fig 12). The reason why four of the clay samples are comparatively more fine-grained than the vessels is most likely due to the manner in which the samples were taken. The clay used for the manufacture of the test briquettes was "shaved" off the upper-most layer in the sedimentation beakers. In a full-scale production, where the clay is levigated in a larger sedimentation pool/pit/barrel, one may assume that the potter is slightly less selective. Thus, the result of the sedimentation test indicates that when the clays are treated in this way any of them could have been used for the manufacture of Late Creamware vessels.

The fired test-briquettes of clay FCSG-7 were tested with HCl. The samples fired to 650 and 700°C show a weak

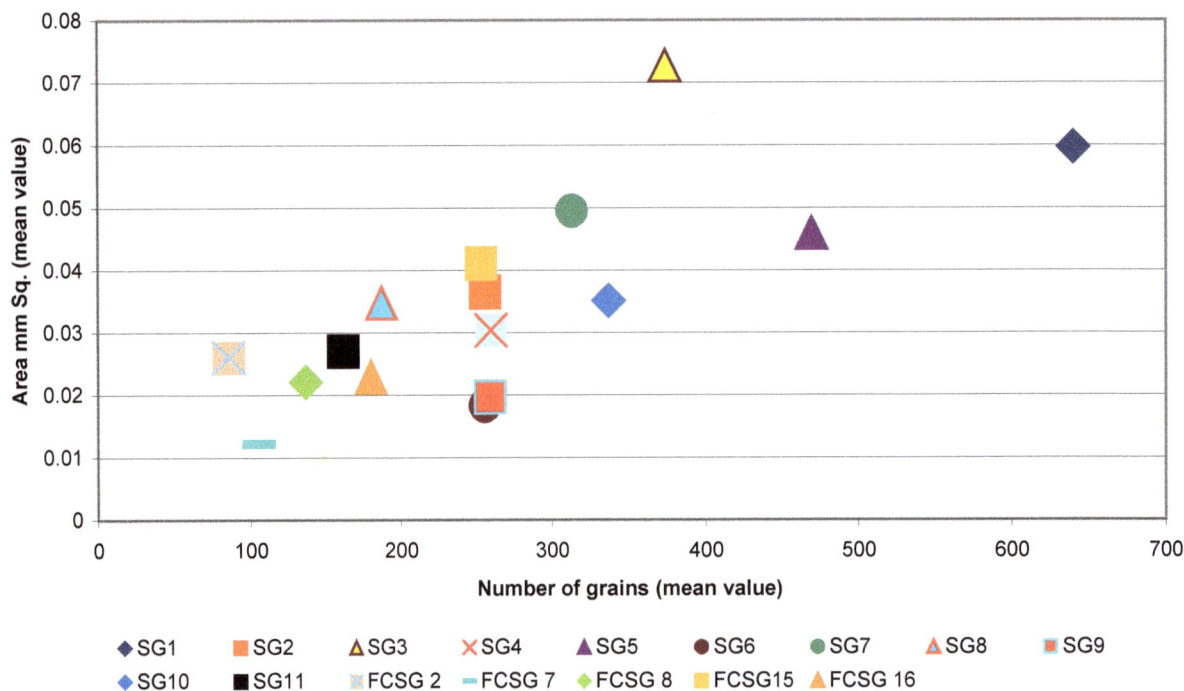

Fig 12. Scatter-plot showing the relation between area in mm² (mean value) and number of grains (mean value) for grains in the size interval <0.1≥0.01 mm for fractionated clays and the sampled sherds. Most of the fractionated clays fall in the lower left corner of the plot.

Sherds	Fe-species	CS (mm/s)	D/ε (mm/s)	H T	w+ (mm/s)	SP %	T (est) °C
sg-1	Fe^{3+}(Clay)	0.342(11)	0.942(19)		0.327(15)	69.6(20)	802
	Fe^{3+}(Hem)	0.327(33)	-0.154(33)	50.56(22)	0.288(58)	30.4(56)	
sg-3	Fe^{3+}(Clay)	0.333(13)	0.864(22)		0.325(18)	88.2(29)	716
	Fe^{3+}(Hem)	0.329(39)	-0.146(39)	51.22(27)	0.133(61)	11.8(43)	
sg-5	Fe^{3+}(Clay)	0.3378(84)	0.885(14)		0.317(11)	75.4(16)	775
	Fe^{3+}(Hem)	0.370(32)	-0.131(32)	50.41(22)	0.272(53)	24.6(42)	
sg-7	Fe^{2+}(Clay)	1.07(27)	2.23(54)		0.331(98)	24.2(60)	
	Fe^{3+}(Clay)	0.34(11)	0.82(22)		0.309(39)	54.3(48)	
	Fe^{3+}(?)	0.49(13)	0.10(13)	47.66(90)	0.43(24)	22(12)	
sg-11	Fe^{2+}(Clay)	0.958(57)	2.51(11)		0.241(85)	6.9(21)	
	Fe^{3+}(Clay)	0.357(16)	0.859(26)		0.382(25)	53.7(22)	
	Fe^{3+}(Hem)	0.392(28)	-0.088(28)	51.31(20)	0.136(53)	8.4(34)	
	Fe^{3+}(?)	0.439(67)	-0.068(65)	47.08(67)	0.57(17)	31(12)	

Table 1. Mössbauer parameters of some sherds from San Giovenale with the centre shift (CS), quadrupole splitting (D), quadrupole shift (ε), line widths (w+/w3) given in mm/s; while hyperfine field (H) is given in Tesla (T) and the relative intensity of the Fe-species is given in %.

reaction to the acid. To further investigate the carbonate content of clay FCSG-7 it was analysed by using a LEO Multi-carbon analyser. Clay sample FCSG-15 was used as reference sample (se above).

The results of the Mössbauer parameters are listed in Table 1. Three representative spectra are plotted in Fig 13. The data shows that the sherds could be grouped into two groups. The first, composed of SG-1, 3 and 5, is characterised by two Fe-bearing phases, a fully oxidised clay mineral, Fe^{3+}(clay), and hematite, Fe^{3+}(hem). The second, composed of SG-11 and 7, is characterised by a partially oxidised clay mineral, containing both ferrous and ferric iron, Fe^{2+}(clay) and Fe^{3+}(clay), respectively. An unidentified magnetic mineral, Fe^{3+} (?), with hyperfine magnetic field (H) less than that of hematite was also found in the second group (Fig 13 and Table 1). The Mössbauer parameters of Fe^{3+}(clay) are similar for all sherds in the first group but the relative intensity of Fe^{3+}(clay) and Fe^{3+}(hem) varies, probably indicating that

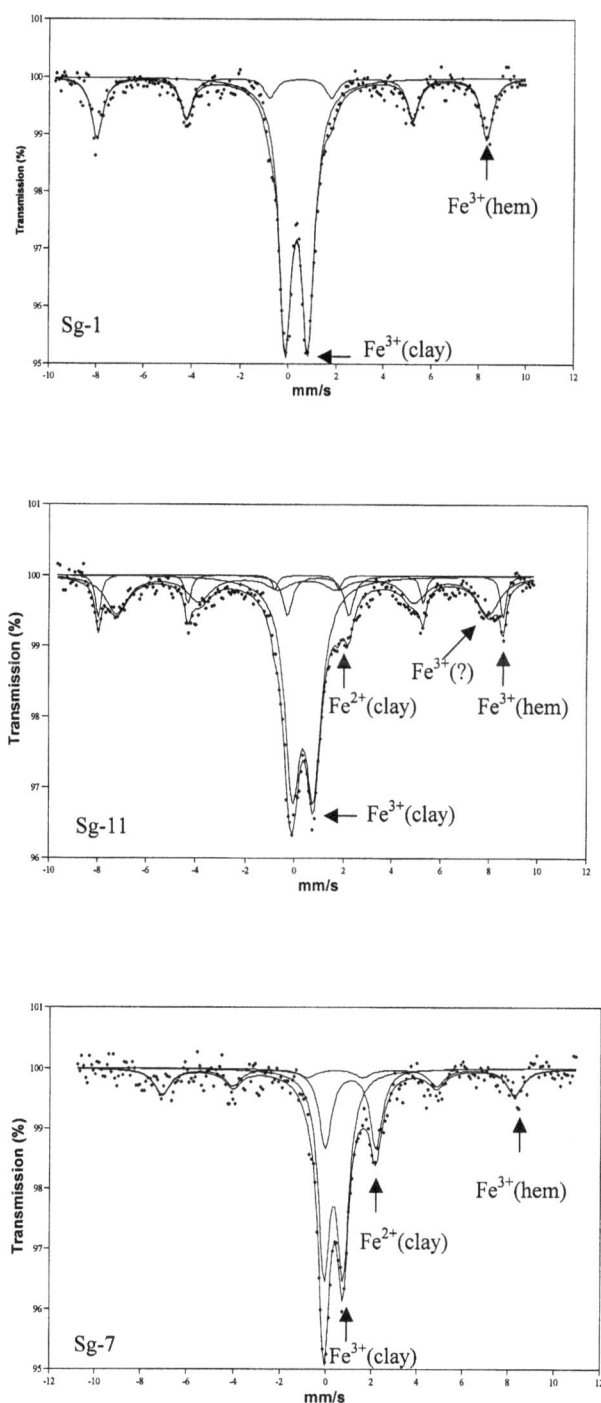

Fig 13. Representative Mössbauer spectra of three sherds from San Giovenale.

the source rocks were similar but fired at different temperatures.

In the second group the Mössbauer parameters of Fe^{2+}(clay) and Fe^{3+}(clay) in the clay, are different as are the relative intensities of the Fe-species. The firing temperatures in SG-7 must have been lower than in SG-11 since the amount of Fe^{2+}(clay) is four times more. It is also possible that the difference in the relative intensity between the two sherds in the second group could be due

to the presence of carbonates in the raw material used for firing. But the presence of Fe^{3+}(hem) in SG-11 and not in SG-7 indicates that the former was fired at a higher temperature than the latter.

By comparing the Fe-species and the amount of hematite in the two groups, the first group represented a higher firing temperature. Moreover, in the second group sample SG-11 must have been fired at higher temperature than SG-7, since it contained hematite while SG-7 did not. As an example of using Mössbauer spectroscopy for estimating the firing temperature of sherds, sample SG-1 was heated in an oxidising atmosphere at different temperatures and the resulting Mössbauer parameters are listed in Table 2. Some spectra are plotted in Fig 14 as an example. The conversion of Fe^{3+}(clay) to Fe^{3+}(hem) with increasing temperature is plotted in Fig 15. The change in the slope in Fig 15 shows that at temperatures less than 800°C no Fe^{3+}(clay) was converted to Fe^{3+}(hem). Comparing the degree of conversion of Fe^{3+}(clay) to Fe^{3+}(hem) in Figs 13 & 14 show that SG-1 was fired at temperatures close to 800°C. The conversion lines between 800°C and 1000°C were fitted using linear fit and the conversion of Fe^{3+}(clay) to Fe^{3+}(hem) as a function of temperature (T) can be written as: Fe^{3+}(clay) $= 242.011 - 0.215T$, with 0.99 correlation coefficient and 0.66 standard deviation. The amount of Fe^{3+} in clay in Table 1 was used in the equation above and the estimated firing temperatures of the sherds in group 1 ranged between 716°C and 802°C. The estimated temperatures are based on the assumption that group 1 sherds had the same source rock.

The firing temperatures for the samples used in the carbon analyses were chosen as the result of the Mössbauer spectroscopy analysis, which indicated a firing temperature of the pottery at 800°C. One sample of each of the clays FCSG-7 and 15 was fired at a lower temperature than 800°C (700°C) and one at a slightly higher temperature (825°C) and one at distinctly higher temperature 900°C for 45 minutes (Table 3).

The raw clay (FCSG-7 raw) contains a total of 3.04% carbon (both organic and inorganic). Only 0.66% of the carbon has left the clay when it was fired up 700°C. Thus, it can be assumed that the vast majority of the carbon derives from inorganic carbonates. In sample FCSG-7 there is a clear decrease of CO_3 in the clay powder fired at the higher temperatures compared to the lower ones. At 700°C there is 2.38% CO_3, and at 825°C the contents of CO_3 has decreased to 0.137% and at 900°C the contents have decreased even further, to 0.059%. The contents of CO_3 in the reference sample FCSG-15 are very low, and there are no marked differences between the varying firing temperatures. The result of the carbon analyses of the calciferous clay (FCSG-7) corresponds to the result of the HCl-test and the analysis of the thin-sections of these samples.

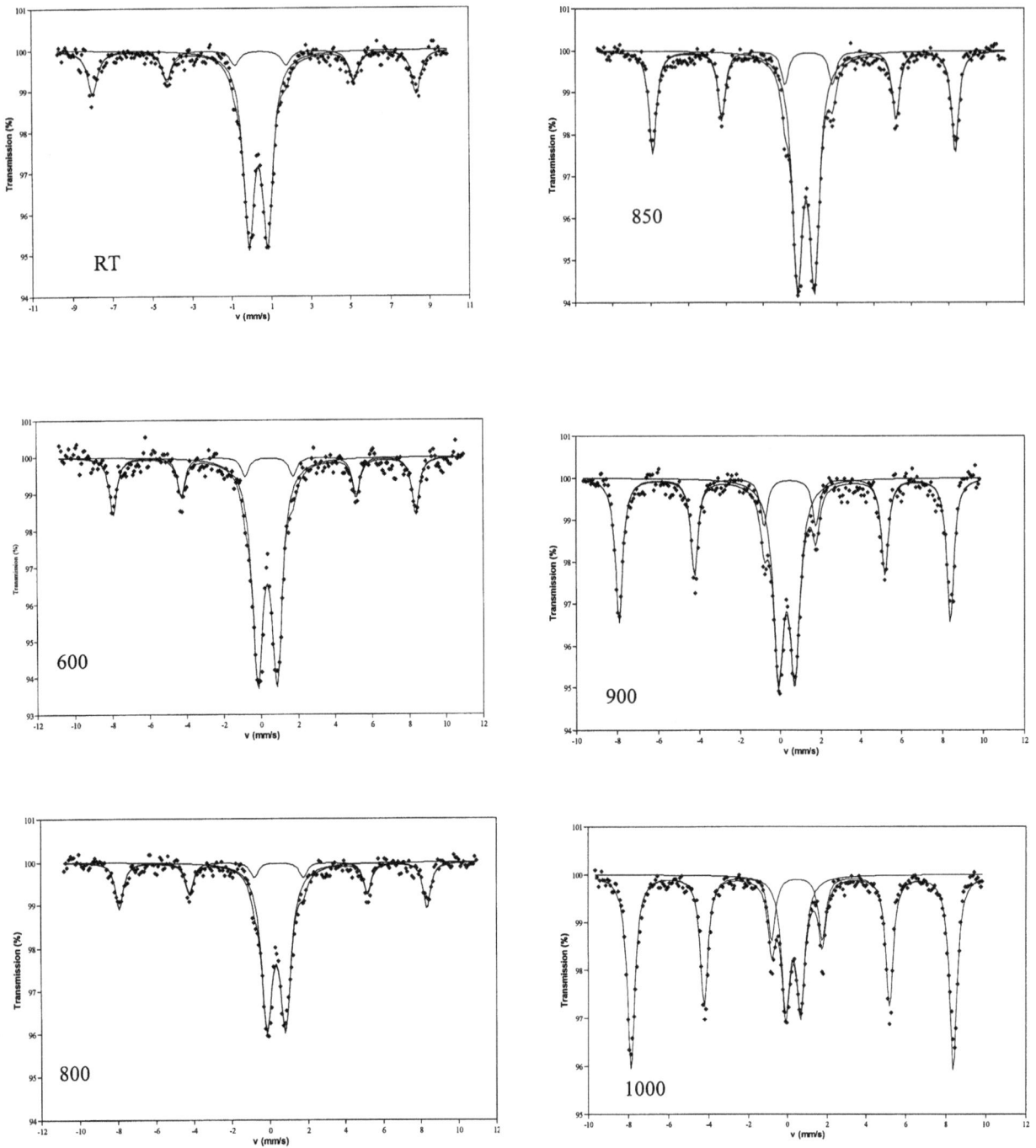

Fig 14. Representative Mössbauer spectra of SG-1 at three different temperatures.

In order for clay to transform into ceramic a firing temperature of 500°C is quite sufficient. At this temperature most of the crystal water has dehydroxylated and the original clay mineral structure is partially destroyed. However, a firing temperature of around 800°C that has been estimated for the Late Creamware vessels must be considered as fairly low for high quality earthenware ceramics. Earthenware fired in a kiln is most often fired at temperatures between 900 and 1000°C. The question is then, is it possible that these vessels were fired in an open fire? Apart from the firing temperature –

800°C is a common firing temperature in an open fire – are there other indications of such a firing procedure? Several of the Coarseware pots as well as Late Creamware vessels that have been found during the excavations at San Giovenale have dark patches on the outer surface. This type of patches on ceramics indicates smoking of this part and is often caused by pieces of firewood that have been leaning on the pot during firing (Fig 16). Furthermore, practically all sherds of the thick walled Coarseware but also some sherds of the thin walled Late Creamware have a dark core, indicating that

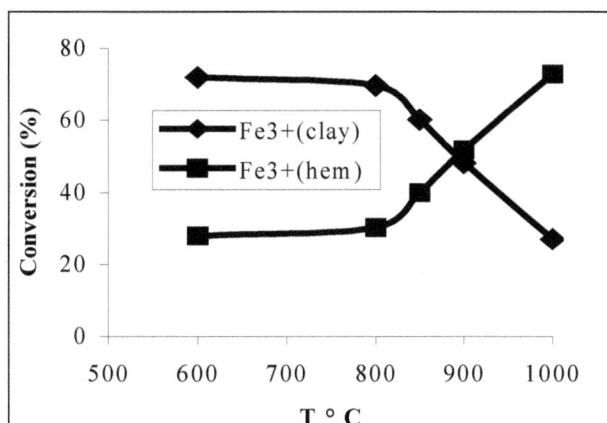

Fig 15. The change in the intensity of Fe3+ associates with iron in clay minerals and iron in hematite, respectively.

Fig 16. Sherds from San Giovenale that has with dark patches, which most likely are the result of a reducing atmosphere e.g. when a piece of firewood has been leaning on the pot during firing.

Temp °C	CS (mm/s)	D/ε (mm/s)	H (T)	w+/w3 (mm/s)	SP
600	0.339(12)	1.034(21)		0.340(16)	72.0(21)
	0.339(29)	-0.126(29)	50.50(20)	0.239(47)	28.0(47)
800	0.339(12)	0.973(20)		0.344(15)	69.7(19)
	0.348(25)	-0.136(24)	50.32(17)	0.246(40)	30.3(43)
850	0.3194(97)	0.911(16)		0.328(13)	60.1(14)
	0.356(13)	-0.128(13)	50.349(91)	0.231(22)	39.9(32)
900	0.312(13)	0.806(21)		0.302(17)	48.2(16)
	0.366(10)	-0.112(10)	50.473(71)	0.209(17)	51.8(36)
1000	0.291(11)	0.741(19)		0.261(15)	27.10(93)
	0.3726(52)	-0.1076(52)	50.369(36)	0.2283(87)	72.9(24)

Table 2. Mössbauer parameters of sample SG-1 heated at different temperatures for 24 hours. The symbols are identical as in Table 1.

Sample	firing temp. (°C)	weight (g)	carbon (%)
FCSG 7	0 (raw)	0.2144	3
	700	0.2253	2.38
	825	0.2271	0.14
	900	0.2559	0.06
Reference sample			
FCSG 15	700	0.2412	0.07
	825	0.2559	0.05
	900	0.2447	0.06

Table 3. Carbon analysis of samples FCSG-7 and reference sample FCSG-15. The table shows the strong decrease in carbon content of sample FCSG-7 in the temperature interval 700° – 825°C.

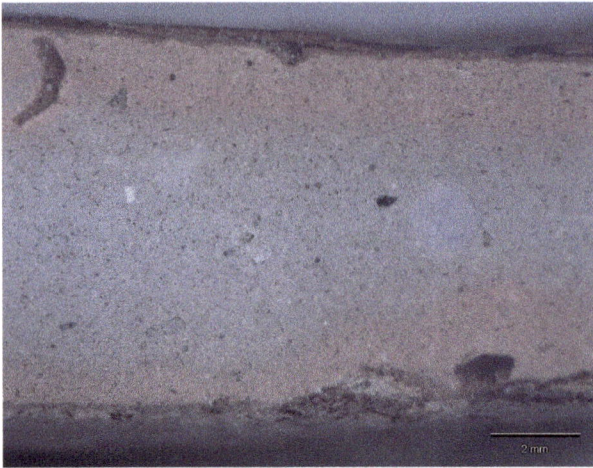

Fig 17. Vessel SG-7 with a not yet oxidised core. This is an effect of a short firing time.

Fig 18. A replica of a Late Creamware plate made by the fractionated clay FCSG-7 and fired in a kiln at a temperature of 800°C. Height 6 cm, Foot height 2.5 cm, Rim diameter 12.5 cm, Foot diameter 5.8 cm.

this part of the ware is not yet oxidized, which is an effect of a short firing time (Fig 17). The dark patches on the surface and the non-oxidised core are both very typical signs of a firing in an open fire. The absence of remains of kilns from the Etruscan time in the region of our study further supports the assertion that firing was done in open pits.

If the carbonate content of the clay CSG-7 had been tested prior to use by the ancient potters they would normally have avoided it if (as in this case) a non-calciferous clay was easily available. But since the test-briquettes of the clay produce a strong ceramic ware after firing even at these comparatively low temperatures the problem of breakage may never have occurred. However, there are still questions to be answered concerning the calciferous clay FCSG-7. Why does it behave this way? Is it the type of carbonate? Is it the relatively rich amount of iron in the clay? Is it the type of clay minerals in the clay? Is it the grain size of carbonates and other minerals

in the clay? Further analyses may hopefully help solve these questions. A small test briquette may not have the same thermal qualities as a vessel. As an experiment to further investigate the possibility that this clay can be used for pottery production a replica (full-scale) of a Late Creamware vessel was made and fired in a kiln at a temperature of 800°C for 30 minutes (Fig 18). The vessel withstood the stress of both the rapid firing and cooling, nor were there signs of cracking or any other effect of hydration and carbonation of the calcium. The buff red colour of the plate is also very similar to several of the analysed vessels. Thus, the experiment fully supports the theory that clay CSG-7 could have been used for the production of Late Creamware plates.

Acknowledgments

Our gratitude is extended to the Swedish research council (Vetenskapsrådet) for their generous grant, making this project possible. Thanks are also due to the staff of the Swedish Institute in Rome for all their assistance. The samples were taken in collaboration with the *Soprintendenza alle antichità dell'Etruria meridionale* with the assistance of dott:sa Enrica Foschi.

References

Bazzichelli, G. 1877. 'Bieda. (Scavi a San Giovenale di O. Rispoli di Corneto)', *NSc*, Ser. 3:1 (1876-77), 151-154 (= *Atti della R. Accademia dei Lincei. Memorie della classe di scienze morali, storiche e filologiche*, Ser. 3:1 (1876-77), 467-470.

Cousins, D.R. & Dharmawardena, K.G. 1969. Use of Mössbauer Spectroscopy in the Study of Ancient Pottery, *Nature*, **223**, 732-733.

Fuglesang, D. 1998. Two unpublished chamber tombs from San Giovenale, *OpRom* 22/23 (1997/98), tomb 2, 78-89.

Fuglesang, D. forthcoming. *The underground room and the late house V in area F*, forthcoming.

Gierow, P.G. 1969. *San Giovenale I:8. The tombs of Fosso del Pietrisco and Valle Vesca*, Lund 1969 (ActaRom-4, 26:1:8), FP IV, 14-17.

Lindahl, A. 2002. Microscopical analyses of ceramic thin-sections of votive terracottas from Tessennano, Vulci, Tuscania and Tarquinia. In Söderlind, M. PhD thesis, The late Etruscan votive heads from Tessennano, A study of Production, Distribution and Sociohistorical Context. *Studia Archaeologica 118*. Rom. s.393-423.

Olinder, B. & Pohl, I. 1981. *San Giovenale 2:4. The semi-subterranean building in area B*, Stockholm 1981. (ActaRom-4, 26:2:4).

Pohl, I. 1985. Nuovi contributi alla storia dell'abitato Etrusco di San Giovenale nel periodo fra il 500 ed il 200 a.C, *PP* 40, 43-63.

Pohl, I. Forthcoming. *San Giovenale II:5. Two cisterns*

and the well in Area B (ActaRom 4, 26:2:5), forthcoming.

Rancourt, D.G.1994. Mössbauer spectroscopy of minerals: I. Inadequacy of Lorentzian-Line doublets in fitting spectra arising from quadrupole splitting distributions. *Physics and Chemistry of Minerals,* **21**, 244-249.

Threipland, L.M. & Torelli, M. 1970. 'A semi-subterranean Etruscan building in the Casale Roseto (Veio) area', *BSR* 38, 1970, 62-121.

CHAPTER 9

Feasting in later Iron Age and Early Roman Britain: A Ceramic Approach

Sarah Ralph

Introduction

The effects of the Roman conquest of Britain and the ensuing processes of Romanisation have been studied for many years (Haverfield 1906; Hingley 1996; Millett 1990). Material culture from Late Iron Age (LIA) and Early Roman sites has mostly been studied from a Romano-centric viewpoint, *i.e.* assuming that people eating Roman foodstuffs were Roman or desired to be more like the Romans. This period (*c.*100 BC to AD 100) witnessed the arrival of a whole series of accessories relating to the etiquette of eating and drinking. These included a range of ceramic and metal vessels, particularly jugs, cups and strainers, as well as fine tablewares and of course amphorae, which held (among other things) a new drink – wine. Food and drink are deeply implicated in the politics and construction of cultural and social identity and a feast is one of many opportunities where food and its consumption can be studied. They are occasions where food is consumed of a different quality and quantity to that of everyday meals. This difference in the food offered or shared reflects a common understanding of the closeness of various types of social relationships. They can express status and social distance, political power and family bonds. This paper will look at the introduction of new ceramics at this time and reconsider the use of 'Roman' material culture associated with food and drink in the context of feasting and propose why feasting is an invaluable analytical tool in the study of social complexity during this period.

Feasting

The very foundations of archaeological investigations are the residues of food preparation and the consumption of that food; animal bones, pottery, plant remains (micro and macro), landscape exploitation, settlement patterns and grave goods. Food and drink are forms of material culture and, as with all archaeological materials, they cannot be divorced from the social and cultural context in which they were produced, consumed and discarded (Miracle 2002, 65). Food plays an 'active' role in the creation of socio-cultural contexts and the negotiations of power enacted within them, and must be viewed as more than just a source of nourishment. It is a language through which a society expresses itself and therefore the activity of eating can be used, consciously or otherwise, by the social group or the individual within the group, as a symbol to communicate a message. What and how we consume is socially, culturally, economically and politically motivated (Meadows 1999, 105).

Feasts can bring together a group of people, they can commemorate an event and they may also be used to reinforce status. However, I would like to focus on the political aspect of the communal consumption of food and drink. Feasts provide an arena in which social relations are symbolically represented, i.e. these are idealised representations; the way people believe relations exist or should exist rather than how they are in reality. As a result, they offer the potential for manipulation by individuals or groups attempting to alter or make statements about their relative position within that social order as it is perceived and presented (Dietler 1996). Individuals can create, maintain and even contest positions of power and authority within structured systems, and in pursuit of their own conflicting interests, they may be able to transform the structures of the systems themselves. As a result, feasts are subject to manipulation for both ideological and personal goals (Dietler 1996, 89).

This paper considers feasting from a ceramic perspective, looking at the ways in which certain types of pottery can be used as an indicator for feasting and how this particular form of material culture was manipulated in the context of feasting in later Iron Age and Early Roman Britain.

Iron Age and Early Roman Britain

The period 800 BC to AD 100 was a time of considerable change in Britain. From 500BC onwards the archaeological record becomes generally fuller and more visible. More sites are known and all classes of material culture increase in number. Fine metalwork and weaponry are deposited in watery places, on dry land, and in graves in increasing numbers from this period too.

The adoption of wheel turned pottery has often been seen as one of the key defining features of the Late Pre-Roman Iron Age in Southern Britain. A distinctive style of wheel turned pottery, sometimes labelled 'Belgic' or 'Aylesford-Swarling', appeared in parts of Hertfordshire, Essex, Kent and West Sussex during the first century BC. This innovation is one of the major changes that took place in these areas during this period. This period also witnessed marked changes in settlement, ritual, material culture and political organisation. There was the emergence of a moneyed and urbanised state level of social organisation. A greater distinction between spheres of practice defined as sacred or profane is seen in the separation of ritual away from settlement, involving the construction of shrines and formal cremation cemeteries (Hill 1995). A number of rich 'chiefly' graves are associated with this new form of burial rite. Settlements with specialist functions emerged too and occupation expanded into previously marginal areas and was accompanied by a concern with demarcating large tracts of land, as expressed in the emergence of new forms of settlement, such as *oppida*. There were imports of ceramic, metal and glass vessels associated with eating and drinking, as well as exotic foodstuffs and Mediterranean wine. These demonstrate an increased concern with the semiotics of the meal and the use of eating and drinking as an active vehicle for social distinction. The appearance of Roman pottery is often seen as integral with the aforementioned changes.

Feasting and Vessels

Feasts, like other types of commensality, help to create and reinforce social connections and do so within a context in which distinctions among people can be emphasised and elaborated through the use of particular kinds of foods and beverages, serving equipment and etiquette of seating, serving and eating (Appadurai 1981; Dietler 1996). Pottery is a primary means of addressing feasting, as it is practical (preparation, storage, serving), socially symbolic (decoration, style) and ubiquitous in the archaeological record. Blitz (1993), through a study of consumption at Mississippian sites, demonstrated that while pottery types and styles may remain constant between domestic and communal activities, vessel sizes might diverge. Within the public context of mounds, vessel size was noticeably larger than in the strictly domestic contexts due to the need to prepare and serve large quantities of food (Blitz 1993, 90). However, it must be noted that the need to prepare and serve large quantities of food could be met by an increased number of standard sized domestic vessels. Knight's (2001) research into Woodland period platform mounds in eastern North America concluded that vessels used in feasting activities did not exceed the vessel sizes of those found in ordinary domestic contexts. Further evidence from the Mississippian Moundsville polity demonstrates that pottery that was used as diacritical markers in feasting activities was dependent on the level of the political hierarchy of contemporary sites (Welch & Scarry 1995, 413-414). The differences in pottery consumption highlighted in these three New World examples are related to the level of hierarchical social and political integration at the sites. Despite the presence of the same pottery styles and types, their usage differs markedly.

Food, pots and politics are intimately linked. The study of ceramics can be turned from more traditional uses, such as markers of chronology and exchange, to explore the complexities of commensal politics. Ceramic vessels serve in the mediation of political power. They offer many provocative insights into the negotiation of power relations and the process of politics in past societies and can be used to move beyond the understanding society based purely on their structure and typology.

Pots are tools, as proposed by Braun (1983) and are used for storing, preparing, cooking and serving food and drink: the 'foodways' of societies. This term refers not only to food preparation technology and the types of foods consumed, it also encompasses the social aspects of food such as the conventions of the meal; how cooking and eating reflect and reproduce the structure of family life; the use of meals to incorporate or distinguish, express or compete for status. Viewing pottery in this light allows archaeologists to move away from the more technological and functional ceramic analysis, and develop the notion that the need for specific types of ceramic vessels is directly related to how specific cultural foodways require vessels to prepare and serve certain foods and drinks in specific ways.

Feasting could have influenced the technological or stylistic design of container crafts. Containers that appear at feasting events may in turn influence the ritual process of informal meals within households. After all, they do not go into hiding after feasts are over and design changes bought about by feasting events can reverberate beyond these occasions – therefore expanding the influence of feasting behaviours across multiple domains of social action. Practical qualities are tied to the preparation and consumption of foodstuffs. These are determined by the context of use (public vs. private), the contents (liquids vs. solids) and the social composition of such events (individuals vs. extended families and households). They also depend on the transfer of knowledge and access to specific manufacturing materials and can be associated with specific cultural groups or identities. The role of pottery in enhancing the social occasion of eating and feasting has been suggested as a reason for its original adoption in many societies. It is argued that in Mesoamerica, the adoption of ceramics was as a result of aggrandisers borrowing foreign ceramic technology for personal advantage in displays of competitive feasting (Clarke & Blake 1994). Here, ceramics were initially adopted more for their power to impress than for their culinary potential in food preparation.

Wobst (2000) has referred to human artefacts as 'material interferences' or as 'material intentions to change'. He views artefacts as linked to peoples' intentions to change something from what it was to what they thought it should be (Wobst 1997), or to prevent change that would take place in the absence of those artefacts. The term 'interference' emphasises that people entered artefacts into contexts they wanted to change (or that would change in undesirable) directions if artefacts did not interfere) (Wobst 2000: 42). Humans artefactually interfere where they cannot or choose not to accomplish (or prevent) change by other means, i.e. non-artefactual ways such as speech, gestures (Wobst 1997; 1999; 2000). In their social role as material interferences in the social field, artefacts are designed to influence how people interact (Wobst 2000, 47). They bring about change in how people evaluate each other and themselves. They provide individuals with a 'tool' to change the reading of individual intent, and they provide group members with material scales to evaluate the individualisation or 'groupification' efforts of their cohort members (Wobst 2000, 47). Such material interferences are always placed into a context to change it (be that matter or people or people's perceptions of people or matter), or to modify the inherited readings (Wobst 2000, 47).

I therefore propose that the adoption of new ceramics in later Iron Age Britain is related to the activities of those individuals and groups, whom wished to change or alter their real or idealised position within society. These actions were being played out in the context of feasting – the new arena for power politics.

Ceramic development in south eastern Iron Age Britain

During the later Iron Age, particularly in south eastern Britain, the political, social, economic and physical landscape was changing. The demand for a range of ceramic and metal vessels, particularly jugs, cups and strainers, as well as fine tablewares and mortaria has been suggested to reflect a desire amongst the British elite to emulate Roman fashions in the preparation and consumption of food and drink (Trow 1990, 103). It is assumed that 'barbarians' would automatically wish to emulate the 'civilised cultures' of the Mediterranean whenever they had the benefit of coming into contact with it, and that the gradual absorption of Mediterranean goods, practices and beliefs is a natural and unavoidable process. However, I would argue that the pattern of cultural borrowing was not one of general emulation, but rather highly limited, specific and coherent. After all, what and how we consume is socially, culturally, economically and politically motivated and therefore one cannot view the appearance of Mediterranean goods as an inevitable process. The presence of Roman goods does not necessarily equate to Roman-style practices, or to the adoption of a Roman way of life (Hawkes 2001, 102).

It is important to observe the changes occurring in ceramic assemblages within the context of the socio-political and economic transformations of the later Iron Age – changes which I believe to be related to the activity of feasting. In order to comprehend the use of ceramics in feasting, it is important to understand what the actual ceramic changes were and when they were taking place during this period.

It is immediately obvious that a wider range of different shaped ceramics were available in the Late Iron Age (LIA), when compared the narrow range of simple open containers of the Middle Iron Age (MIA), which were used in all aspects of food storage, preparation and serving. Some functional differences did exist among these hand-made MIA pots, e.g. burnished vessels were used more often for serving than cooking compared to plain vessels which were used more for cooking than serving. Larger vessels were used primarily for storage/cooking whereas smaller sized vessels were used for serving and cooking. The MIA is characterised by essentially multi-purpose pottery vessels.

Specific forms of vessels with specific functions appear during the later Iron Age, accessories all relating to the etiquette of eating and drinking. Hill (2002) identified two broad phases in the development of LIA pottery. The first (before *c*.20/10BC) is characterised by the appearance of new 'tall' and constricted forms alongside open bowls/jars, which were themselves now made in new shapes. These tall forms included a range of beakers, necked or cordoned jars and pedestalled urns. The next phase (after *c*.20/10 BC) is marked by assemblages with visually distinct types of vessels with specific forms and surface finishes, each with specific functions. These include burnished carinated open bowls/jars such as *tazze* and necked or cordoned bowls, all of which are special serving forms (for illustrations see Hill 2002). At the same time the 'cooking pot' with a combed surface became increasingly common, along with very large storage jars, with similar surface treatments. Roman dinner services are imported such as Arretine, *Terra Nigra* and *Rubra* and *Terra Sigillata* wares. *Terra Sigillata* was never abundant in Iron Age Britain, but the earliest assemblage currently known comes from Braughing-Gatesbury (a sub site of the large Iron Age complex at Braughing). By the mid-first century BC ceramic assemblages were marked by a range of distinct vessels, a visual and perceptible distinction between kitchen wares and serving wares, and an emphasis on tall forms. This range of distinctive pottery forms widens further in later assemblages (*c*.10 BC onwards), with the addition of platters, cups, beakers, flagons, flasks.

The changes that took place in later Iron Age pottery assemblages should not imply that eating and drinking were unimportant in the MIA, rather these transformations illustrate that the specific forms and social roles of eating and drinking were altering both at the level of the big social event and the daily preparation and serving of meals. It is worth noting that in later Iron Age Britain, alongside changes in ceramics, there is also evidence for a wider range of metal and wooden vessels in this period, e.g. buckets, tankards, paterae.

Feasting and Drinking

As well as the introduction on new vessels associated with eating, an array of equipment related to drinking appeared at this time too. This is noteworthy considering this period also witnessed the arrival of new form of alcohol from the Mediterranean – wine. Along with feasting, drinking is a prime political and economic tool.

Drink is a social lubricant in both formal and informal feasting contexts, simultaneously facilitating social interaction and reinforcing institutionalised status distinctions within a society (Abercrombie 1998). The distribution and consumption of alcohol would have played an important role in Iron Age society. The vessels required for the preparation, distribution and consumption of these beverages were a vehicle for inter- and intra-group competition, and underwent considerable change, both symbolically and materially through time (Arnold 1999, 71).

The rarity value of wine, as well as its relatively, long shelf-life compared to ale, added to its appeal. The presence of amphorae and associated feasting and drinking paraphernalia in some of the rich 'chiefly' burials of this period (e.g. Welwyn) would appear to support the idea that wine was a valuable status commodity.

The new tall forms (as mentioned above) were probably designed for drinking alcohol, as shown by Okun's research (1989) in the upper Rhineland where a high proportion of tall drinking forms characterised pre-Romanised assemblages. Handmade tall, neckless or slack shouldered open jars are known from sites in south east England, e.g. Gatesbury Track, Braughing and Baldock. Single examples also occur in MIA assemblages at Wendens Ambo and Little Waltham. These jars are replaced later by wheel made, undecorated, cordoned necked and other tall jars in the later first century BC and later by beakers. The functions of pedestalled urns are unclear, but Hill (2002) suggests that they are connected with drinking. They are replaced by beakers as grave goods in the first century AD. If this was a direct replacement with a vessel of similar function, then these other 'tall' vessel forms may have been associated with drinking or serving liquids too. However consuming drink from a pedestalled urn or a later beaker would have required practice so as not to spill the contents. Constricted forms, narrow necked jars and flasks were another prominent addition – forms again probably used for holding and serving alcohol. These forms comprised only 1.4% of assemblages dating before c.125-100BC, but comprise 10% of those dated c.100-10BC and 12.2% of those dated 10BC to AD 43. These new LIA assemblages occur on settlements and also in the cremation burials that become common in the first century BC.

New pottery, new people, new places
Settlement expansion into previously under utilised areas or marginal areas is a key feature of the later Iron Age. This is certainly true of southern East Anglia which had very little permanent settlement at the start of the later period, but towards the end of first century BC it contained different styles of pottery, coinage, cremation burials and new types of settlements: e.g. oppida. Movement into areas with previously little permanent

occupation may have allowed greater freedom to escape from deeply sedimented practices and their related structures of authority; the creation of new social practices and categories of action and things as an active strategy of challenge (Barrett 1991). This movement into new areas would have generated a need to create new identities in order to bring together peoples from diverging backgrounds and negotiate socio-political and economic relations. Feasting provides the arena in which to generate these new relations and allow individuals and groups to establish their position within this new social context. Feasts can bring together a group of people, but they also offer the potential for manipulation by individuals or groups attempting to alter or make statements about their relative position within that 'new' social order as it is perceived and presented. These events provided individuals with the opportunity to create, maintain and even contest positions of power and authority.

The selection and utilisation of a limited and specifically sourced material culture from the Mediterranean, i.e. eating and drinking equipment, as well as a new form of alcohol, wine, would certainly have made an impression on the attendees and aided in the creation of certain relations between individuals and groups. The movement into 'virgin' territory where no boundaries or restrictions were already set in place would have been enticing to a number of people. However, the arrival of peoples from differing backgrounds would have created a social vacuum. New relations between these various individuals would have to be renegotiated. Material 'interferences' (to use Wobst's terminology) were required to tackle and alleviate the situation. The appearance of new forms of material culture associated with eating and drinking would suggest that feasting provided the arena in which carry out the 'interferences' or 'commensal politics' required in order to establish fresh relationships, be they social, political or economic. These negotiations may have taken place on the micro level, e.g. family and kin relations, or on the macro scale, such as individuals or groups wishing to establish themselves in society.

Feasting provided the occasion with which to tackle the social tension or void created by the movement of peoples into this area. As a result these political consumption events allowed particular individuals to emerge who, in order to maintain their position, sourced new feasting paraphernalia (hence the emergence of new material culture in the region). This continuous pursuit for power affected changes and structures of society and transformed the social, political and economic landscape – the emergence of coinage, new settlements.

The engine for change from egalitarian to ranked societies has been said to be as a result of self-interested competition among political actors vying for prestige and social esteem. These political entrepreneurs have been called 'aggrandisers' and overtime some have become chiefs with institutionalised authority. These individuals are most evident in the newly emerging burial rites of this period. Many of these graves are dominated by feasting paraphernalia. A funeral was of course a time when individuals repaired the torn fabric of a community and re-created society. The funerary meal expressed the importance of the meal in wider society and its use as a specific 'tournament of value' (Appadurai 1986); a key arena in which households could both express and compete for social status. One of the richest is from Welwyn (Hertfordshire) which contained five amphorae and a bronze strainer and dish. Further finds included pedestal urns, bowls, cups, beakers, platters, flagons and a tripod vessel. There was also a cup belonging to a class of silver drinking vessels popular in the Mediterranean world, and among the Romans in particular, during the last century BC and the first century AD.

These burials are just one example of the types of people who may use the activity of feasting for personal goals. It must be noted that not all feasting is hosted by aggrandisers to further their own positions of authority, nor is all aggrandising carried out in the context of feasts. Feasting has many different contexts and may be organised at the corporate or individual levels.

East Anglia – A case study
East Anglia provides an interesting case study for there was no simultaneous change to LIA styles of pottery across East Anglia from c.125 – 7 5BC. Rather, some northern parts of the region still used MIA tradition pottery after the Roman conquest. It is important to ask why southern East Anglia developed LIA tradition pottery so early and why other areas continued with MIA tradition pottery for much longer? If changes in pottery forms, deposition and production can be linked to wider aspects of social discourse, feasting may provide an analytical tool with which to understand these ceramic variations.

These ceramic variations within the region could indicate significantly different foodways in different cultural environments. A striking feature of early first century AD ceramics in northern East Anglia is the relative lack of differentiation and categorisation. There are few shapes and little decoration. In contrast to southern East Anglia, the northern area displays little evidence for social differentiation or hierarchy in the pottery or wider aspects of the foodways these ceramic tools were a part of. It is not because those groups in northern East Anglia were peripheral that Gallo-Belgic pottery or amphorae are extremely rare in these areas. Rather, there was little demand for these forms – be they made locally, in southern East Anglia or further afield. Nor was there the demand for exotic foodstuffs and beverages that were eaten and drunk from them. Whatever changes took place in these areas in cooking and serving meals, the setting and social contexts of such meals, and the larger social discourses they sustained or changed, did so within the existing foodway traditions (Hill 2002, 158).

Categories are a product of peoples' thinking on and practical engagement with their worlds and these are subsequently expressed through the use of new types and forms of pottery in specific contexts. The increased demand for these new types of pottery forms could be suggested to be linked to the introduction of the potter's wheel, which would have been employed to meet this demand through the production of indigenous imitation wares. When technologies become affordable by a large number of people in communities, elites or incipient elites may completely abandon these technologies for the production of new prestige items. Alternatively, elites may find ways to embellish the value of objects through either expensive hand-crafted decoration or technical elaboration (Hayden 1995, 263).

Although concentrations of imported prestige items might reflect increasing wealth, the absence of such imports need not indicate a lack of prosperity. Social, political or religious motivations might cause the deliberate exclusion of imported prestige items. Caesar, for example records that in Gaul the Nervii banned the import of wine and other luxuries, which they believed would impair their Courage (Bell. Gall. II, 15, 4). The patterns of pottery use in northern East Anglia should not be seen as a product of backwardness nor isolation. These were dynamic societies with contacts between each other and with those to the south. Rather, the maintenance of these ways of life was probably a conscious choice. East Anglia provides an example of an area in which the manifestation of wealth and influence was articulated through insular traditions rather than imported exotica. The conquest period settlement at Thetford, Norfolk, despite requiring the mobilisation and large-scale consumption of both material and human resources in its construction, it is impoverished in term of imported finewares. Groups in northern East Anglia accommodated and transformed selected elements of the new ceramic traditions but social discourse was carried out in a different field of consumption – the consumption of large amounts of precious metals and coins in hoards. Generally, the paucity of imports in Suffolk and Norfolk stands in stark contrast to the remarkable concentration of gold-alloy neck-torcs and coin hoards recovered from the area.

Discussion
At the end of the Iron Age, eating and drinking habits were changing for people. This is demonstrated by the appearance of new objects and foodstuffs. Food (and drink) is socially defined and its consumption maintains life and social relationships. It also signifies identity, power, authority, domination and resistance. It is often assumed that the 'barbarians' of northern Europe would automatically wish to emulate the 'civilised cultures' of the Mediterranean whenever they had the benefit of coming into contact with it, and that the gradual

absorption of Mediterranean goods, practices and beliefs is a natural and unavoidable process. However, as shown in south-east Britain and particularly East Anglia, the pattern of cultural borrowing was not general emulation, but rather highly limited, specific and coherent. East Anglia clearly illustrates this point, with only certain forms of new eating and drinking paraphernalia being utilised within certain areas of this region.

The later Iron Age period witnessed an expansion of population into previously uninhabited areas. This movement would have brought together a myriad of people from a variety of social, political and economic backgrounds. A situation, such as this, would require a renegotiation of relations and the creation of new identities. A feast, given its importance in commensal politics, provided the occasion for individuals and groups to re-establish a social discourse. In order to successfully manipulate the outcome of these events, 'material interferences' took place in the form of new ceramics from or influenced by the Mediterranean and offered alongside a new form of alcohol, wine. As Wobst (2000) notes, humans artefactually interfere where they cannot or choose not to accomplish change by other means. In acquiring this social role, artefacts are designed to influence how people interact, thus bringing about change in how people evaluate themselves and others. The introduction of these new ceramics into the context of feasting was a pro-active move by individuals or groups to manage or alter the social vacuum created by population movement of the later Iron Age. These items served several functions; a sense of indebtedness was created between host and guest, and it allowed hosts to distinguish themselves from other potential hosts or even attendees, this in turn could have led to an element of competition between these individuals who demanded new vessels and drinks in order to out-perform each other and create further social debts. In striving to alter their own positions within society and achieving personal goals, their actions potentially had the power to alter the structure of society at large.

It is interesting to note where these new ceramic forms and alcoholic beverages associated with commensality are found in the archaeological record. They are found on the new settlement types of this period – oppida, and as part of grave goods assemblages in the newly emerging burial rite – cremations. Both these features are themselves located in these newly inhabited areas of south eastern Britain, especially the southern region of East Anglia, and are thought to be connected with the rise in complexity and the emergence of powerful individuals. Each of these features is interconnected – all creating a knock-on effect of change, which I believe was articulated through the mechanism of feasting. Of course feasting was not the only avenue/outlet for aggrandisers and as the archaeology of northern East Anglia aptly demonstrates consumption can take many forms and the peoples of this region chose to carry out their commensal

politics through the consumption of precious metals deposited in hoards.

The ceramic evidence for later Iron Age East Anglia emphasises the variation in adoption of imported pottery. Much like the Mississippian examples showed (Blitz 1983; Knight 2001; Welch & Scarry 1995), despite 'Roman' forms of pottery appearing in Britain, the contexts in which they are used differ. When used in a different context, the ceramics takes on new identities, i.e. ceramics taken out of the Roman context and placed within the feasting context of Iron Age Britain and used by different people, creates new identities. These new identities are then used by people to transform and manipulate the social structure. Therefore just because the ceramics are Roman in nature, it does not necessarily equate the users as Roman. The North American examples also highlight how social structure can affect differential use of pottery too. East Anglia aptly shows this where 'material interferences' took several forms and varied both temporally and spatially.

The transformation of the pottery repertoires during the LIA would have affected all meals, not just special occasions. Feasting has many levels and can occur in a variety of social contexts and scales, ranging from the community at large to the family or kin group. A meal, its preparation and consumption are seen as one of the key areas in which the structure of the family (its form, division of labour, gender relations, expectations, forms of authority) are made manifest and reproduced. Preparing and eating meals are one of the ways in which a society's norms are expressed, inculcated, reproduced and challenged.

Conclusion

Feasting would have occurred throughout the Iron Age as a means to maintain, alter or establish a variety of relationships within society. During the later Iron Age the movement of people and the prospect of the Roman invasion turned feasting into a powerful mode of commensality. People now had to redefine themselves in these new situations and a feast provided the opportunity for people to gather, create identities and alliances – something particularly important given the imminent of arrival of the Roman army. The consequences of these events are changes in material culture and more importantly changes in the political structure of society and the emergence of aggrandisers, all of which in turn affected one another.

One needs to recognise that inter-cultural consumption of objects or practices, the process which instigated the encounter with the Mediterranean and Roman Gaul, is not a phenomenon that takes place at the level of cultures or abstract structures. It is an active process of creative transformation and manipulation played out by individuals and social groups with a variety of competing interests and strategies of action embedded in local political relations, cultural perceptions and cosmologies. Focusing on the process of consumption can provide a useful and sensitive means of penetrating indigenous agency and experience in the encounter. Demand for goods is never an automatic response to their availability. It must be understood as an aspect of the political economy of societies that follows the culturally conditioned political logic of consumption in specific historical circumstances (Appadurai 1986; Miller 1995). The evolution of tastes and desires in the realm of consumption is a powerful indicator of local experience of global colonial processes (Dietler 1995, 97).

In conclusion, I would suggest that feasting provided the opportunity for individuals or groups to augment their existing power and prestige or create new relationships. Imports obtained from the Roman and Mediterranean worlds through new trading contacts held by these few privileged individuals, provided the means in which to differentiate oneself from the rest of the community and raise one's status in society. Individuals and groups actively sourced new ways to consume food and drink in order act as 'interferences' in the changing social, political and economic climates of the later Iron Age. These new ideas and objects could then be manipulated and displayed through feasting; the new arena for power politics.

References

Abercrombie, T.A., 1998. *Pathways of Memory and Power: Ethnography and History among an Andean People.* Madison: University of Wisconsin.

Appadurai, A., 1981. Gastropolitics in Hindu South Asia. *American Ethnologist,* 8, 494 – 511.

Appadurai, A., 1986. *The Social Life of Things: Commodities in Cultural Perspective.* Cambridge: Cambridge University Press.

Arnold, B., 1999. Drinking the feast: alcohol and the legitimation of power in Celtic Europe. *Cambridge Archaeological Journal,* 9(1), 71 – 93.

Barrett, J.C., 1991. Bronze Age pottery and the problem of classification. In J.C. Barrett, R. Bradley, & M. Hall (eds.). *Papers on the Prehistoric Archaeology of Cranbourne Chase.* Oxbow Monograph 11, 201 – 30. Oxford: Oxbow Books.

Blitz, J.H., 1993. Big pots for big shots: feasting and storage in a Mississippian community. *American Antiquity,* 58 (1), 80 – 96

Braun, D., 1983. Pots as tools. In J.S. Moore & A.S. Keene (eds.). *Archaeological Hammers and Theories,* 107 – 34. New York: Academic Press.

Clark, J.E. & Blake, M., 1994. The power of prestige: competitive generosity and the emergence of rank societies in lowland Mesoamerica. In E.M. Brumfiel & J.W. Fox (eds.). *Factional Competition and Political Development in the New World,* 17 – 30. Cambridge: Cambridge University Press.

Dietler, M., 1995. The Cup of Gyptis: Rethinking the colonial encounter in Early Iron Age western Europe and the relevance of world-systems models. *Journal of European Archaeology* 3(2), 89 – 111.

Dietler, M., 1996. Feasts and commensal politics in the political economy: Food, power and status in prehistoric Europe. In P. Wiessner & W. Schiefenhövel (eds.) *Food and the Status Quest, an Interdisciplinary Perspective,* 87 – 125. Providence: Berghan.

Hayden, B., 1995 The emergence of prestige technologies and pottery. In W.K. Barnett & J.W. Hoopes (eds.) *The Emergence of Pottery: Technology and Innovation in Ancient Societies,* 257 – 65. Washington: Smithsonian Institution Press.

Haverfield, F., 1906. The Romanisation of Roman Britain. *Proceedings of the British Academy 1905 – 1906,* 185 – 217.

Hawkes, G., 2001. An Archaeology of Food: A case study from Roman Britain. In G. Davies, A. Gardner & K. Lockyear (eds.) TRAC 2000. Proceedings of the 10th Annual TRAC. Oxford: Oxbow Books, 94 – 103.

Hill, J.D., 1995., *Ritual and Rubbish in the Iron Age of Wessex.* BAR British Series 242: Oxford: British Archaeological Reports.

Hill, J.D., 2002. Just about the potter's wheel? Using, making and depositing Middle and Later Iron Age pots in East Anglia. In A. Woodward & J.D Hill (eds.). *Prehistoric Britain: The Ceramic Basis,* 143 – 60. Oxford: Oxbow Books.

Hingley, R. 1996. The 'legacy' of Rome: the rise, decline and fall of the theory of Romanisation. In J. Webster & N.J. Cooper (eds.) *Roman Imperialism: Postcolonial Perspectives.* Leicester Archaeology Monographs 3, 35 – 48.

Knight, V.J., 2001. Feasting and the emergence of platform mound ceremonialism in eastern North America. In M. Dietler & B. Hayden (eds.) *Feasts: Archaeological and Ethnographic Perspectives on Food, Politics and Power* 311 – 33. Washington: Smithsonian Institution Press.

Meadows, K.,1999. The appetites of households in early Roman Britain. In P.M. Allison *The Archaeology of Household Activities,* 101 – 20. London: Routledge.

Miller, D., 1995. Consumption and commodities. *Annual Review of Anthropology,* 24, 141 – 61.

Millett, M., 1990. *The Romanisation of Britain. An Essay in Archaeological Interpretation.* Cambridge: Cambridge University Press

Miracle, P., 2002. Mesolithic Meals from Mesolithic Middens. In P. Miracle & N. Milner (eds.) *Consuming Passions and Patterns of Consumption* 65 – 88. Cambridge: McDonald Institute Monographs.

Okun, M.L., 1989. An example of the process of acculturation in the Early Roman frontier. *Oxford Journal of Archaeology,* 8(1), 41 – 54.

Trow, S., 1990. By the northern shores of the ocean: some observations on acculturation process at the edge of the Roman world. In T. Blagg & M. Millett (eds.) *The Early Roman Empire in the West,* 103 – 18. Oxford: Oxbow Books.

Welch, P.D. & M.C. Scarry., 1995. Status-related variation in foodways in the Moundville chiefdom. *American Antiquity*, 60(3), 397 – 419.

Wobst, H.M., 1997. Material authenticity and autochthony, before and after markets. In *Fulbright Symposium: Indigenous Cultures in an Interconnected World.* Pre-printed papers, non-paginated, Museum and Art Gallery of the Northern Territory: Darwin, Australia.

Wobst, H.M., 1999. Style in archaeology, or archaeologists in style. In E.S. Chilton (ed.) *Material Meanings: Critical Approaches to Material Culture,* 118 – 32. Salt Lake City: University of Utah Press.

Wobst, H.M., 2000. Agency in (spite of) material culture. In M-A. Dobres & J. Robb (eds.) *Agency in Archaeology,* 40 – 50. London: Routledge.

CHAPTER 10

Abstracts of Lectures Given at the Conference but not Presented in this Volume

Edited by
Alex Gibson

Dean Arnold
(Professor of Anthropology, Wheaton College, Wheaton, Illinois)

Changes in Production Organization and Pottery Technology in a Maya Community 1965-1997

Among other uses, archaeologists utilize pottery to study social and technological change. But, do all aspects of pottery production change at the same rate? Or, do some aspects change more quickly than others? If so, which aspects change the most and which are the most conservative and why? What do the changes in pottery reveal about the changes in the society? Using an ethnoarchaeological approach, this paper explores the changes that have occurred over a 32 year period in a contemporary community of potters in Ticul, Yucatan, Mexico and relates those changes to the study of archaeological pottery in general. While almost all of the production process in Ticul has changed in more than three decades, the population of potters, the kind of temper used, and the most common forming techniques have remained the most conservative aspects of production while vessel shapes, demand and market have changed the most. The theoretical and practical implications for these conclusions for pottery production elsewhere will be explored briefly.

Louise Bashford
(Dept of Archaeological Sciences, University of Bradford)

Organic Residue Analysis of Neolithic Pottery from Causewayed Enclosures at Kingsborough Farm, Eastchurch and Chalk Hill, Ramsgate, Kent

Organic residue analysis of archaeological material has taught us much about the nature of organic substances surviving in pottery vessels and the likely functions of different vessel types. Residue analysis is not routinely applied to archaeological ceramics, and these methods have not yet realised their full potential for archaeological research. Some of the applications of modern residue analysis were applied to stratified archaeological samples using early Neolithic pottery from two causewayed enclosures in Kent.

Different characteristics were noted in the residues from the two sites which may have implications for vessel use, food preparation, site function and spatial analysis. Stratigraphic sampling of one assemblage led to indications of changes in vessel use over time. Possible dietary variation was ascertained through isotopic analysis, which confirmed the presence of mixed adipose residues in the earlier sherds and of dairy fats in later sherds, indicating increased use of arable resources. The project concluded that further detailed study is required to test the validity of the results.

Ina Berg
(University of Manchester)

A Comparative Look at the Use of the Potter's Wheel in Bronze Age Greece

Analyses of Aegean Bronze Age pottery follow the standard dichotomy in dividing assemblages into wheelmade and handmade pots. This procedure causes two methodological problems. First, it ignores manufacturing methods that combined several techniques in the making of one vessel. And second, it assumes that all wheelmade pottery is made uniformly with the fast wheel. However, already in 1959 did Foster ('The Potter's Wheel' Southwestern Journal of Anthropology 15, 99-119) draw our attention to the fact that unpivoted turntables can be used to reach rotation speeds sufficient for the making of small vessels or parts of vessels (esp. rims). Combined with a recent analysis of the pottery assemblage from Phylakopi on Melos (Greece), which has demonstrated that potters did not achieve the expert level of competence (cf. Roux & Corbetta 1989 The Potter's Wheel), this contribution intends to throw doubt onto our assumption of a uniform use of the potter's wheel and wishes to open up the debate to explore the great diversity of manufacturing processes employed by Bronze Age potters.

Louise Brown
(Old Scatness Jarlshof Environs Project /
University of Bradford)

Towards an Integrated Approach to on-site Artefact Management: a Case Study from Old Scatness, Shetland

The research-led excavations at Old Scatness, Shetland span the last ten years. This time-frame, coupled with the project's research agenda, have enabled the development of recording methodologies and strategies to deal with the amount of artefacts and samples taken from the site. With a pottery assemblage consisting of over 40,000 sherds it has been imperative that these have been managed in such a way as to maximise the potential of the assemblage. Such an assemblage provides the unique opportunity for the implementation of new and further research, to date the majority of this work has been the analysis of residues. It ultimately will also play a part in the reassessment of the Iron Age type-site of Jarlshof, less than a mile from Old Scatness.

Cole Henley
(Royal Commission on the Ancient and Historical Monuments of Scotland)

The Art in Artefact: Exploring Pottery Decoration in the Neolithic of the Outer Hebrides

The analysis of ceramic decoration in the Scottish Neolithic has a rich history which, along with chambered cairns, has been central to our interpretations of this period. Since the work of Piggott in the 1930s, the form and decoration of Neolithic ceramics in Scotland have largely served as tools for relating sites to particular chronological and regional types, to the extent that we still refer to, for example, Grooved Ware and Impressed Ware sites. Yet despite the inherent value that such broad categories present to our understanding of this period, at a site - and perhaps also a regional - level such a view of pottery decoration can be problematic.

In this paper I wish to explore the ceramics from one site in the Outer Hebrides, Eilean Domhnuill, and examine why it was that pots at this particular site were so elaborately decorated. Through reference to the rich archaeological record at this site, contemporary sites in the region and also anthropological analogy I wish to suggest that in order to understand the decoration of these vessels we need to attempt to understand the function of applying decorative motifs to ceramic vessels and the functions that such vessels might ultimately have served through their use and deposition.

I hope to argue for an agency for ceramic decoration, at least for this one site, and relate this to broader developments within the region at this time; a period where society would seem to be increasingly concerned with the construction and maintenance of elaborate social boundaries, of which ceramic decoration was just one aspect.

Carl Heron, Marcus Forster, Ben Stern[1], Oliver Craig[2] and Soren Andersen[3]

1 - (University of Bradford)
2 - (University of Rome)
3 - (National Museum of Denmark, Centre for Maritime Archaeology)

The Contents of Late Mesolithic/Neolithic Ceramics from Denmark

In order to investigate issues of dietary change and the exploitation of marine resources during the Mesolithic/Neolithic transition, c. 4,000 BC, a number of potsherds from six sites in Denmark have been analysed for the presence of organic residues. Samples have been selected from Tybrind Vig, Bjornsholm, Norsminde, Ringkloster, Ertebolle and Store Amose. These samples have been subjected to GC, GC/MS and compound-specific GCIRMS to understand the origin of the lipid extracts. The presence of specific biomarkers combined with carbon and nitrogen isotope ratios provides a valuable means of identification. The significance of these results will be outlined.

Mel Johnson
(CFA Archaeology Ltd)

Skilmafilly, Aberdeenshire: Recent Work on a Bronze Age Cremation Cemetery

Abstract: Excavations undertaken by CFA Archaeology Ltd on the route of the St Fergus to Aberdeen Gas Pipeline during July 2001 revealed a well-preserved Early Bronze Age cremation cemetery, located at Skilmafilly in Aberdeenshire, to the west of Peterhead. The burials consisted of 28 un-urned and 11 urned deposits of cremated human bone in pits, arranged in a tight cluster. The urns comprise both Cordoned and Collared urns. A tiny vessel was found inside one of the urns along with the cremation.

The un-urned cremation deposits have been dated at

Groningen University, using the technique of AMS radiocarbon dating of cremated bone developed by Dr Jan Lanting. Eventually all of the cremated bone deposits will be dated. This makes Skilmafilly by far the most comprehensively dated Bronze Age cemetery in Britain. Furthermore, its dating will add to what we already understand about the chronological relationship between Collared and Cordoned urns from the dates recently obtained by the NMS /Dating Cremated Bones Project/. The results obtained so far provide a tight clustering of dates, with an overall range from around (or just before) 1900 BC until around 1600 BC. Assuming that the urned cremations will fall within the same date range, this is consistent with the known period of currency of Collared and Cordoned urns in Scotland.

Mark Knight, Duncan Garrow & Emma Beadsmore
(Cambridge Archaeological Unit)

Refitting Mildenhall Pits

The excavation of 236 Early Neolithic pits at Kilverstone, Norfolk, produced 12356 worked flints and 2469 potsherds all in excellent condition. The size and context of the assemblage bears a remarkable resemblance to that from the type site at Hurst Fen. The exceptional contextual detail that accompanies the Kilverstone material gave us an important opportunity to look again at the relationship between a distinctive regional style of earlier Neolithic pottery and a site comprised entirely of clusters of pits. Our particular approach to this relationship involved laying out the entire assemblage, both pot and flint, in order to find connections between and across contexts. This paper provides an interpretation of these refits.

Ann MacSween
(Historic Scotland)

Kintore, Aberdeenshire: Pottery from a Multi-period Plough-truncated Site

A large scale excavation in advance of development at Kintore near Aberdeen (Carried out by Murray Cooke - AOC Archaeology on behalf of Bett Homes) has produced a sizeable assemblage of prehistoric pottery spanning the Early Neolithic to the Early Iron Age. This paper will present the initial results of the analysis of the assemblage which includes the first Grooved Ware to have been found in Aberdeenshire.

Sarah Percival
(Norfolk Museums)

Context, Style and Regionality, the Grooved Ware Pottery from Flixton Park, Suffolk

Excavations at Flixton Park, Suffolk have produced over 33kg of prehistoric pottery predominantly Grooved Ware. The site is located on a gravel terrace on the southern bank of the River Waveney close to the Norfolk/Suffolk border (NGR TM 30288631) and was first identified from aerial photographs which revealed a complex landscape of enclosures and monuments visible as crop marks. Proposed gravel extraction prompted a series of 'rescue' excavations undertaken by Suffolk Archaeological Unit, which revealed a timber circle, ring ditch and pit deposits. Flixton Park occupies a north-east to south-west ridge of gravel terrace on the southern slope of the River Waveney. The riverside location of the site is typical of the topographical location of Grooved Ware sites which are consistently found in riverine or coastal. The location of the site offers good visibility across the river valley and the relative height of the setting, 16.26 metres O.D., suggests that the site would in turn have been highly visible to anyone utilising the river valley.

Excavations within the area formerly occupied by Flixton Park began in the early 1990s when a ring-ditch believed to be of Early Bronze Age date was recovered (FLN008). Following the excavations a geophysical and desk-top survey of the whole of the northern area of the park was commissioned. The survey revealed a second ring-ditch plus a number of other features within the area threatened by gravel extraction. Full excavation covered an area of 4,320 square metres including the ring-ditch and an extensive area to the north. The earliest features identified were a series of pits containing Grooved Ware and a substantial timber circle with an approximate diameter of 18m originally comprising 36 postholes. Radiocarbon dating of a charcoal sample from the fill of one of the postholes indicated that the structure was in use c.4470BP (Waikato/5428, 1σ, cal. BC 3344-2944, cal. BP5293-4893; wk.no.Waikato/5427, 1σ, cal.BC 773-406, cal. BP 2722-2355). The postholes of the timber circle also contained Grooved Ware of the Durrington Walls sub-style as well as struck and burnt flints.

In addition to the timber circle the excavations revealed a large ring-ditch, 20m in diameter which cut through the timber circle directly to the north. The ring-ditch also contained Grooved Ware but this was highly abraded and was interpreted as being residual perhaps being redeposited when the ring-ditch cut through the timber circle. Charcoal from a single, unurned cremation found within the fills of the ring-ditch produced a radiocarbon date of 3700BP.

The aim of the paper is to present a synthesis of the data from the various excavations examined within the existing pottery reports and to present a re-evaluation of the Grooved Ware sub-styles as identified by Longworth with particular reference to material from Flixton and other East Anglia sites.

Alison Sheridan
(National Museum of Scotland)

Radiocarbon Dating of Scottish Beakers: Results from the NMS Dating of Cremated Bone Project

Since 2001 the National Museums of Scotland Archaeology Department has been running various radiocarbon dating programmes, designed to establish a firmer chronological basis for (*inter alia*) Copper and Bronze Age pottery from Scotland. Having first focused on cinerary urns (as reported on in the 2002 Conference and published in Gibson's 2003 *Prehistoric Pottery…* volume), attention has since focused on Food Vessels and Beakers. This contribution presents the new dates for the latter, plus a critical re-evaluation of the existing Scottish Beaker dates. This provides useful new information to feed into Stuart Needham's broader typological-stratigraphic-associational study of British Beakers (which he discussed at the 2002 Conference).

Ann Woodward
(University of Birmingham)

Pottery in a Later Bronze Age Landscape

Excavation of a multi-period 55 hectare site at Bestwall Quarry, Wareham, Dorset have been undertaken over the last 14 years by a local amateur archaeology group, in advance of sand and gravel quarrying. Publications are being prepared by the group in association with a series of professional consultants and finds specialists, funded through the Aggregates Levy Sustainability Fund. The later Bronze Age landscape comprises a large-scale field system with a series of eight individual Middle Bronze Age roundhouses, usually located in field corners. In the Late Bronze Age a more restricted area of settlement was established.

The pottery assemblage is large (15,800 sherds) and contains many feature sherds, full or part vessel profiles and measurable rim diameters. The Middle Bronze Age ceramics include examples of vessels from three different regional styles of the Deverel-Rimbury tradition: Avon/Stour Valleys, Dorset Downs and Central Wessex.

However, the Late Bronze Age assemblage is very uniform and belongs to a highly characteristic 'Dorset' style which has also been identified at Eldon's Seat and Sherborne.

Dating of the various assemblages has been undertaken using a series of 38 high precision radiocarbon dates, while the questions of sourcing of inclusions, pottery production and exchange have been investigated by means of detailed fabric codings, thin section petrography, and ICP analysis. Perhaps the most significant discovery has been the identification of waster sherds in both Middle and Late Bronze Age contexts; this confirms that some at least of the pottery was being made on the site.